Advance Praise for
"Tell Me More": Listening to Learners Explain

"In this tightly conceptualized and well-crafted book, Duckworth and colleagues make a significant contribution to educational theory, research, and practice. They illustrate, with powerful and lively teaching examples, how theory related to the construction of knowledge by students can be implemented in the classroom. The rich and deeply textured examples of teaching and learning in this important book also reveal how gifted teachers can be astute and perceptive researchers. This book is a singular contribution to the literature on teaching and learning."

—**James A. Banks**, University of Washington, Seattle

"Duckworth has given us case studies of 'mid-wife' teaching at its very best. First she describes her own classroom where she coaches beginning teachers to give birth to their own ideas. She describes in great detail how their ideas are drawn out, nourished, articulated, and tested. We see the fledgling ideas actually developing and gaining strength. Then we see Duckworth's students becoming teachers who, in turn, draw out and nourish the ideas of still younger thinkers. Duckworth is a gifted coach who articulates her craft with the greatest care and insight. She gives her readers the sense they themselves are attendant at the birth of ideas and we in turn feel blessed by being witness to the miracle of creation."

—**Mary Field Belenky**, co-author of *Women's Ways of Knowing*

"Duckworth's book, *"Tell Me More": Listening to Learners Explain*, is a fascinating and pioneering account of people working together over many weeks, struggling to invent the ideas they needed to understand diverse phenomena in fields as diverse as physics, poetry, or geography. What is extraordinary about Duckworth's approach is that it depends entirely on the participants' will to understand. The teacher does not tell the students what to learn or even what questions to ask. Duckworth's moving account takes on the quality of six or seven beautiful narratives: everything depends on a collective comprehension of Duckworth's proactive approach and style. This book is a must read for teachers and others who want to come to grips with fundamental problems facing all undefeated educators: What is thinking? How does it grow? How can learners, including the teachers, help each other?"

—**Howard E. Gruber**, Teachers College, Columbia University

"I read each chapter of this volume over and over, hoping by sheer "rote learning" I could translate what it offers into my own daily practice, rather then rushing ahead to my own "right answers" whether it's about a particular child or a particular school or system. These essays in their concrete dailiness give us a vision of what's possible, some crafterly advice regarding how to proceed, and the courage to try.

"The trustworthiness" of our fellow citizens' minds, which Lisa Schneier proposes in the final chapter, is surely a hard idea to hold onto, and maybe even quixotic. But it's the only stance possible in the education of our children. This collection of accounts by working teachers makes this proposition abundantly compelling and offers some quite useful entry points for actually doing so—in each classroom or home workplace—tomorrow."

—**Deborah Meier**, Principal, Mission Hill
Elementary School, Boston

"This book by teachers for teachers about learning raises the fundamental question: How can learning be made exciting for both students and teachers? Their innovative approach specifies a process of mutual inquiry and discovery that begins with a real problem in all its complexity and emphasizes close observation and listening to the development of ideas. Detailed case studies of classroom dialogue, with students at various ages on topics ranging from physics to poetry, document the value of their approach and show how other teachers can adapt it to fit their particular contexts and carry it into their own practices."

—**Elliot G. Mishler**, Harvard Medical School

"This rich collection of stories by teachers in a variety of settings learning about teaching, and about learning, is a gift to those of us who love teaching, who believe in children's and adults' capacity both to teach and learn, and who see the potential for human liberation through education. Using detailed accounts of their work, the authors show the interesting, and often surprising, process and outcomes of what Duckworth calls "reciprocal stirring of ideas" among learners and teachers and the intricate relationship among ideas, feelings, and action. This book provides a close-up view of a foundational Freirean principle of learners constructing their own knowledge based on prior experience, new information, and meaningful dialogue with others. It also raises questions such as, what kind of knowledge must we have about the subject matter and our learners, and how much of our own vulnerability as teachers must we be willing to expose, in order to engage fully in Teaching and Learning."

—**Margo Okazawa-Rey**, San Francisco State University

"This compelling collection vividly portrays Eleanor Duckworth's notion of 'the having of wonderful ideas,' an educational practice, as you will see, typified by passionate teachers and engaged students, together collaborating in the 'collective creation of knowledge.' Every teacher and every student of teaching can profit from studying this book."

—**William F. Pinar**, Louisiana State University

"Spend time with Eleanor Duckworth and you will become a better educator. Her life's work has been studying the habits of engaged learners. In this delightful volume, she and her co-authors show how the best teaching grows from a close look at how we and others are learning."

—**Ira Shor**, City University of New York Graduate School

"TELL ME MORE"

Listening to Learners Explain

Edited by
Eleanor Duckworth

TEACHERS COLLEGE PRESS

Teachers College, Columbia University
New York and London

"miss rosie" copyright © 1987 by Lucille Clifton. Reprinted from *Good Woman: Poems and a Memoir 1969–1980,* with the permission of BOA Editions, Ltd.

Published by Teachers College Press, 1234 Amsterdam Avenue, New York, NY 10027

Copyright 2001 by Teachers College, Columbia University

Library of Congress Cataloging-in-Publication Data

Tell me more : listening to learners explain / edited by Eleanor Duckworth.
    p. cm.
   Includes bibliographical references and index.
   ISBN 0-8077-4041-1 (cloth : alk. paper) — ISBN 0-8077-4040-3 (pbk. : alk. paper)
    1. Learning, psychology of—Case studies.   2. Teacher-student relationships—United States—Case studies.   I. Duckworth, Eleanor Ruth.
   LB1060 .T46 2001
   370.15'23—dc21   00-053269

ISBN 0-8077-4040-3 (paper)
ISBN 0-8077-4041-1 (cloth)

Printed on acid-free paper
Manufactured in the United States of America

08 07 06 05 04 06 02 01 8 7 6 5 4 3 2 1

Dedication

We dedicate this book to Jean Piaget (1896–1980) and Barbel Inhelder (1912–1996), two giants whose theory and clinical research dominated the field of cognitive psychology in the twentieth century. Their work uncovered the powers of children's minds. The work described herein is built, both in theory and in practice, on a foundation they put into place.

Contents

Acknowledgments

The authors are grateful to Angela Valenti for remaining on top of all the necessary corrections, coordinations, and communications, between the United States, Canada, Puerto Rico, South Africa, and Australia. She worked throughout with thoroughness, resourcefulness, and good cheer.

And we are grateful to Susan Liddicoat for her insight, encouragement, and remarkable patience as our editor.

Introduction

Eleanor Duckworth

We teacher-authors of this book are passionate about human learning, and we trust that the stories in our chapters show why.

The chapters focus on various learners coming to understand various subject matter over days, weeks, or months. In each case, the author sought to engage learners in a subject matter and to follow the evolution of the understanding and the engagement over time. In each case, there is a narrative implicit in people's developing knowledge that is engaging to read. Taken together, the stories deal with learners of all ages, in a range of settings, and learning about a variety of subject matter.

Chapter 1 contains a description of part of a course in science teaching and learning, which entails the teachers becoming learners themselves and attending to themselves as learners. The chapter tells the story of adults who, through experiments of their own devising, learn about what makes things float and sink. (The main intent of the course was for them to learn about the nature of learning and teaching science. Learning about their own science learning was the heart of the course, but the chapter mentions only marginally how this experience touched them as teachers.)

That course in the teaching and learning of science in particular, one that I taught in Geneva for 4 years, served as the basis of a course that I now teach, designed for teachers of any subject matter (see Duckworth, 1996, pp. 122–168). Titled simply Teaching and Learning, it again features the teachers' own learning, but now in a variety of fields—science, math, poetry, history, and music, among others. Whatever the subject matter that they usually teach, they all become learners in the variety of subject matter addressed in the course. I introduce this variety in order to have each student have the experience of learning anew, both in areas in which they feel comfortable and in areas in which they do not. Since their time is spent with several different types of subject matter, their learning in any one of them is less deep than the learning about density that I write about in chapter 1. But their learning about teaching and learning, the real subject matter of the course, proves significant.

Throughout the course, we are considering the question, If we really believe that learners construct their own knowledge, what can we do to help?

Chapter 7 documents the growth in understanding about teaching and learning that takes place in such a course. Teaching in South Africa, Namane Magau engaged a group of teachers as learners, and gave them practice in engaging other people as learners, in the interests of their addressing that question. The subject matter of her chapter is the teachers' learning, not about science, math, or poetry, but about teaching and learning.

Between these two chapters are the following: Lisa Schneier in chapter 2 writes about a group of six 9th-grade students in a Boston high school as they engage with poetry; she presents a careful account of their work as they read their first poem together. In chapter 3 Hallie Cirino describes three preschoolers together learning to write stories. Ileana Quintero in chapter 4 describes a 9-year-old who was one of a group of elementary school students learning to map their neighborhood in San Juan, Puerto Rico; in this case, hearing the child's words is less important in following her development than seeing her maps. In chapter 5 Mary Kay Delaney, a teacher of political science, describes her work with two high school students learning about the nature of the American presidency; a lot happens in very few sessions. In chapter 6 Isabella Knox, a medical doctor in a neonatal intensive care unit, supports the learning of a medical student in that unit.

All these authors were in a teaching relationship with the learners they write about. This does not mean that they were necessarily in an *institutional* teaching relationship, although some of them were. It also does not mean that the authors were involved in explaining a subject matter to the learners. What it does mean is this: The author assumed a responsibility for sustaining the learners' continued interest in, and developing understanding of, the matters they explored together. It is *through* helping learners learn that we come to see what is involved in learning.

The author cannot simply be an observer of someone else's teaching. She has to be an active participant—a learner or a teacher. In all of these chapters, the author is the teacher. As a teacher, she is in a position to follow through on her hunches about what the learner is understanding, and what would be best to try next, in order to sustain interest and develop insights. The teacher-author must elicit and maintain the learners' interest in the subject at hand. She must keep the interest alive in the areas she thinks are fruitful to explore, probe for deeper or clearer responses, encourage the learners' confidence, and pose the next challenge. All this is in the service of searching for the sense the learner is making and of facilitating its evolution—a sense usually very difficult to seize, because it is usually very different from the teacher-author's own. At the heart of the teacher's decision-making is her understanding of the learners' sense at that moment.

There are thus two fundamental aspects to this kind of work: engaging and maintaining the learners' interest in making sense of the material; and finding out what this developing sense is. The two are interrelated. The attention we give in trying to understand the learners' sense plays a large role in keeping their interest engaged. (Many learners have told us how rare it is to have someone attend so closely to their thoughts and feelings about ideas.) And the intensity of their involvement plays a large role in their eagerness/willingness to say (or draw or write or otherwise express) what sense they are making. As Lisa Schneier has said: "If we listen, they will hear their own answers."

Two experiences influenced me in the development of this work. For one thing, I came into education through a science curriculum development project, the Elementary Science Study (1970). The premise of that curriculum work was that in order to learn about the material world of ice cubes, frog eggs, shadows, pendulums, or whatever, learners need the things themselves, not words about them. This premise has guided me ever since, and it guides the work in each of these chapters, no matter what the subject matter. To learn about babies, the learner pays attention to babies; to learn about teaching and learning, the learners pay attention to new situations of teaching and learning.

As important as that experience was, the major, and earlier, influence was the work that I did as a research assistant with the Swiss student of children's thinking, Jean Piaget, and his coauthor, Barbel Inhelder. Through this work I learned to investigate children's understanding by having them take their own understanding seriously, pursue their own questions, struggle through their own conflicts. To do this, I learned to talk with children in a way that kept them interested in the discussion and invited them to say what *they* thought about the topic. And I learned the importance and the challenge of *listening* well enough to understand what they were saying.

When I started teaching, I found that this was at the same time a way of engaging people—young and old—in pursuing their own learning. Finding someone who was interested in their thoughts, people became avid learners, even in fields that had not interested them before. My ways of trying to follow their thoughts turned out to be excellent ways to excite their learning.

With Piaget and Inhelder, I was caught up in issues of how people learn. One of the elements that most intrigued me in their work was the realization that ideas are inaccessible to learners in the absence of other prerequisite ideas. As I moved into education, it became fascinating to me to see how learners managed to move on from ideas that they held to more complex ways of understanding. It is this interest, as well as a passion for teaching, that has driven the development of this work.

We authors try to set up relationships between learners and a part of the larger world. We ask what they notice, what they make of what they notice, what interests them, what confuses them, what they make of what others say; we ask them on what grounds they think what they do, and whether they could say it more clearly; we make a hunch about what is behind what they say and check that hunch with them; we draw attention to seeming contradictions; we introduce new elements that we think may capture their interest in a different way.

References

Duckworth, E. (1996). *The having of wonderful ideas* (2nd ed.). New York: Teachers College Press.
The Elementary Science Study. (1970). *The ESS reader*. Newton, MA: The Education Development Center.

1

Inventing Density

Eleanor Duckworth

This is a story about the collective creation of knowledge: its multiple beginnings; its movement forward, backward, sideward; its intertwining pathways. The setting is a course in science teaching at the University of Geneva.[1]

A major part of this course was engaging the students in finding something out for themselves, through their own investigations of everyday phenomena; and then drawing pedagogical themes from this joint engagement. The major subject of study varied from group to group; we would try two or three kinds of activities until something caught on. In this group, the first one happened to catch on: why some things float and not others. It caught on partly because of some tantalizing phenomena that occurred in the very first session and partly because the members of the group (with one exception) were willing to acknowledge that they didn't know, couldn't remember what they ever might have been taught, about what makes things float. It was their willingness to be perplexed, and to struggle publicly with their own perplexities, that created the story.

The story covers eight weekly sessions. In addition to the work on floating and sinking, which took 1 or 2 of the 3 hours per session, we also watched the apparent motions of the moon, trying to fit observations with theory; we discussed assignments that the students carried out in their classrooms; we read Piaget and Inhelder; and we discussed their classroom teaching.

The class sessions were not tape-recorded. I was not setting out to do a study. But from the start I found the sessions with this group fascinating, and it happened that I was able to spend as many hours as it took to write down everything I remembered. I have re-created the story from those notes.

In addition to myself as the teacher of the course, the characters are the following:

Regular participants:[2]
Claire, Danielle, and Lise—kindergarten teachers; an inseparable trio
Colette—teacher of high-school-aged girls in their last year of a non-academic, not even vocational, program
Evelyne and Henri—a married couple; she taught nursery school, he usually taught 4th grade, but this year, as part of a special project, Henri was working in Evelyne's classroom
Ingrid—a Dutch student, doing a master's degree in education; having no class of her own, she did the weekly assignments with Jacques
Jacques—teacher of 5th-grade children in an immigrant neighborhood
Jeanne—2nd-grade teacher
Pierre—5th-grade teacher

Irregular participants:
Anna—South American doctoral student in education
Bertrand—African master's student in education
Helen—Canadian doctoral student in education
Stuart—American doctoral student in psychology, who carried out assignments in the International School
Robert—French physicist, visitor to one session

First Week: Early Ideas, Imaginative Explorations, Rubber Bands, and the First Reference to the Air Hypothesis

I asked the students to do what interested them with the following materials: plastic dishpans and pails; water; glass, plastic, and metal containers, with and without covers; escargot shells; nuts and bolts; odd pieces of wood, some hard, some soft; straight pins; corks; scrap metal; Styrofoam; rubber bands; plastic bags; toothpicks; aluminum foil; and a balance, consisting of a piece of pegboard with a plastic pan hung from each end (see Figure 1.1).

They were game, this group. It's not easy to create something respectable to do with such a nondescript collection of materials; and it is very easy to feel foolish.

The kindergarten group—Claire, Danielle, and Lise—started by putting things in containers and floating them (I overheard one of them say she was going to put some corks in a tin to make it lighter), before settling on seeing how many bolts they could place on a small raft. Starting with a square plastic cover, they examined whether it mattered if the bolts were

FIGURE 1.1. Pan balance

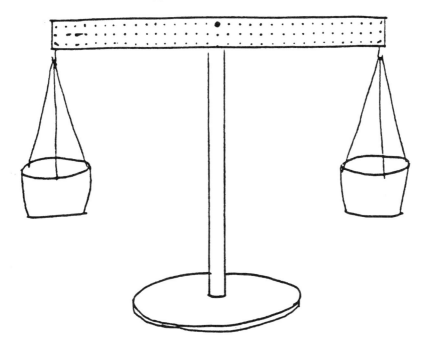

placed in the middle or around the edges; whether the size of the raft mattered; whether the material it was made of mattered; whether having a rim mattered. This group also screwed cup hooks into corks to see how many metal washers a floating cork could carry.

Colette, Pierre, and Henri were, by the time I saw them, holding pieces of wood by the corner, just barely, to hold them upright without affecting the depth of their floating, and trying to determine why some of them floated more deeply than others. The pieces of wood were of highly irregular shapes. They examined the pieces to see whether they were the same kind of wood, used the balance to compare their weights, and compared their volumes by pushing them down in a clear plastic bag of water, noting the height of the displaced water. When they later gave an account of this work to the assembled group, they said that they had concluded it was the volume of a piece of wood (as assessed by the water rise in the plastic bag) which determined how deep it floated. Among the evidence they presented were two pieces of wood that they said had the same volume, when it was clear to the eye that they in fact had different volumes. The three were nonplussed when I mentioned that; realized that their final conclusion was undermined; became dismayed over the difficulties of doing anything dependable; cast aspersions on the homemade balance as an example of everything that made the situation impossible (though when I stoutly defended my balance, Colette acknowledged that they were only looking for excuses); but did not think to question the wisdom of measuring volume by water rise in a deformable container.

Another group blew air into a plastic bag and added weights inside it, to see how many it would take before it would sink in a pail of water. They reached the point where it sat on the bottom of the pail and stuck out above the surface of the water. I asked them if it was then sinking or floating. There were differences of opinion. The idea occurred (though not at all easily, and perhaps it came from me) to put more water in the pail. They managed to cover it with water, but then could not decide whether it was touching the bottom. It moved when they stirred the water, but that was not convincing evidence.

After the break the whole class took up this group's problem: how to tell whether the plastic bag was touching the bottom of the pail or hovering just off it. There was no consideration of the relative likelihood of one or the other, or of whether an object ever stays put under the water, without going either up or down. They wanted to determine what this bag was actually doing; and after stirring the water, they couldn't think of how to tell. As a temporizing measure, until someone came up with a better idea, I suggested using a mirror. Somewhat to my surprise, it turned out to be helpful: holding the mirror on the bottom of the pail and looking down through the water, they could see, first, that the middle of the bag was not touching, and then that the points of it were (see Figure 1.2). ("Because of the distribution of the density," explained Pierre.)

When they saw its points just barely touching, they added more water, thinking that might float it off. It didn't. They wished they could add a lot more water, put it in a swimming-pool-ful of water, to see if that would float it. I proposed making a very tiny object that just barely sank in a cup of water, for which a pail of water would then be a lot—close to the equivalent of a swimming-pool-ful of water for the bag. They thought that that was a good idea. I made a tiny object of cork and clay, which sank very slowly in a cup of water and came to rest on the bottom. Predictions then were half and half that it would float in the pail. It did not float in the pail.

This idea that more water might support more weight then was modified—though nobody made this explicit—to the idea that more horizontal surface contact between water and object (later referred to as "the bearing surface") might support more weight. They found two identical small containers and weighted them with equal weights, distributed so that one

FIGURE 1.2. Weighted air-filled plastic bag in pail of water

floated upright and one floated flat (see Figure 1.3). Both sank, but the flat one sank more slowly. Everyone felt that that was inconclusive.

At one point during these experiments (which took some time to accomplish, given the nature of our materials), Pierre said that things floated if they had air in them and sank if they did not. I had expected this hypothesis at some point, since it always comes up. I knew, also, that there was no very direct way of countering it. I cut a small piece off a plastic bag and put it under the water. It floated up. I couldn't tell what most of the group thought, but Pierre said, rather weakly, that there were tiny invisible pockets of air in the plastic, which accounted for its floating.

The year before, I had discovered with my students a remarkable feature of our collection of rubber bands, to which I now turned. I tossed in a green one, and it floated. "Capillarity," said Pierre (a word commonly used in French, whereas we would say "surface tension"), "like a needle." I teased him for seeking refuge behind a word, and also pushed the rubber band underwater to show that it rose. (It did not occur to me, however, to show the contrast with a needle, which can be made to sit on the surface of water, but sinks once you push it under.) I then tossed in a blue rubber band, which sank. They were intrigued, and produced a color hypothesis, as a joke. (I said I liked that better than "capillarity"; I am not sure they understood why I did.) They pursued the color hypothesis and saw that indeed, the red, green, and yellow bands systematically floated, and the blue and white bands systematically sank. They were fascinated. Some-

FIGURE 1.3. Equal weights, one upright and one flat, sinking

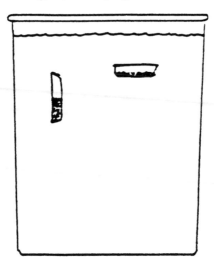

one tied together two rubber bands of different colors to see which won. They also tried a plain brown one. (It floated.)

In the midst of this, Claire, quietly by herself, tied a knot in a yellow band, as a better way to find out whether floating was influenced by the amount of "bearing surface." The yellow band still floated, and she was distinctly pleased with this neat test. She caught my eye at that point, to share her pleasure.

Second Week: Investigations Become More Systematic and Explanations Seem Elusive

During the early talk—of moon observations and work in classrooms—Colette said that her adolescent girls had not much patience for playing around. Above all, they wanted to know the answer. That took me aback—I didn't know to what question. To all the students in this course, it was obvious: why some things float and some sink.

What had I had in mind, then, if not that question? Not that there was some single nuggetlike answer. Rather, that whatever people thought about floating, it would be fleshed out, called upon to account for some surprises, attached to real-world complexities. I had hoped they would come to agree that this part of the world is more interesting and less simple than they had thought. And I had hoped that they would be able to see what it was like to figure out some of the complexities for themselves.

I asked whether there was anything from last week that they would like to pursue. They said rubber bands. Colette said, without elaborating, that a colleague of hers had commented that the dyes must have different specific weights. What she said seemed plausible to some, and nobody had any other idea. But it did not seem to anyone to be an answer.

I then proposed three problems as possible activities for the session, in order to develop some surer familiarity with floating and sinking phenomena.

1. For rubber bands, I asked them to try to quantify the various degrees to which the different colors sank or floated.
2. I posed a similar problem more generally: Do two sinking objects of the same weight need the same amount of some floating material to make them float?
3. And then I proposed taking some object that sinks and modifying it so it floats—specifying ahead of time which point on it would be uppermost as it rose to the surface.

Claire, Danielle, and Lise worked on the third problem, but started with a floating object rather than a sinking one. To arrange for a given point to be highest, while the object sinks, they found they had to add a weight underneath, "in continuation" of the point.

I encouraged them to do the problem as originally posed, and they tried the reverse procedure. Taking a stone, they specified the point on it that they wanted to rise, and they tied a piece of Styrofoam on the opposite side. They found that the Styrofoam turned the stone over, so their point rose last rather than first. They eventually placed the Styrofoam directly on the point that they wanted to rise first, but they were not satisfied with this solution, since the point was not the first point on the total object (stone-plus-Styrofoam) to get to the surface. Later, in discussion with the whole group, I asked if it would be possible to make an object such that the "floater" would not be topmost. They thought then of putting some floater on both sides, but wondered whether it would float up sideways. We were all interested in going further with this, but put it off.

The rubber-band group put their efforts into ordering the five colors. By racing them, ascending and descending through water, and by putting them in saltwater, they were able to tell that the whites were greater "sinkers" than the blues, and the yellows were greater "floaters" than the greens and reds. But they could not yet distinguish between the reds and the greens. The colors were size-coded, as it were: There were five different sizes, one size per color. But the sizes did not coincide with the floatability: The best sinkers (the whites) were the smallest, but the best floaters (the yellows) were not the biggest. To distinguish between the greens and the reds, their next idea was to tie one of each of them to a white one—one red tied to one white, one green tied to another white. When both now sank, they tied two of each of them to a white one. The green now sank, and the red still floated. They concluded that red was a better floater.

The fact that the reds were bigger didn't seem to enter into consideration. And yet they still felt puzzled. I think it was because they had established that the size of these rubber bands was not responsible for their floatability, and yet they were vaguely aware that in this case the size of the red might affect how much white it could lift. They felt they needed to know something about the nature of the material itself. I had already been suggesting that they cut equal-sized pieces from the green and red bands and use them in their experiments. Now I said that it was precisely in order to understand better the nature of the material that I had been suggesting that. They seemed, then, to find sense in my suggestion and carried it out. (The green carried more white than the red.) Of course that investigation did not tell them much about the nature of the different-colored rubber. But it did neatly establish the order of the colors, and they then felt quite satisfied with what they knew—the nature of the material seemed not, after all, to have been what was bothering them.

In the group discussion, I raised the question of how they might go further, and quantify the relationships between the colors. Several of them were particularly sharp, as together they thought through what they would have to do. They could, for example, use the tie-together-one-that-floats-with-one-that-sinks technique, provided they established equal-sized pieces. Or they could time the ascents and descents, as they had started to do, but through greater depth; or through the relatively shallow depths available here, but a hundred times over, taking averages.

Three different groups worked on the third problem. They all found, with some surprise, that different sinking objects of the same weight might need different amounts of floating material to float. The most striking instance was a small weighted plastic container that needed 15 times its weight in Styrofoam to float it. Pierre was in this group, and he maintained that an object floated or not according to the "volume of air" it contained. I tried to support any skepticism that Henri and Jeanne seemed to be tending to feel, by exclaiming that surely the Styrofoam did not have 15 times the amount of air. (Pierre had not claimed it did, but I wanted to push the matter.) Pierre's first reaction was that it could have, maybe not 15 times the volume, but 15 times the quantity. (The 15 factor, in fact, applied to weight, which might have been what he had in mind when he said "quantity.")

Later, in group discussion, he said that maybe five times was taken up by air; the rest was something else. I asked about the role of air in the rubber bands. Colette suggested that perhaps one dye had more air in it. They talked about how to know whether there's air in something. Someone asked whether there was air in water, and Pierre said, of course there is, that's how fish breathe. Jacques asked, how do we know it's air, maybe we should talk of a vacuum, or maybe it's oxygen. Maybe it's just how much space there is between the molecules. It's not molecular, Pierre said.

The "bearing surface" was again considered. Claire said that couldn't be a factor, because of her experiment the week before, tying a knot in a rubber band. Jacques agreed with her, but saw that he wanted to contradict himself—What about those water bugs that can stand on the surface of water because they have broad feet? Stuart said that his kids had found that aluminum foil floats in a sheet, but sinks in a small packet. Some thought that they themselves floated more easily flat than in a ball, but there was disagreement on this.

I tried to summarize the factors they seemed to be considering—surface, air, volume. All three times that I tried this summary, Pierre broke in whenever I said "air" to specify "volume of air." I finally paid attention, and asked why he thought that should be specified. I did not manage to understand what he was thinking, and ended up saying "quantity of air."

We came back to the question of whether there was air in Styrofoam. Danielle pointed out that you can crush Styrofoam, and she proceeded to do so. She managed to flatten it dramatically, and it still floated. She said that it was still a bit spongy, by way of saying that there was still some air in it. They compared its speed of rise from the bottom of a pail of water with a noncrushed piece and found no difference. Pierre, among others, said, "Of course." I told him that I thought he would have expected the opposite—that with less air, the crushed piece should be less of a floater. He saw what I meant, and responded (as the week before with respect to the balance) by saying that you really couldn't count on these makeshift materials for any dependable experimental findings.

At the very end of the class it occurred to me that if the Styrofoam was crushed underwater, bubbles should come out. About half of us were together after class to try it. Oddly enough, it was not clear whether any came out or not. We then squeezed with a vice. Bubbles were obvious this time. (But not, it seemed to me, with the volume one would have expected.)

Third Week: We Encounter Mysterious Pill Bottles, Statistical Rubber Bands, Floating Balloons, and Sinking Wood; and We Make a Detour

Colette had brought in two plastic pill bottles that one of her girls had given her. With no water in them, they floated. Full of water, they still floated! Only Pierre refrained from being surprised. He said, of course there's air in the water. Henri balked at this; he said he wasn't convinced it was due to air.

Jacques then upstaged even this puzzle, with a collection of colored rubber bands that he had bought and experimented with. Apart from the white, which systematically sank, the other four colors had a statistical tendency to sink or float, but you couldn't count on any one. Moreover, out of 10 blue bands, say, all 10 might be floating after half an hour, only 4 after an hour and a half, but 7 after four hours! Total mystification. I borrowed them to study at length myself.

We needed a change by then. That things that are lighter than (the same volume of) water go up and things that are heavier than (the same volume of) water go down did not seem to be an idea that was establishing itself easily through the collection of phenomena we had been studying. So far, they were tantalized and intrigued enough to keep pondering and to try to make sense of what they saw. That was the best possible position from which to proceed; but it seemed to me we needed to go down a different path in order to see similar questions from different angles. I proposed that we stop a frontal attack for a while, and go around the edges. They agreed to that, though they were clearly impatient to know "the answer."

The end run that I took was not the best, although a number of fruitful developments took place in spite of it. It consisted of focusing on air and water (and perhaps it came partly from wanting to catch the bubbles squeezed out of the Styrofoam). I knew that there were surprises in the interactions of air and water, tubes and containers, and that most of the surprises were explained if one only kept in mind that when put together, air goes up and water goes down. It seemed to me that this useful, simple principle might then be helpful in thinking about more complex objects. For some reason, it did not occur to me that I was highlighting the air hypothesis.

The surprises did occur, and the simple principle did emerge, but this work in general did not contribute to the developing ideas about floating. I shall mention only one main pursuit that related quite explicitly to the problem that was on their minds.

Among the materials available that day were balloons. I did not usually have a specific purpose in mind for materials that were available, but the balloons had been intended to make bubbles underwater, or to fill with air, or somehow to relate to what I had intended as the work of the day.

Jacques, Ingrid, and Anna, however, classically turned the materials to their purposes—filling them with water to see whether they would float! Colette's pill bottles must have been the inspiration for this enterprise. It was as if they set out to astonish themselves, and astonish themselves they did. The balloons did float; half full of water, almost full of water, and completely full of water, feeling very heavy indeed, they did float. Ingrid thought to try a balloon by itself, working hard to get every bit of air out of it, although she didn't think to empty the air underwater. It floated. She hadn't predicted that, nor the opposite. She accepted the outcome with interest, and pondered it. Most of the others didn't take much interest in it, but one person (was it Claire?) went on to tie it in knots, and noted that it still floated.

Later, when reporting to the rest, Anna said that the balloons floated more or less high according to whether there was more or less water in them. Almost everyone was astonished that they floated at all, especially Colette: "It feels so heavy!" Pierre, once again, was not surprised; of course, he said again, there's air in the water. It seemed to me that others besides Henri were unsatisfied with that refrain.

At the break, I brought out a gallon jar in which there had been a piece of wood in water since the year before. The wood was resting on the bottom. There was great interest in this. They wanted to know how much it had weighed when it was dry (I didn't know). They thought that it must have soaked up water, but did not understand why this water-filled wood sank while a water-filled balloon floated. As for what should be done with it, Claire said to take the wood out and let it dry. Pierre asked that it be kept as it was for a while, so he could try to float it, with air.

A couple of other remarks that evening bear reporting. In the face of our most dramatic instance of the reality and intractability of air, Ingrid wondered what happens when a boat turns over and sinks. For water to go in, the air has to go somewhere else. Where does it go? No one knew.

At another point I heard Jacques and another wondering together whether an object that sinks in a dishpan would do the same in a huge amount of water. I, of course, thought we had dealt with that the first week, with the tiny object that still sank in a bucket, having barely sunk in a cup.

At the end, I asked if they were still willing to pursue tangents, or if they were too impatient. They were impatient, but they said they'd stick with me.

Fourth Week: We Look for "Proper Places"
of Different Liquids and Try to Refloat the Wood

Two major activities took place in this session. I introduced a variety of different liquids, and most people worked with them. Henri and Pierre, however, preferred to try to float the old piece of wood. I shall describe their work first.

They believed that the water it had been in for a year must by now be airless, so they started by blowing bubbles through straws into the water. When this did not float it, they removed the wood to some fresh tap water, and again blew bubbles into the tap water. When the whole group gathered to hear about their progress, they made a third try—replacing fresh tap water with a solution of saltwater. Henri and Pierre's idea seemed to be the following: Although the wood was placed in new water, the old water was still what saturated it; since the old water was airless, they would have to get it out of the wood, before new, aerated water would enter it and make it float again. Recalling some version of osmosis, they reasoned that the saltwater would draw out the old water from the wood, and it would then be replaced by the new water, which would be aerated.

Most of the other members of the class, especially Danielle, seemed to think that this was pretty crazy—although Pierre's "scientific" talk of the osmosis phenomenon made some of them take it somewhat seriously.

Jacques said that a kid had told him that a clothespin had floated and then sunk because water had gone in and taken the place of the air that was there. He proposed this as a plausible hypothesis in the present case, but was not sure it applied. Ingrid wondered (again!) if a whole lot of water to float it in would make a difference. There was no very strong reaction to this thought; nobody took it as a suggestion for an experiment to be done at this point. Ingrid also said that entire logs are sometimes found sunk in lakes, where the water is not airless. Pierre and Henri said, yes, but they're rotten. Someone said that this one was, too, and I pointed out the stink. It was left inconclusive.

Pierre also said in this discussion that oxygen is what matters, not air. He asked if there was any oxygen in the top of the jar when I opened it. I said I was not sure, but thought not. And I pointed out that I didn't know whether what might have been there would have been oxygen or air or carbon dioxide or nitrogen or what. Pierre was sure that only oxygen would make a difference to floating.

The wood was left in the saltwater so the osmosis procedure would have time to work. Ingrid asked how long it had taken to sink. Since it had taken 2 or 3 weeks, she thought that one week was too short a time for this experiment. I pointed out that wasn't necessarily the case, since this procedure was not the reverse of the procedure that had brought about its sinking. They tended to agree with that.

As far as the liquids were concerned, I had brought salad oil, mineral oil, salt, liquid detergent, alcohol, molasses, and a heavy syrup. I had also brought, as coloring agents, ink, red food coloring, and iodine; and (for economy's sake) very skinny test tubes to work in. In addition to various liquids, there were various solids, in tiny bits—plastics, toothpicks, Styrofoam, seeds, rice, rubber, hardwood; and two large containers, one of salad oil and one of heavy syrup, in which they could try floating the solid bits.

They made a variety of intriguing or lovely effects with the liquids, most of which I shall not try to describe. At the beginning, at least, none of the work was directed toward answering any specific question. They tried to get to know the materials.

They shook liquids together and watched them separate from one another. They watched drops from one liquid rise or sink in another. Ingrid tried to dissolve each liquid in molasses. Alcohol was the one she did not try: all the other liquids were more similar to molasses, in something like "thickness" or "heaviness," and since none of them had dissolved, she thought it unnecessary to try alcohol.

In the general discussion, we looked at Evelyne's six-layered bottle. When she had made it, earlier, she had not known what each of the layers was, so I had asked her to try liquids two at a time. Now, redoing some of her pairs during the discussion, we found that alcohol tended to stay under the salad oil; but when we used a very skinny tube (nobody mentioned this necessary condition) and put oil in first, alcohol stayed on the top. The Claire-Danielle-Lise group said that the oil was "a barrier," and this was generally accepted, along with the observation that other liquids didn't form barriers—liquids went right through them to their proper places. (I do not recall who introduced the terminology of "proper places," but chances are that I did, since it is probably an anglicism.) They did, after this evening's work, have a general idea of which liquid went where.

In spite of this notion of proper places, some wondered whether one could make alternating bands of alcohol and oil. Some wondered whether, if one used a great deal of a liquid, it would sink down underneath a liquid that it otherwise floated on. Some thought it would not, though I did not take note of their reasoning.

At the end of the discussion, Evelyne said she did not see why weight mattered with liquids and not with objects. This was the first time I was aware of anyone (with the possible exception of Ingrid in her molasses work) thinking in terms of weight. I did not think to ask what she meant by that—what made her think the weight mattered, since nobody had weighed anything. I said, instead, that this was just the question to leave on, and we did. Nobody, all evening, had tried to float any solid objects.

Fifth Week: We Become More Familiar with the Liquids, and We Dry the Wood

The waterlogged wood was still not floating—neither in its saltwater, nor in new water. There was still a great deal of skepticism on the part of most of the group—especially Danielle—about why on earth it would. It seemed to me that Pierre was not sure whether he thought it was the water in the wood or the water around the wood that had to be changed. Danielle said that it didn't matter what kind of water was in it, there was water in it, and that's why it sank. Someone else, again, compared it to wood on the bottom of rivers and lakes. Pierre again said, but that wood is rotten; and it does matter what kind of water is in it, if this were oxygenated water, this piece of nonrotten wood would float. Lise said that then this piece of wood, once dried out and floating again, would not sink provided its water was changed every day, or stirred, or had air blown into it. Pierre and many others agreed that this would be a test of his ideas. So they set out, now, to dry it, after first weighing it wet, out of general interest in the comparison of its wet and dry weights. Claire and Henri did the weighing.

In the interest of having them develop a yet more solid feeling for the buoyancy of different liquids, I directed their attention to eight different questions:

1. What are the proper places of these liquids with respect to each other?
2. What is the lowest possible place for saltwater—that is, when it is as salty as it can get?
3. Which liquids form "barriers" and in what conditions?
4. Which liquids mix with each other?
5. On which liquids do the various solid bits float?
6. Does the amount of a liquid influence its proper place?
7. Can you make alternating stripes with two liquids?
8. How come we talk about weight with liquids, when we ruled it out with solids? (Evelyne's question)

Other points of interest arose, of course, both in individual work and in the discussion. These included the difficulty in separating certain liquids from oil, if they had been thoroughly shaken; characteristic ways in which different liquids move; what remains of various liquids after evaporation; curving interfaces; whether colors leave one liquid and enter another; and whether molasses is after all a liquid.

At one point, Evelyne had a container in which some drops went up and some went down, through a middle liquid. She said she thought that going up were air bubbles surrounded by alcohol and coming down were air bubbles surrounded by syrup. Pierre, beside her, maintained that they were solid drops—not air in the middle. His major reason was that if it's air it can't go down.

Henri reported that he had worked on trying to alternate layers, using syrup and salad oil. While on the whole the syrup was under the salad oil, a slim amount of syrup stayed on top. He had tried to thicken that layer, but it never got thicker; as he added syrup, it went down through the oil, leaving the small amount on top. It was not clear upon inspection whether this was a thin layer, or simply a ring around the edge of the tube. He had concluded that it was a layer, because when he posed a grain of rice in the middle, it was braked, before it went rushing down through the oil; he ascertained that in a tube of oil alone, without syrup, it did not linger at the top, but went immediately rushing down.

According to Henri, the grain of rice went through the oil and came to rest on the syrup. As we passed the tube, however, it went on down through the syrup to the bottom; Colette expended some effort trying to get it back to rest on the top of the syrup.

Claire, Danielle, and Lise tried floating different objects in different liquids. They prepared a set of plastic cups, each with about an inch of one liquid. They were disappointed, in general, not to find more differences from one liquid to another. Perhaps due to this dull outcome of their well-planned investigation, they began, after a while, to use grains of salt as objects, and drops of liquid, also. They seemed to acknowledge at the end that they were changing the liquids when salt or other liquids dissolved in them, but as they worked they were giving no thought to that fact.

Ingrid reported that saltwater could be made to be heavier than liquid detergent, but not heavier than syrup. In her tube, which contained, from bottom to top, syrup, saltwater, detergent, and freshwater, she dropped grains of salt, in the attempt to make the top layer slightly salty. It did not work; the grains went right down through all the layers.

Colette, working to establish the liquids' proper places first put alcohol followed by mineral oil, and then put mineral oil followed by alcohol. She convinced herself that alcohol stays on top. She then put in equal quantities of six liquids: syrup, ink, water, alcohol, salad oil, and mineral oil. She was not explicit about any reason for comparing equal quantities, but it was a first tiny step in a direction that led to important consequences later. There was a visual elegance to the array, even though three of the liquids mixed with one another. She had, from the bottom up, a layer of syrup, an obviously triple layer containing a mixture of ink, water, and alcohol, a layer of mineral oil and a layer of salad oil. Its orderliness was very appealing (see Figure 1.4).

FIGURE 1.4. A layer of syrup, a mixed triple layer, a layer of mineral oil, a layer of salad oil

Just before leaving for the night, Pierre tried to float the waterlogged wood, which seemed dry. It sank, in tap water, but more slowly than it had when they first tried it, he said. Claire had weighed it partway through the session. It seemed dry then also, but there had been no difference in the weight.

As we left, Jacques said we should get a physicist someday to answer all this. I said—with considerable hubris considering that I have no formal physics training—that I thought we could answer most of it ourselves.

Sixth Week: We Get a Physicist and Narrowly Escape Disaster

"Zut, alors! Robert a tout fichu en l'air tout ce que j'essayais de faire avec Pierre." (Zut, alors! Robert totally wrecked everything I was trying to do with Pierre.)

Robert was a physicist friend and colleague from a French university who was himself interested and engaged in working with teachers on the teaching of science from a Piaget-and-Inhelder perspective. We had often talked about our pedagogy. Specifically, I had been telling him about the investigations of this group, week by week. I knew our pedagogical approaches were different, but I had not realized how little he understood of what I tried to do. It did not occur to me to give him special instructions about how to behave this evening, especially since I had told him about it each week. As I introduced him to the group, I said I was asking him to promise not to "explain" anything; but that was the extent of my instructions.

Pierre spent the whole of the experimental period with Robert. I do not know what he asked nor what Robert said, but there was a lot of questioning and explaining taking place. My attempts to break them up became rather comic. Once I said, don't sit here next to Robert, he'll lead you into conversation. Robert said, I didn't say a word, it was him. I said, I know, but he's my student, I want to be polite to him. Jacques found that very funny. I think it was he who most appreciated the comedy of the evening.

In this session I wanted them to work more systematically with solid objects. I had prepared a tube in which I had liquid detergent, mineral oil, and alcohol—three liquid layers, with solid bits at both interfaces, as well as on the top and on the bottom (see Figure 1.5). They liked it a lot. Rather

FIGURE 1.5. Three liquids and four kinds of solid bits

than asking them to try to do something similar, I gave them much more focused instructions. Most of them had not yet paid attention to the fact that a given solid object might float in one liquid and sink in another. I knew what complications arise with more than one liquid at a time and judged that the previous two sessions had been amply characterized by such complications. Now I wanted the activity to be simple enough to provide some regularities. I asked them each, or in each group, to take one liquid and classify the solids according to whether they floated or sank in their liquid. Halfway through, I asked them to do the same with a second liquid.

I had given them yogurt containers to use, because their width would allow objects to pass each other, going up or down through the liquids. Everyone used them but Pierre, who used a test tube. As a result, the small objects had no room to pass one another; everything stuck together in the oil, and his findings turned out not to be useful.

Right at the beginning of the experimenting, he put a piece of chalk into his liquid, and as it sank a trail of bubbles rose to the surface. I asked him where he thought they came from. "It's a chemical reaction of some sort, isn't it?" he replied.

Near the beginning of our summarizing discussion, Robert intervened to ask what I meant by *proper place*—was it Aristotelian? I said it was our terminology. He said, yes, but for what? I produced an account that satisfied him, but I was rather short with him, which I did not feel good about in the context of the class. In general, instead of trying to explain to him what we were about while we were about it, I tried to proceed, cutting him short in order to minimize the damage, intent on telling him afterward what a nuisance he had been and why.

A variety of solid bits had behaved inconsistently, and we had difficulty deciding where they belonged—matches, straws, wood, aluminum foil. The best discussion concerned the question of what might make an object not go to its proper place: It might be pushed by another object on its way to a different place, and then get caught there; there might be bubbles attached to it; it might have a coating (*une carapace*) around it of some other liquid it had traveled through; sometimes they stopped at the surface of a liquid, unless you pushed them through it.

I asked them to go back to working out the four troublesome kinds of solids, with these factors in mind. They worked again for some time, but with inconclusive results. Many of them worked with aluminum foil, the hardest of all to understand. A sheet is so thin it does not break through the surface of the water, and a ball is full of air pockets—so in both these forms it stays on top of water, though the proper place of aluminum is on the bottom. Some were led to speak again of the "bearing surface."

Nobody ever drew a connection between the aluminum foil, floating needles, water bugs walking on water, and their observation that sometimes solid bits stayed at the surface of a liquid unless you pushed them through. With hindsight, I now wish I had drawn more attention and thought to that phenomenon right then. We never again came back this close to a discussion of surface tension.

This part of the evening's work, then, did manage to establish, in spite of a few confusing contradictions, the idea that both liquids and solids have their proper places in the floating order.

We then moved on to the now-dried piece of wood. Henri and Claire weighed it, as we all watched, putting the dry wood on one side and its wet weight (measured in pieces of steel) on the other. The equal-arm balance showed clearly that the wet weight was greater. Henri had the nice idea of finding the amount of water that corresponded to the difference in weight; it amounted to about half a yogurt container. (We wondered whether we had done this weighing accurately.)

It was my suggestion then to attach the weights to the wood to see if it would sink. It did, but not with a thump, as one of them pointed out. Someone said that that was how it had sunk when they first took it out of the water, but I am not sure that was true.

I had the idea of floating a fresh piece of wood in the old water, which we had kept. Everyone agreed that that would be a test of Pierre's hypothesis that the wood had sunk because there was no air in the water that it was trying to float in. We found a dry piece of the same kind of wood. And it floated in the old water. In spite of our agreement ahead of time about the significance of this experiment, there was a great lengthy discussion about these results, including discussion of various kinds of water and their role in floating wood.

This in fact became the very worst part of the evening, from my point of view. If there is any basic principle in my teaching, it's that people are to feel free to express their thoughts about what is going on and why, and that those thoughts are to be taken seriously. A number of the ideas that had been put forth throughout these weeks were quite fanciful, but we had always given them due attention and tried collectively to devise experiments that would check them out. Robert, by contrast, referred to several ideas as harebrained (*de la fouthèse*), whereas Pierre's ideas, which were no more clear, but expressed in scientific words, Robert reinterpreted until they made good sense; and then he gave them his support. I was too distressed to follow, let alone remember, what was said.

I did make some efforts to redirect the discussion, which included asking the group what they thought was the proper place of this wood—

floating or sinking. This did not lead to any great insight, even though they compared it, quite properly, with chalk, which floats for a while and then sinks, and said that you would have to know what timescale you were talking about. When they reached this point, Pierre observed that time was working against his hypothesis; no failures could be taken as conclusive because they were being carried out in a short timescale.

Near the end, Robert asked if he could say two things. I replied that he should judge, hoping that by now he had enough of my approach on which to base his judgment. I was wrong. First he lectured them on how it's all very well to do experiments, but it's not good enough, the point of experiments is to check a hypothesis; now Pierre has hypotheses, which makes the experiments they give rise to worth doing; but most of the rest of them—. Again, I wished he would go away. I did not try to develop my view that before you can form a hypothesis you have to explore, to develop a familiarity out of which hypotheses can grow; that the trouble with the science most of us have learned is that it is made far too neat—neat hypotheses, neat formulas, neat answers—before we have any sense of what the questions and perplexities are, so the science we learn never touches what we think about the world around us. Nor did I point out that Pierre's hypothesis was his greatest liability! In common with large numbers of people, Pierre didn't want not to know, and he had a hypothesis wonderfully suited to that purpose: If an object floats it's because it has enough air in it, if an object sinks it's because it doesn't have enough air in it. He could explain anything. And at the same time, he could hold himself back from any perplexities that might lead him to figure out something new. My hardest job was to move Pierre beyond that hypothesis. I wished that Robert would go away.

He didn't, however. His second point was to describe a procedure for finding the density of flour. Now, nobody had mentioned density all evening—neither the word nor the notion had figured yet in our talking about the issues. But he hadn't noticed this. He understood that a key to our questions was the notion of density, and he wanted to tell us about a neat technique that involved that idea—whether or not it had any relation to floating and sinking. (It didn't.)

I was, again, beside myself at this intrusion. This group of intelligent and willing adults had spent 6 evenings working toward an understanding of floating and sinking. It would make all the difference in their feelings about the accessibility of science if it were their own ideas and explorations that took them to this understanding. If Robert, discussing his fancy technique for establishing the density of flour, took that possibility from them, convinced them that they should have known all along that it was a simple matter of "density," they would lose most of the benefit of their struggle.

I was also beside myself when, in the course of his account, he described how wood, with its fibers and open tubes, differed in structure from Styrofoam, with its closed air pockets. (I had told him, in our week-to-week discussions, about the attempts to squeeze the air out of the Styrofoam.) *"Merde, merde, merde,"* is the close of this paragraph in my notes. And I would not know until the next session what the effects of these lectures had been.

But a better moment came already this evening. Robert based part of his explanation of the density of flour on the formula $p1v1 = p2v2$. Most of them had the confidence—which I like to think came at least in part from their experience in this course—to admit good-naturedly, if with some small embarrassment, that the formula meant nothing to them. Robert was astonished. Hadn't they taken physics? Of course they had! The formula nonetheless meant nothing to them. Robert explained it and continued with his account, but it was not clear that any of them followed.

Later in the evening, during the part of the class that dealt with their work with children, Henri gave a long statement on the virtues of "this method" compared with "the other method," and he referred to Robert's formula as something that they had all learned at some time by lecture and memory.

At some other point in the evening Jacques made a comment to the effect that experimenting was better than lectures, and Robert responded sympathetically to this criticism of lecturing, saying that what one remembered, in spoken discourse, was not what one heard but what one said. We all liked that. To me it seemed that it could have led Robert directly away from the kind of explaining he had been doing all evening.

Seventh Week: I Start My Journal, "Super Class, Super Great Class. (In My Opinion.)"

I started this class by telling the students how troubled I had been by Robert's visit. They were very sympathetic. Jacques said he was very like a Frenchman, having to show what he knew. Henri and Evelyne said something to the effect that he was always explaining, and why couldn't he not explain. Ingrid, who had left early, asked, oh, did he finally get a chance to talk, poor man, I thought he must have been very frustrated.

I said that I felt especially bad about having, essentially, withheld from them the chance to talk to a physicist—as Jacques in particular had said he would like to be able to do. Jacques, however, hardly seemed to remember; he more or less shrugged it off. I also said that I had become angry at him afterward for a few things; they laughed and said they weren't surprised. I said we had often talked about our pedagogy, and I had not realized that I should have explained more to him before his visit; they said it's hard to understand. Pierre, Danielle, and Lise, very unfortunately, were not present this evening.

After this discussion I felt much better. They seemed, above all, amused by the clash of fundamental views of how to help people learn science. I never would know for sure how Robert's interventions influenced their ideas about floating and sinking, but it seems to me that the net result was more confusion than clarity. He certainly hadn't made them feel there was nothing more for them to do.

This evening everyone worked together, standing around one high table. Colette said she wanted to do a final class with her students this week on floating and sinking, and she wanted to be ready. So we rolled up our sleeves. Henri said quite firmly, to start us off, that he believed it was air that made things float. Ingrid demurred right away; she did not think there was air in Colette's plastic pill bottles that floated. She spoke of "specific weight" (the French equivalent of *specific gravity*) but could not quite say what that meant.

I asked about the liquids: Did they think there was more air in alcohol than in syrup? They thought not, led by Henri. Henri said he thought that for liquids it was weight that mattered. I took a large amount of oil and a small amount of water, and pointed out that this oil would weigh more than the water. He then said he meant the weight for the same quantity. Colette had mentioned that her students had measured out equal amounts and weighed them. We had never done this in our class (Colette had layered equal quantities, but not weighed them), so she brought out their results. The girls had weighed one deciliter of each liquid. The order of the weights was the same as the order in which they floated on one another (with one exception). Colette was surprised; she had not noticed that her students had found a correlation between these two orderings. The group as a whole took the girls' work as convincing evidence that weight-for-a-given-amount was the relevant factor for liquids.

I went back to whether air was a necessary hypothesis for objects. Bertrand said he thought that for objects it was a question of the material they were made of. I asked what it was about the material that mattered; someone suggested that it was the amount of air it contained.

Colette very tentatively and very quietly wondered if it was the same for objects as for liquids. I asked her to say that again, since no one had heard it. She did, but nobody took it up.

A short while later, Claire said she thought Colette was right, and I tried to pursue the idea. I brought out a balloon full of water, floated it, and asked with what they would compare its weight. This proved more confusing than helpful. Colette suggested comparing it with the weight of the water in the tub. Some others said, no, it doesn't matter how much water is in the tub.

My idea with the balloon had been vague. To make a connection with their thoughts, I was groping as much as they were, and I moved toward the helpful questions stumbling as much as they did in moving toward the helpful ideas. In any event what I thought we needed next were two objects of the same volume and different weights. The objects I came up with were two identical capped bottles. I left one filled with air and put enough water in the other until it just barely floated.

I was now thinking of these two bottles as, themselves, objects with equal volumes and different weights. The water in one of them was meant to make it heavier than the other and just happened to be a liquid. I hadn't meant to draw attention to the contents in their own right. However, when I asked again, as with the water-filled balloons, with what we should compare the bottle that just barely floated, it was soon clear that nobody thought of the bottle-with-contents as a single object. It did serve a different purpose. Evelyne picked it up and looked at it closely—clearly looking at the water, not at the bottle-with-contents-as-object. She started to say that we should now fill this bottle with the various different liquids, one after the other—and then she stopped in confusion. It was a germ of an idea, not yet clear. Claire took it the next step. She said they should now try to see how much syrup they would have to put in the other bottle to make it also just barely float, and then how much alcohol, in yet another identical bottle. A few were about to try that, when some others said they already knew it would take less syrup than alcohol. They were about to let that drop, when I said—offhand, and really as a joke—that there would be more air in the one with the syrup. They laughed at my devilry, found this thought totally perplexing, and decided they had better do it. Lo and behold, when they did it, both bottles just barely floated, but one had more air! That was the single greatest blow to the air hypothesis!

Someone suggested weighing the two liquids, which led Claire to point out that this was already a balance. They had taken great pains to see that they floated at the same level, (namely, just barely), and since the bottles were identical, that meant the amounts of liquid weighed the same (see Figure 1.6).

While this work was going on, it became clear to me that to pursue Colette's idea that maybe it's the same for objects as for liquids, what we needed was not a just-barely-floating object but a sinking object, an object

FIGURE 1.6. **Equal weights of syrup and alcohol**

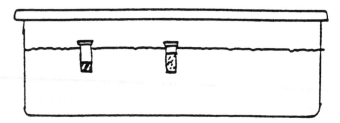

whose weight-volume characteristics would be different from the water around it. I tossed a rubber stopper into the water, and it sank. To follow up on Colette's idea, I asked, what we should compare it with? Once again, their ideas first took off in a quite different direction from what I had had in mind. Claire remarked, as she looked at the stopper, that objects don't weigh the same in water. There was considerable discussion of this phenomenon, the nicest comment being Stuart's explanation of why a pail of water is easier to lift under water: Under water you're only lifting the pail, while out of the water, you're lifting the water too. Jacques, during this discussion, lifted the stopper from the bottom of the pail through the water and a little distance into the air. He said he could feel a slight difference, though he said you would need to do it with something bigger (or did he say heavier?) to be sure.

Evelyne and Colette, during this time, had been struggling together to remember what they had once learned of Archimedes' principle. Jointly, haltingly, they produced the words: A body in water loses in weight the weight of the amount of water it displaces. I said to myself, well, there it is, they've done it by remembering. But it led absolutely nowhere! Everyone heard it, laughed at how far away it was from their struggles, and went back to work on their problem.

Claire made the first suggestion about what to compare the rubber stopper with, building on her interest in weight and ways of weighing things. She suggested measuring out its equivalent weight of water, then seeing whether it floated in syrup, and, if so, measuring out its equivalent weight of syrup. Although I was privately thrilled by this suggestion, it was not received with much interest by the group. We know it will take less syrup than water, people said. Others recalled that Colette had reported her students doing something similar with three rolls of Scotch tape (admittedly an unusual standard of weight): They had found out how much of each liquid it took to make the weight of these three rolls. Although Claire was hesitant about her idea, she stuck with it: Her one response to the reference to the girls' experiment was, we don't know whether the three rolls floated. It turned out that the stopper did float in syrup, and a couple of other people became interested in Claire's suggestion. Without being clear why, but, I think, with some sense it might be a good thing to do, they decided to do it. Claire did the weighing, and we ended up with syrup in one plastic cup, water in another, and the rubber stopper in a third, all weighing the same. People seemed to recognize that it was a neat little setup, but nobody knew what to do with it (see Figure 1.7).

As they were talking about it, my attention was caught by Jacques, fingering some materials hidden from most of us behind a bucket on the table and muttering to himself. After some time, he described a plan. In three identical goblets, put equal amounts of alcohol, and put these equal weights of syrup, rubber stopper, and water into these three equal amounts of alcohol (see Figure 1.8). All three will sink in the alcohol, we know, and then we can see how the alcohol level will rise in each case. (The amount of alcohol needed to be enough to cover the rubber stopper.) Few, if any, followed Jacques's reasoning. Why alcohol? they asked. They'll mix anyway, someone said. We already can see that the water will make it go higher than the syrup, they said. What will that tell us; we already know they all have the same weight. Jacques finally convinced most of them that it was true we knew the water would push the alcohol level higher than the syrup would, but we didn't know about the rubber stopper; he thought that since it sinks in one and floats in the other, it would push the alcohol to a level somewhere between the levels of the other two. He barely mentioned volume, and nobody ever talked about a relationship between weight and volume. But he certainly knew what he wanted to do and why.

It came out very close—especially between the rubber stopper and the water—but they read it as confirming Jacques's prediction. It was a good moment.

FIGURE 1.7. Equal weights of syrup, water, and rubber stopper

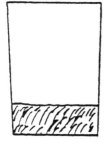 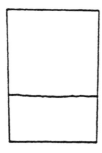 

FIGURE 1.8. Pouring equal weights of syrup, water, and rubber stopper into equal volumes of alcohol

I noted that Evelyne was still very perplexed. I did not quite follow what she said, but it concerned trying to keep straight the idea that, of weight and volume, one was kept constant across these three items (syrup, rubber stopper, water), and the other went in an ordered series, from less to more.

After much time given to considering the significance of what Jacques had done, someone (it might have been myself, or perhaps it was Claire) wondered about another object, which would float on water. Would it make the alcohol rise higher? We decided to make such an object, the same weight as the rubber stopper, and proceeded to make it from cork and plasticine. It took some time, of course, assembling it and checking until it weighed just what the stopper weighed, and then checking to see that it floated on water. Two goblets with the same amount of alcohol were readied. Jacques knew that this object, made to float on water, could not be counted on to sink in alcohol, and he was prepared to hold it down with the point of a needle if necessary. The moment was even more intense than during Jacques's original experiment, because by now almost everybody at least knew what they were looking for, if not why. It did sink. And when the alcohol level this time was the highest of all, the pleasure was great.

After it was done, Anna said that they hadn't needed to put the last object in the alcohol, because they knew its volume was bigger. How did they know? I asked. By looking, she replied. We took them out then, the rubber stopper and the invented object, to compare them, and most thought it was not obvious. I had actually asked them, before they put it in the alcohol, whether it looked larger, and nobody had paid any attention, including Anna. I believe that she was now so convinced of the idea that she simply convinced herself that you could see it.

Ingrid remained perplexed. The prediction worked for that object, but why should we assume it would work for another? We should make another object, the same weight as the stopper, that floats in water, but that is smaller than the stopper. There was considerable interest in that idea, but we had worked hard, and it was time for a break and to switch to other aspects of our class.

I noted that nobody ever spelled out what these experiments meant. There was hardly a mention of different volumes for the same weight, and certainly not a mention of trying different weights of the same volume. There was just a greatly satisfying sense for most of the students that they could produce something systematic and, to that extent, comprehensible. A couple of them mentioned that they still didn't know why the experiments turned out that way. It took another whole evening of work before most of them could relate this elegant experiment to the other phenomena they had been trying to understand.

At the end of the class, Jacques and Colette lingered, along with Helen and Anna. I asked Colette if she was ready to put things together with her girls. She said she thought the answer was specific weight. I asked her what that meant to her. She buried her face in her hands to think; what she came up with was not clear to me and I could not remember it. I asked how she now understood her pill bottles. She said something to the effect that they were light, without saying in relation to what. Jacques said if you melted them down and made a cube of them, that cube would float. He said it was like the balloons—full of water or not, they floated, so they floated. Colette said, so the plastic floats, whether full of air or full of water. I brought out the balloons, which were still in the cupboard—one full of water, and one two thirds full of water, but we did not get out a pan of water to float them in. Anna remembered that the amount of water in the balloons made a difference to how high they floated. Jacques said they floated at about the level of the water inside them. And when I asked Colette if she remembered how high her pill bottles floated, full and empty, she said she would have to do it again, but she thought that full of water they floated just at their caps, while full of air they sat on top. She tried now once again to say what specific weight meant to her: You have to state the weight per cubic meter, or something. It was still quite vague and, notably, showed an effort to repeat a school formula. In an attempt to turn her attention to what we had been doing, I muttered something about weight per anything, but she did not pick it up. I said that float or sink was a pretty crude measure—and also arbitrary. There was some acknowledgment of this point, but it was not a striking idea for anybody. I was annoyed with myself for not having given more attention to Anna's early observation about how high or low an object floats.

There were two other nice insights in the course of the evening's work. They seem related, but they were separate insights coming at separate times in the discussion. At one point, in considering the ordering of liquids that float on each other, Colette said, "And air is the lightest of all."

And in the discussion of proper places, Jacques said that a balloon filled with a gas lighter than air will float up until it gets to a place where the air is not heavier than it, and then stop, having found its proper place.

This class, by the way, was the last time the wood was mentioned. Colette, who had been absent the previous time, asked what had happened as it dried. They told her that it now floated, and that the loss of weight represented so much water. Jacques explained that they had been told about long openings in it that were initially full of air, which water replaced over time. Nobody went to look at it.

Eighth Week: Lingering Confusion, Consolidation, and Further Questions

In this session, I was, to begin with, greatly disappointed. In spite of my knowing that structuring complex ideas is never straightforward, I had expected that the previous week's breakthrough would have left clear marks of excitement and understanding. Excitement and understanding did emerge as the evening went on, but things were far from clear.

Jeanne and Evelyne remarked that the last had been a tough session—exhausting. Jeanne said she was more confused at the end of it than before. A number of people had tried to look things up in books in the meantime, or talk to more-knowledgeable friends. Colette, for example, had looked up plastic in a chemistry book, and found there was some oxygen in it—though she was not sure that meant that there was air in it. Helen had included discussion of this problem in her weekly telephone call to Canada. She said she thought they were so close now that people had to know. (And I had gone away thinking that now they did know.)

Henri summarized his understanding. There were three parts to it: One liquid floats on another if it weighs less, given the same amount; for solid objects the relationship between how big it is and how heavy it is matters; and the amount of air matters.

Considerable discussion followed about the role of air before Jacques said he thought he could account for everything with one hypothesis. He said it clearly—if two things weighed the same and one took up more space, it would float on the other—but he said it hesitatingly, so some did not follow him. Most did follow the second time he said it, but did not leap to agree. Colette in the meantime had also looked up *specific weight* in a book, and said that she saw a relationship between what she had read there and what Jacques had just said. She was able to say what she meant by specific weight this time; but of course in the standard definition, on which she based what she said, it is volume that is held constant, and weight that varies. Henri pointed that out that it was in that way different from Jacques's hypothesis. Someone else said it didn't matter; it amounted to the same thing. Henri repeated his point, but agreed that it came to the same thing, and nobody voiced disagreement.

Colette, during this discussion, said that her colleague had told her that the only importance of air was that it had an effect on the specific weight of an object. She did not say this very clearly; nobody followed up on it.

I drew Jacques's experiment on the blackboard for those who had been absent the week before. It went slowly, but we finally arrived at Ingrid's question: Could you make an object of the same weight as the rubber stopper that floated on water and that was smaller than the rubber stopper? At this point everybody went to work, some on that problem and some on more general ways they wished to check Jacques's theory.

Claire, Danielle, and Lise, with Helen watching, carried out an investigation based on one that Claire had read about in a book. They had a plastic ball that they could open to fill with plasticine. This they did, weighed the ball, put it in a container brimming with water, gathered the water it caused to overflow, and compared the weight of that water with the weight of the ball. The ball, which had sunk in the water, weighed more. Then they removed some of the plasticine, until the ball just barely floated, and found that it now weighed the same as the overflow water (see Figure 1.9).

The third phase of the experiment was a little confused, I think. When they removed the rest of the plasticine, and the ball floated high on the water, it displaced a good deal less than its whole volume. The book talked of weighing the amount of water that the ball now displaced, but this had, so far, no basis in anything that the students had done, nor any of the questions that they had had. That led to some confusion on their part about what

FIGURE 1.9. A glass full to the brim and water; a ball with much plasticine, or a little plasticine, or no plasticine

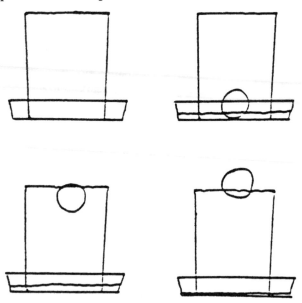

they were doing, why they were doing it, and what they might expect to find. I believe that they were weighing the amount of water now displaced by the floating ball and expecting this water to weigh more than the whole ball, confounding the book's experiment with Jacques's experiment. And I believe that they convinced themselves that that was the case—not hard to do with the difficulties of accuracy presented by a small high-floating object and a wide container.

Jacques chose to check his theory with a ball of aluminum foil. I was annoyed at his choosing this difficult-to-manage item (I thought I should have noticed in time to steer him into using another material), and it was problematic. But with his using a vice to squeeze out enough air so it sank, and using a narrow test tube so a water rise would be most easily visible, it did confirm his predictions.

Pierre was more interested in talking out ideas than in experimenting. Now he *was* perplexed—and productively so. He engaged Stuart and me in a discussion of the nature of density. We are 15 people in this room, he said, that's the density of people in this room. I said, that's the number. He said, but take another room, with a different number of people, that would be a different density—the number of people for the surface, that's what density is, isn't it? So we can say the same for objects, can't we? That's why there's more weight for the surface. That's why they can have the same size and one be heavier—it's denser. At one point, when he took a hollow plastic ball and spoke of the amount of matter for the surface, I finally exclaimed, "For the volume." He said, yes, surface or volume. It's not the same thing, I said, and he replied, yes, volume. I was not sure what that meant to him.

But he clearly was thinking about his questions here, and I clearly failed to follow a practice which I am quite sure would have been useful. Instead of picking up on what wasn't quite right—he was speaking of surface where we had been working with volume—I could have picked up on what was profoundly right in what he was saying: That's why they can have the same size and one be heavier—it's denser.

Alas, I was extremely tired during this class, feeling neither patient nor inventive, and I did not manage to find the ways to help him think through the ideas he was finally grappling with. Simply asking him to say more about that one thought would surely have helped.

Pierre was also concerned with experimental issues: You can never do a proper experiment, never check on what makes it float, because all the factors are intertwined; you can't keep both weight and density constant and change only volume, for example, so you can't do a well-controlled experiment. He and Stuart kept up this discussion as I left—Stuart developing the view that you could nonetheless do a well-controlled experiment.

The most intriguing set of experiments was the work on Ingrid's question, carried out by Evelyne, Henri, and Jeanne: Could we make an object that floats on water and takes up less room than its equivalent weight of water? First they used a snail shell, stopped with plasticine, and floating. It turned out to be bigger than its equivalent weight of water. Then they tried to make many objects smaller than it, that would also float. They tried cork with plasticine, Styrofoam with coins, cork with coins. All of them, at the same weight as the snail shell, and smaller, sank. I overheard many statements that started, "What we need now is . . ." and then responses of two sorts—either no, then it would be too big; or no, then it would sink. Henri concluded that it was impossible. Jeanne and Evelyne did not. Jeanne exclaimed, "Everything's possible in science," and considered that they just did not have the right materials. They needed the right kind of plastic—like Colette's pill bottles.

After this working time we assembled again, and this second discussion was rather more encouraging. At the beginning of the discussion several people said that things were clearer now. Jeanne volunteered that she now understood Jacques's experiment. Ingrid then said very slowly and hesitatingly approximately what Jacques had said at the beginning, adding that it depends on the liquid. Again, she had to repeat it, in order for people to follow what she was saying, but then many indicated agreement. She herself was very surprised that it depended on the liquid. She had not seen the point of doing different liquids until last week; she seemed quite moved by the depth of her present understanding of this matter.

Lise, at this point, said that it does not depend on the liquid, and a very long discussion ensued in order to clear up that disagreement. It turned out that Lise was referring to the fact—which came to her group as a surprise—that the plastic ball, submerged, displaced the same amount (not weight) of syrup or detergent as it did water.

In the course of that discussion, in listening to the students describe their experiment, Ingrid predicted that an object that just barely floated would weigh the same as its volume of water. She was delighted that their experiment confirmed that.

Jeanne, Evelyne, and Henri described their attempts to make an object that floated on water and that took up less room than its weight of water. I asked the whole group who among them thought it was possible. Jeanne and Evelyne did. They were doubtful about it, given everyone else's views, but they did not see why not.

I asked Henri what he thought now about his three hypotheses. He said he still thought they were right, and he repeated them. This time, the weight-volume relationship was stated clearly, and the air hypothesis became "And then if there is more or less air, that makes a difference to the weight-volume." He thought, too, that he could take any object now and predict whether it would float or not: weigh it against water, then put it and the same weight of water in equal amounts of another liquid and see which takes more room . . . and so on. There was general agreement.

Jacques and Stuart both seemed clear that the air hypothesis was not necessary. Jacques said it quite clearly—it was taken care of in the weight-volume relationship. I did not sense a universal rallying round, but a general sense that he was probably right. We kept coming back to it, though.

Ingrid, who said that until now she had never understood the balloons—they were heavy, so why didn't they sink—came back to them in this final discussion. She quoted a girl in Jacques's class who had said, "Water goes with water and the balloon floats." She said that she had not understood at the time what the child meant, but she did now, and liked it a lot. Jeanne admitted that she did not understand this, so we brought out the balloons again. Watching them float at different heights, according to the amounts of water and air in them, everybody came to understand what the child meant. They noticed again that the water levels were even, inside and outside of the balloon. They noticed also—it was the first time it was mentioned—that the air was always at the top; Stuart said, "Air floats," which they liked. Ingrid said that if the balloons were filled with syrup, instead of water, they would sink. And full of oil, I asked. They would float, but higher.

And what if there were a vacuum inside, Ingrid now asked. (Ingrid used the French *vide*, which means both "vacuum" and "void.") I took a capped jar, full of air, which floated, and asked what it would do if we removed the air. Most people thought it would sink. They mainly seemed to agree it would weigh less, but thought it would sink anyway. Claire gave the major clue to this reasoning: She thought that perhaps the volume would now be different. I did not find out for sure what she meant by that, but my sense is that it is a view of volume that takes into account how much of the volume is filled with matter. If a jar has air in it, then the whole system is full of matter, and each part of the system takes up space. If it doesn't, then the inside, left to its own devices, would not take up any space and the only "volume" is that of the glass itself and of its cover. It is a notion of volume partially contaminated by a notion of density. (This interpretation seems to me consistent with the way everyone looked at the bottle I had prepared in the previous class—the bottle weighted with some water, which I had intended to be seen as a single object, bottle-with-contents. Nobody thought to look at that as a single object, having weight and volume—the contents demanded too much attention in their own right.)

Ingrid tended to think that making a vacuum would be changing the conditions enough so that a different theory might be needed; after all, theories hold in certain conditions, and often you find that outside those conditions they must be modified.

Jacques predicted that it would still float; he fit the situation easily into his general one. (Though I do not know if he thought it would float higher.) But apart from him, and perhaps Stuart, there was no certainty, no way to think about this question, in relation to the work they had done.

At another point we had a small glass bottle, which, filled with air, sank. Someone suggested filling it with Styrofoam instead, but everyone came to agree—I noted that Jeanne was among the most adamant—that it would not float then either; it would be still heavier.

Pierre continued to think about the air hypothesis. Couldn't you say that air had something to do with it, more air floated more? Jacques made a very clear statement to the effect that it simply wasn't necessary, with which I finally allied myself. I wish I had asked Pierre to go back to his thoughts about density, and say how he saw the air hypothesis fitting in with those. Or I wish I had had him think about the vacuum jar from the point of view of his thoughts about density. But I did neither. And Pierre was not swayed by Jacques and me.

In one of the last points of discussion, we came back to boats. Claire asked how come plasticine sank, in a ball, but floated when posed on the water shaped like a boat. Then she answered her own question—it's now taking up more space in the water. Everyone seemed to understand and agree, and she was very pleased with herself. It seems to me now that this would have been a good time to ask her again what she thought about the volume of the vacuum jar. But I missed it at the time.

It is only now—while working on *revisions* of this account—that I have noticed that, with the exception of Robert's lecture and Pierre's solo discussion, the term *density* never appeared. *Specific weight* did. But whenever anyone referred to Jacques's experiment and the relationship between weight and volume, the term they used was *weight-volume*. I do not even know whether Pierre knew that weight-volume was density and wanted to understand that better or whether density represented something different for him. I have the same question about what Lise wrote in the postscript that follows.

So the group "invented density," but gave it their own name. I expect that at least some of them did not know that what they had invented was the idea of density; and that for them the word density still represented something else, that they may or may not have thought they knew something about. I wish I had caught on to that in time to say simply, "What we've been calling weight-volume is what is ordinarily referred to as density."

Postscript

A few weeks later, each of the 10 regular participants wrote a brief paper about their learning about floating and sinking.

Claire, Danielle, and Lise all seemed to have internalized Jacques's experiment (to which of course, Claire had made major contributions) and to feel they had gone one step further with their experiments the last day.

In addition, Danielle wrote of her understanding why one small jar sank while one large jar floated:

> I found that strange, and was sure that it was because there was a lot of air in the big one, and less in the little one, but I couldn't go any further. Then we left that, to work on the "proper weights" [sic] of liquids: we came to realize that the weights of the liquids, in relation to the volume they occupy are different according to the liquids, which implies that they can float on each other. So, in alcohol, the lightest of all the liquids that we saw, objects float, but less well than in water, which is heavier in relation to the volume it

occupies. I thought then maybe, in spite of the air in it, the big jar would sink in alcohol, thus, that there was a parallel to make between the weight in relation to the volume of the object and the weight in relation to the volume of the liquid.

Claire wrote a wonderful account of the ups and downs of her coming to the conclusion, once and for all, that the "bearing surface" is not a factor in floating. She ended:

> In retrospect I realize . . . that in fact the shape doesn't change anything about the property of the object etc. If the volume is the same, the shape can be as different as can be and that doesn't change anything, it's the law of conservation of quantities. For a given volume, we can give it any shape, and that will not change anything about its property, if it floats, it will float, even with another shape etc.

Lise wrote of the same issue (referring to the same experiments they had done together) in slightly different terms. She also wrote:

> If syrup is heavier than water, we know that it has a greater density than water . . . but in fact why is it so and what exactly is density. It seems to me that we never talked together about what density is.

Colette described four stages. First was "'fog': what are we looking for? What is expected of me?" Then "'clearing': enumeration of different factors . . . and verification of their relevance." She wrote, "I was able . . . to assure myself that none of these factors alone was the cause. I confess however that for a long time I attributed a predominant role to air." The third stage was "'confusion': the appearance of terms and principles from physics, and the impossibility of relating them to the factors we had been working on." And finally, "comprehension, but I must admit that I am not sure that I would have reached it without the theoretical explanations I was given."

For Evelyne, comprehension did not come. Here is part of what Evelyne wrote:

> Everything went well until the second to last lesson. The more I manipulated, the more I was satisfied, and the more I had the impression that all these different approaches would soon lead me to understand the problem of floating. Yes, I would have liked to consult books and good old Archimedes was in my mind. But each

time I decided against it because I was afraid I would lose my ardour for manipulating, and would fall back into book knowledge. This concern was accentuated when our visitor chose to dazzle us with $p1v1 = p2v2$.

At this time in December I felt generally that I was becoming less receptive, in the class and elsewhere. And when Jacques had a wonderful idea, it certainly was that for him and maybe for others (cf. Henri) but for me it was the coup de grâce. In an instant, everything collapsed and everything I had brought to bear in the preceding sessions was wiped out. I had the impression that all was but wind.

In the disorder, Henri tried to help me out, but no matter how much he explained to me, made me drawings, and repeated it to me in different forms, nothing was internalized. I seem to understand for the moment, but when I have to re-explain it, I get muddled, and nothing is coherent any more. . . .

Personally, it [the situation] doesn't discourage me at all. It is perhaps the best proof that I still need time to continue to manipulate, while I try to form hypotheses. Because while in the first session I was able to "play" without any clear goal, now I feel very deeply the need to know what I want to. So now I have to begin to form hypotheses, so I can verify them. All this will make me relate my different manipulations to each other, so as to find the link among them.

Henri wrote:

The first time, it seems to me, that I began to feel an answer to the floating problem was when Jacques Bonnard did his experiment with the stopper, syrup, water and alcohol, and he observed, at equal weights, the volume of the first three in alcohol. This clicked for me. From then on I only tried to confirm or invalidate [these ideas].

He gave an extremely clear account, with no mention of air, of how to predict whether a given object will float in a given liquid.

Jeanne wrote little about what she now felt she understood of floating and sinking (she wrote more about pedagogical insights). But she did write the following:

These discussions, above all the [last two] were for me steps forward. Sometimes my mind was completely muddled and then the next week glimmers would appear. For example, after Jacques' experiment I was disequilibrated and the discussion the next week was helpful. I have the impression of having understood . . . why one object sinks and another floats.

She also had the following interesting comment:

I have opened my eyes to a lot of notions that hadn't interested me before. For example: why in a mountain chalet does the condensation form on the outside window, while in my Geneva apartment it forms on the inside window? One question leads to another and another. You start asking about everything.

Ingrid wrote:

I think that alone I never would have taken the next step. I do not remember how we came to the idea of weighing the object and taking a quantity of liquid that has the same weight as the object and seeing whether the object has a greater or smaller volume than the quantity of liquid and thus predicting whether the object floats or sinks.

She was the only one who referred to the aluminum foil, and acknowledged not understanding a number of phenomena (those that in fact depend on surface tension).

And Pierre? Here is some of what he wrote:

In the beginning I had ideas stemming from previous personal experiences and physics courses in high school. I have to say that these ideas have not changed; rather they were refined, reinforced by becoming more real as a result of the manipulations during the course.

As the sessions went by, I was more and more convinced that the phenomenon . . . results from a set of intertwined factors and that it was just about impossible to isolate some factors without bringing in others. This was also confirmed for me by our physicist-visitor.

Currently, as far as the experiments carried out in this course are concerned, it seems to me that the factors involved in floating/sinking are the material the object is made of, the air it contains, the form and the mass of the object. When I speak of the form, I am thinking of a very thin needle.

Thinking back on everything I've done, I note that I observed many things, but I don't have the impression of gaining understanding of fundamental aspects of the phenomenon of floating.

Jacques I have saved for the end. He wrote at length about the phenomena that particularly caught his interest (starting with the rubber bands), and how they affected him, before moving on to consider the effects of working as a group.

The experiments of the others, their discoveries, their conclusions, the discussions that we had at each session were for me the stimulus to keep going with the search, the opener of new tracks to follow, the confirmation or disconfirmation of my own findings.

His inclusion of details of time and place, as he closes this section, makes it sound like a moment of historic importance.

And I think that if, the 13th of December, 19——, in the Dacha [our small classroom building] between 7 and 9 p.m., everyone present (at least I hope so) came to grasp the principle of floating, we can attribute a part of the success to each of us.

And after considering many of the elements that went into the class and his involvement in it, his final paragraph expresses again his own excitement.

Each Tuesday evening, all propositions, good or bad, right or wrong, could be made, and never was any value judgment brought to bear on them. Everyone had the occasion to have wonderful ideas and to be proud of them. To the point (please forgive me if this appears somewhat presumptuous) that I currently have the very validating feeling of having myself discovered the principle of floating.

Commentary

• The idea of density was clearly a collective construction, extending even as far as to include some of the group members' students. It was not simply a matter of pooling results. It was far more a matter of intellectual exchange in the search for understanding—an exchange in which one person's idea stirs another's. The seventh session is the most striking example of this kind of reciprocal stirring of ideas, but it characterized each session, and Jacques's closing comments speak to it eloquently. Often the contributions are made backward or sideward: One person's idea is not immediately taken up as such, but suggests something else to another. Piaget speaks of *tatonnement,* groping toward an understanding, with stabs in a general direction, guided on the one hand by some feeling about where things aren't quite working right, and on the other hand by a recognition of familiarity with something you know. Transferring back and forth between different minds, the process is more visible here, and there are more different sources of tentative ideas to try out, but I think it may be very similar to what takes place within one mind.

• The work was characterized as much by feeling as by ideas. Playfulness, mystification, laughter, excitement, frustration, trust, confusion, fascination, determination, appreciation of visual beauty, enjoyment of one another—all of these were involved in keeping the work going.

• I am impressed that powerful ideas are so meaningless and hard to recognize before the frame has been built into which they can fit. A special case is that of critical experiments that turn out not to be critical. In the first class, we conducted a critical experiment to see whether an object that sank in very little water would float in a larger container of water. The object sank in both, but the question kept coming up for weeks. In the sixth session, everybody agreed that a certain experiment would test Pierre's hypothesis that the wood had sunk because there was no air in the water in which we tried to float it. But when the experiment was done, the results gave rise to endless interpretations.

Perhaps the most dramatic instance of a critical experiment not being critical was the supplement to Jacques's experiment, in the seventh and eighth sessions. The prediction was that an object of the same weight as the rubber stopper and that floated on water would take up more room than the stopper and more room than its equivalent weight of water. For those who followed the ideas, and had some way of understanding the point of his experiment, it was an exciting confirmation. For those who did not, it proved nothing: It worked for this object, why should we believe that it will work for another? The critical experiments themselves cannot impose their own meanings. One has to have done a major part of the work already: One has to have developed a network of ideas, into which to embed the experiment. Jacques did the major part of the work in his mind, assembling the ideas that his experiment then could confirm (and I wager that if the experiment had not confirmed it, he would have redone it until it did)—and when he first did it, he was the only person for whom it meant anything.

• I am intrigued that Jacques's invention took the form of holding weights constant and comparing volumes. Was that largely due to the circumstances of the activities we pursued, or is the notion somehow more readily apprehensible in this form than in the standard "measure out equal amounts and then weigh them"? For liquids, measuring equal amounts is pretty simple, and this procedure did occur both to this group and to Colette's girls. For solid objects of random forms, measuring out equal amounts is no easy job. The liquids served as an intermediary, first for finding equal weights, and then, after one more step, for finding equal volumes. The sequence can be summarized as follows:

It started when I chanced to put different liquids in identical pill bottles to make two objects of the same volume and different weights—the classic approach to thinking about density. The liquids in the bottles weren't meant to be the object of attention. But Evelyne then had the idea of somehow comparing various liquids in these identical bottles. Claire had the idea of putting, in each of several identical bottles, just enough liquid, a different one in each bottle, to make it float. Then another person questioned the weights of these different amounts of different liquids, and it was agreed that these different amounts weighed the same. Then later, in the presence of the rubber stopper, Claire had the idea of finding *its* weight in different liquids—a big step, which she took after she noted Colette's wondering whether the answer to their question might be the same for objects as for liquids.

It was after all this had been done—with one object and two liquids, all of equal weight, lined up before him—that it occurred to Jacques to look at how much room the object took up compared to the room the liquids took up.

• I was also intrigued that density turned out to be such a difficult idea. What is it that is hard about putting those particular ideas together? Evelyne gives us the clue that the difficulty is in developing two systematic sets of relationships, while separating them and integrating them both at the same time. A global idea of *amount* must be differentiated into *weight* and *room-taken-up*. Each object has its rank order on each of these scales, which sometimes seem related to one another and sometimes don't. The hard part may be straightening this out—are they dependent on each other or aren't they? And then the two ideas must be integrated back together into an idea that now is different from the original, undifferentiated one.

• I think both Pierre and Evelyne merit special mention. Pierre was the one member of the class who did not, at least during the first six meetings, seem to make himself vulnerable by acknowledging how much he did not know, by putting forth ideas he was not sure of, by expressing his surprise. In the final class, when he was struggling with ideas that he acknowledged not to be clear, I did not do a good job: On the one hand, as I have said, it did not occur to me that he (or others) might not have made the connection between what they referred to as weight-volume, and what the rest of the world called density; on the other hand, I did not follow through with him on the ideas he was grappling with. He came a long way to get to this place, I believe, and I wish I had managed to help him build from there.

As for Evelyne, I was much relieved to read "it doesn't discourage me at all." I note with interest the fact that Henri's explanations did not help her. I find her own account deeply interesting. She had a wonderful time finding out about liquids and floating phenomena, convinced that at some point everything would fall into place. She did not herself work at how they might fall into place, developing her own hypotheses as she went, but I share her conviction that when she does, the ideas will come and the coordinations will happen.[3] I would have loved to be there when it happened.

Notes

1. This chapter is for Claire, Colette, Danielle, Evelyne, Henri, Ingrid, Jacques, Jeanne, Lise, and Pierre, who put themselves on the line as learners in the search for greater understanding of learning and teaching.

2. These name and all the names in later chapters are pseudonyms.

3. In fact, Evelyne's first-person account gives support to the findings of Karmiloff-Smith and Inhelder (1975).

Bibliographic Information

Inhelder, B. and Karmiloff-Smith, A. (1975). If You Want to Get Ahead, Get a Theory. *Cognition*, Vol. 3, pp. 192–212.

2

Apprehending Poetry

Lisa Schneier

miss rosie

1   *when i watch you*
2   *wrapped up like garbage*
3   *sitting, surrounded by the smell*
4   *of too old potato peels*
5   *or*
6   *when i watch you*
7   *in your old man's shoes*
8   *with the little toe cut out*
9   *sitting, waiting for your mind*
10 *like next week's grocery*
11 *i say*
12 *when i watch you*
13 *you wet brown bag of a woman*
14 *who used to be the best looking gal in georgia*
15 *used to be called the Georgia Rose*
16 *i stand up*
17 *through your destruction*
18 *i stand up*

—Lucille Clifton

This is the story of six high school freshmen joining with me in study-ing a poem, "miss rosie." If you are not familiar with the poem, let me suggest that, before reading this chapter, you spend a little time reading it, letting yourself have your own thoughts, feelings, and questions about it. Some of the students' questions will also be yours, and others will take you by surprise. In this way, you will have your own background against which this story can stand.

I need to note that the students did not see the poem as it appears here. I first encountered the poem in a collection of teaching materials, and that copy was incorrectly written with standard capitalization. (The title was capitalized, the first word of the poem was capitalized, the "i"s were capitalized, and the word "georgia" in line 14 was capitalized. The words "Georgia Rose" were also capitalized, as they are in the correct version.) I am not sure what the source of this copy was, though I have tried to investigate that.

This poem was my first encounter with the work of Lucille Clifton; it was through this poem that I got interested in her work. If I had been more familiar with her poetry, I would have known to check the accuracy of the copy of the poem that I had encountered, because I would have known that as a rule she does not use standard capitalization. Her capitalization is purposeful.

I gave the students this capitalized form of the poem, not knowing at the time that it was inaccurate.

I deeply regret the fact that the students and I did not work with an accurate version of the poem. I regret this because the capitalized form I gave to the students violates the true poem; and also because the students and I therefore missed the poem's full impact. I can imagine how interested they would have been in discussing the matter of the poem's capitalization, had they been working with the poem in its correct form.

In the work presented in this chapter, the students' and my quotations of the poem include the capitalizations noted above, since those were part of the poem as we were then studying it.

I conducted this work in the urban high school where I taught. The students and I worked together for 5 weeks on poetry, spending our time essentially on three poems. These were not my students before this work; for my thesis research, I worked with six students of another teacher for their unit on poetry. I was interested in following the students' ideas as they read and studied poems, and in doing this with a small group so that I could focus extensively on what they said. I also wanted to keep them interested in studying each poem over time, giving them room to deepen and extend their initial ideas and feelings about it.

I asked for students from the lowest of the four ninth-grade English "tracks" or skill levels. I did this to counter the possible argument that our close study of text could only be accomplished by the most highly skilled readers or by students who were the most practiced at it already. I also did it to counter the idea that the level or track to which a student is assigned has a correlation with his or her innate ability.

I also asked that the group reflect to some degree the racial and ethnic diversity of the school. Of the six students, one was Haitian American, two were African American, and three were Cape Verdian American. I give this information on the ethnicity of the students because in a society in which the academy has been owned by European traditions and in which students of color are often portrayed as more likely to fail academically than to succeed, it is important to bring to view incontrovertible examples of rigorous academic work done by students of color.

Of the six students, four were learning English as their second or third language.

What you will encounter here is the story of these students, who were inexperienced readers of poetry, and the ways that they responded to the first poem that we studied together. The story focuses on the development of their ideas as I interpreted that development. It turned out not to be a story of ideas developing along six separate pathways. Rather, it is an account of how the students encountered and relied on one another's ideas, whether through conflict, affirmation, or insight, and sometimes without knowing it, as together they built an evolving interpretation of the poem. In many cases, the ideas described here ceased to be attributable to one person, constructed as they were by the students' perceiving and adding to one another's points of view.

This is also the story of my involvement with the students' work, which is significantly an account of the use of Duckworth's methodology extended to the study of poetry. Threaded through this account are indications of how my own role in the group influenced the students, how my own ideas developed about what the students were thinking and doing, and how their thoughts helped me to develop my ideas about the poem under study and about poetry.

It may be startling to some people, as they read the work presented here, to know that I consider it to be teaching as well as research (Duckworth, 1996). It might be startling because what can most strike a reader of this work on the first time through is how different some of the students' ideas seem from those that a more experienced reader of poetry might take for granted. What you see me doing in this work is focusing on or elaborating those seemingly wrong ideas rather than trying to change them. So it might seem that teaching *gave way* to research here, that I gave up opportunities to set the students straight.

What I want to make clear is that I see their responses, their feelings and ideas—*anything* that is a way of taking in the poem—as both the means by which they experience the poem at a given moment and the path through which they will develop a fuller understanding of it. This does not mean that I find the "mistaken" idea and correct it. It means that this idea is seen as a moment in an ongoing, active effort to understand, as an insight with the potential to move further, as not different in kind from my own evolving ideas, and above all as *useful* in its ability to make sense of something, to take account of something in the poem.

For example, Marco, one of the six students, came to the idea that the speaker of the poem was not addressing a person, but rather a farm or a piece of land in order to chronicle its destruction. At first glance, this idea was puzzling, to say the least. But as we questioned it and Marco articulated it more and more to himself and to the rest of us, I began to see that it took brilliantly into account a central aspect of the poem: its description of something wearing out or decaying. (It led another student to decide that this description, so well articulated by Marco, could also hold for the "you" in the poem that most of us saw as a woman: "the *woman* is getting *rotten*.") Marco's idea was also an attempt to explore the boundaries of figurative language, which he knew to be different from other forms of language that he is more familiar with. As he said, the "you" of the poem—whatever is being addressed—"*could* be *anything*."

Sometimes people see this work and think that the lack of explicit correction means that I believe that poetry can mean anything, that whatever a reader takes from it is adequate; or that I only care that the students feel good about their ideas and don't concern myself about the accuracy of these ideas. Neither of these is the case. What I do believe is that the only place any reader can start is with his or her own honest responses, and that as a teacher I can put students into extended contact with the text and one another and find ways to keep them interested in extending those contacts. I believe that the dynamics between the readers and the text will give the guidance that readers need to develop their ideas toward an increasingly full account of the text. Louise Rosenblatt (1978) speaks of the text's "magnetizing" force for the reader. My role is to facilitate this deepening encounter with text, particularly for beginning readers. I see myself standing slightly to the side of that encounter between readers and text, intervening just to keep it going or silently urging it on. If I try to give students the poem by standing between them and the poem, by paraphrasing it, they lose it. They lose the poem. This is particularly true for novice readers, who don't have a confident sense of what can potentially occur between themselves and a text. This doesn't mean that I can't tell them anything, but that the telling is also in the service of developing the authoritative connection between reader and text.

This connection is what I see as the crux of my work as a teacher. I want students to learn to grant authority to their own thoughts and feelings about a text. This is not so that they take their initial responses as a final word, but rather so that each student knows the reliability of his or her *capacity to respond to text* and uses that capacity as the final arbiter of new possibilities for interpretation.

As I said earlier, you are likely to notice ideas here that you do not expect. You are even more likely to catch your breath at the palpable intelligence that creates those ideas and propels them into new ones as the students create their own deep and secure knowledge of this poem.

The following are the names (pseudonyms) of the students and their ages.

> *James,* (15)
> *Juana,* (15)
> *Maddie,* (16)
> *Marco,* (15)
> *Nikki,* (15)
> *Nildo,* (14)

Prelude

I had planned, in our first session, to detail the logistics of the study and to answer the students' questions. It was not my plan, and is neither my practice nor that of the study's methodology, to begin this work with a theoretical discussion of "poetry." I had planned to begin with a poem. We did, however, become involved in a brief discussion of poetry that sprang up as we talked about what we would be doing during the study. I present here what I see as the significant piece of dialogue from that discussion, significant because it provides a glimpse of some of the students' initial ideas and particularly because it introduces the term *exaggeration,* which came to play a central part in our work with the poems.

> *Marco:* They're mostly often about love.
> *James:* They all rhyme.
> *Maddie:* They're like a love letter.
> *LS:* How would it be a poem rather than a letter?
> *Juana:* Make it rhyme.
> *James:* Exaggerate it a little.
> *LS:* Exaggerate it? Like how?
> *James:* Like the clouds. I don't know. Like her skin is like flowers.
> *Nildo:* Her eyes are like the clouds.
> *LS:* Can you explain more about what you mean by exaggerate?
> *Nildo:* Like, they make things [pause] you know, they *exaggerate* [pause] like when they say someone's eyes are so blue like the sky. How can a person's eyes be blue like the sky, you know . . . ?
> *James:* They can [interrupting].
> *Nildo:* Can*not!* That's science fiction.

"miss rosie"

There was a feeling of expectation as we began our first session with "miss rosie." Our initial session was spent talking about poetry and what we would do, but we had not yet looked at a poem. The students had received new, blank notebooks, and we had taken seats around a table in a meeting room off the school library. The room was unfamiliar to them. The tape recorder was unfamiliar also. All of this had been explained, but the setting may have contributed to that air of expectation. Something had been set up. Even as they conversed with their usual animation, teasing one another, they were awaiting the heart of the matter.

I passed out copies of "miss rosie" and asked the students to read it silently. I wanted each of them to be free to form first impressions before hearing it read in any voice but his or her own. There were murmurings from a few students as they began to read by sounding out the words. Then silence. These were moments of first acquaintance, that crucial time when the first connections are made between the reader and the poem. I felt the expectation fade into a somewhat strange completeness, as if the last member of our party had arrived.

But no swift or easy acceptance greeted this poem. Even as the students' waiting attention resolved, drawn by the poem, the poem created from that attention another form of unease:

Nildo: I don't get this.
James: It don't rhyme.
Juana: It don't make sense.
Maddie: It's silly.
Marco: It doesn't make sense.
James: It's stupid. It's exaggerating too much. I mean, it can exaggerate, but it's got to make sense.
LS: You said it's too much exaggeration. What do you mean by "too much"?
James: It's stupid. I don't know. I just don't like it.

I interpreted the comments—as well as the half-puzzled, half-impatient tone that spread from voice to voice—as indicating the students' violated expectations; this poem did not do what they expected poems or language to do. And rather than particular points of surprise or dislocation encountered in the poem, most of these initial comments—"It's stupid"; "It doesn't make sense"—capture the very fact of the violation itself.

I had hoped for some kind of unbalancing, hoped that, by violating their expectations, the poem would draw out those expectations—bring them to light. I had, in fact, relied on the poem to do this. What surprised me somewhat was the blanket nature of their responses, the sense that the poem was to them, at that moment, nothing more than a violation.

But still I felt that we were on fertile ground. James was the most emphatic in his dislike of the poem, his tone the most impatient. But, interestingly, it was his comment that the poem "exaggerate[s] too much" that contained most clearly the seeds of a question, one that he then elaborated as he continued, "It can exaggerate, but it's got to make sense." Referring to the previous day's discussion of "exaggeration," he raises here what I see as a crucial question about the nature of poetic language. He allows the poem room to move beyond the boundaries of prose ("It can exaggerate") while still binding it to the rules of the language as he knows it ("but it's got to make sense").

It was not what he would have said he was doing. The point he was making was that the poem was stupid. When I continued the discussion by asking him to point to a place in the poem where there is "too much exaggeration," he pointed out "in your old man's shoes," saying that the whole poem is too much exaggeration, but that line is "the stupidest spot." He could not say what made him choose this line, and I couldn't guess. But what was clear to me at this point was that they all needed an anchor— something that *did* make sense to each of them, some beginning shape that each could see in the poem.

For this also, as for the unbalancing, I relied on the poem, moving back to it by asking that someone read it aloud. We needed to encounter it in full again, maybe at a slightly different angle. The out-loud reading might accomplish this. Maddie read, somewhat haltingly at first, gaining fluency as she went. The others listened, often following along on the copies in front of them.

The reading moved several of the students to a fuller realization of what was confusing them: The poem had "parts" or "pieces" that did not connect to one another. As I listened to their comments, I began to imagine the morass of disconnected images that the poem was for them:

> *Nildo:* See? This is weird. This is weird. *I don't get it.* What is she
>   doing?
> *Marco:* It's just dumb.
> *Maddie:* That part, the last part don't make no sense. When it says,
>   "when I watch you you brown bag of a woman," first she's
>   talking about sitting next to a [pause] wrapped up like garbage
>   and then . . .

Juana: Now she changed to the brown bag or whatever she's
    saying.
James: It's supposed to be one main thing.
Maddie: That's right.
LS: Supposed to be what?
James: I don't know, she's switching all around, mixing it up.
Nildo: Yeah, he's saying the plot is supposed to be one main thing,
    but this stuff is separating. It's like different stuffs.
Juana: That's right, to be a story . . .

Perhaps the most vivid capturing of the disorientation that they are
experiencing is Nildo's description of "stuff" that is "separating." "It's like
different stuffs." I get the feeling from this of a physical substance that is
supposed to be one object but will not cohere, like a raw egg slipping out
of grasp or boiling water diffusing until beyond recognition.

But the first glimpse of an order or shape also emerges in the preceding
dialogue. Maddie states that "the last part" doesn't make sense. This is the
first time that someone has distinguished some part of the poem from the
whole. The very distinction is a beginning shape. Her comment also implies
that the rest of the poem is now somewhat less chaotic than the last part.

Also worth noting is Juana's reference to a "story" at the end of the
dialogue, along with Nildo's mention of "plot" and the assertions that
the poem is supposed to be "one main thing." They seem to be relying on
the more familiar "story" form of written language as an anchor—as something familiar through which to explore the deviations of the form that
confronts them here.

Nildo, continuing the shaping begun by Maddie, focused on the last
few lines (14–18), building a more specific theory:

Nildo: "I stand up to your destruction [*sic*]." That's what I don't get.
    Why would——?
Juana: "I stand up/ through your destruction / I stand up"
Nildo: Almost two paragraphs over that, it's like sad. And this one
    is beautiful, talking about a beautiful woman, and then they
    say, "I stand up to your destructions"—— Oh, I see it, I get it
    now. Oh *yeah.*
LS: What did you just get?
Nildo: No, I have an idea, I don't know—— [others talking]
LS: Let him tell his idea and then other people can respond to it, OK?
Nildo: Maybe this person who wrote the poem is like a friend—or
    something like that—and she, like, she'll be beside her when
    something goes wrong? Something like that.

LS: I see what you mean. Do you see what he is saying?
Nildo: "I stand up *to* your destruction"

Marco teased Nildo at this point ("Oh, by her side"), and Nildo was laughing when Maddie responded to his idea by saying that maybe one woman is telling a story to another.

LS: James, can I ask you something? Before, you said that things
       don't seem to stay together. Is that what you meant? Can you
       show me what the different pieces are?
Nildo: Oh, yeah.
James: [Looking at the poem] Like around the end, the starting, the
       middle, like everywhere. I don't know.
LS: So just show me one piece and then what another piece is that
       doesn't seem to go with it.

I was trying to get as close to his perspective as I could, trying to see what he saw. I was also trying to introduce into the discussion a closer look at the poem's text.

James: [Still studying the text] Um, the garbage, the garbage and the
       shoes go together, right?
LS: OK, how do they go together, the garbage and the shoes?
James: I mean, they're talking about shoes that are torn up. That's
       what garbage is too, so.
LS: OK, I see. And then which part doesn't go with it?
James: The bottom one. I don't get it. Even after he [Nildo] ex-
       plained it, I still don't get it.
LS: OK, point to where you start not to get it. Where are the lines
       where you start not to get it?
James: Like around where she starts talking about Georgia, "the
       best looking gal in——"
LS: "Who used to be the best looking gal in Georgia"? That one? Or
       the one before, "you wet brown bag of a woman"?
James: That goes.
LS: That goes? How does that go?
James: That's just like garbage. I mean, you know, it's almost the
       same. She's just saying that she's garbage.
Marco: They're still saying that she's garbage.

This movement through the poem with James showed me that the poem had taken an initial shape for him—that more of it cohered for him than he had realized. He became aware that he had developed a guiding idea, that "the end, the starting, the middle, everywhere" were not as disconnected as he had thought. The connection was the implication of "garbage" up to line 13. What still puzzled him were the lines that followed, and in this he joined Maddie and Nildo in their sense of two unrelated descriptions happening in this poem.

The question of how these descriptions could coexist was being set up, the students coming together, adding their voices to this question one by one. They had created an initial, gross ordering of the poem's images by fitting them into two broad categories: images of garbage and decay on the one hand, and the image of a beautiful woman on the other. They do not name the categories, but rather identify them by dividing the poem spatially into two parts. The first two "paragraphs" go together, and the third is separate, something different, disconnected from what came before. It wasn't yet so clearly a question for them as a frustrating confusion, and someone asked if we might try another poem. This one was "too hard to start with." I refused.

I was least clear where Juana and Nikki were in all of this. Marco had followed the preceding conversation closely, agreeing with James. I asked if anyone else saw pieces that didn't fit with one another. Juana, emphatic, chimed in. "I do. None of it makes sense except the first paragraph." She proceeded to read lines 1–4.

What followed I can only describe as a burst of energy. They started to articulate theories that were somehow catalyzed by their focus on the two conflicting descriptions in the poem. All the theories were attempts at reconciling these descriptions.

Maddie began. "For me it makes sense. She's saying something about somebody. She's talking about somebody." I didn't manage to get clear about what she meant before they were all, except Nikki, talking at once. After a minute or two, James's voice emerged above the others.

> *James:* No, no, no! I got an idea. When she says, "the most beautiful gal in Georgia," I think she *used* to be like that and *now* she's old and this garbage there, you know. She *used* to be maybe rich and all that, you know.
> *Nildo:* Oh, yeah. Maybe she is talking about the present and then, you know, first she was talking about present time and then she comes down to her past.

Juana has another idea:

> *Juana:* Maybe this is about two old women. The one is poor and the other one is rich.

> *Nildo:* No, it's only one person.
> *Juana:* "When I watch you wrapped up like garbage"—that woman
> is poor.

Here was another attempt at reconciliation; perhaps these different descriptions refer to different women. Juana turned to Nikki, who had been sitting quietly throughout the discussion. Half curious, half daring, she asked, "What do *you* think?" Very quietly, Nikki responded, "It doesn't match." "It doesn't match?" I asked. "At the end," Nikki said, "it doesn't make sense." In a teasing voice, Marco imitated the questions that I had been asking: "What part? Where in the poem?" Nikki answered seriously, "Where it says, 'used to be called the Georgia Rose / I stand up/ through your destruction / I stand up.'"

> *LS:* Does the rest of the poem make sense to you?
> *Nikki:* I think those do, because it was talking about the same girl
> here and . . .
> *LS:* Where is here?
> *Nikki:* Where it says, "When I watch you / in your old man's
> shoes."
> *LS:* Here she is talking about the same girl as who?
> *Nikki:* As the one wrapped up.
> *LS:* Ah, I see.

Nikki implies that she has just figured out that the descriptions above line 14 ("used to be the best looking gal . . .") all refer to one woman. She here adds her voice to the question of the two contrasting descriptions. She implies that, like Juana, she now sees the poem as describing two people, one in the lines above 14 and the other in the last five lines. I wondered here whether the repetition of "When I watch you" in the poem suggested to them that more than one person is being described. I also wondered whether the phrase "used to" was a colloquialism unfamiliar to some of the students for whom English was a second language. The phrase had been highlighted by James a little while before, but it had not been explicitly defined. There was a dictionary in the middle of our table, but none of the students had used it yet. Perhaps they were not yet familiar enough with the poem to distinguish particular words that confused them. I made a note to myself to check out the students' understanding of that phrase.

Right then, however, I asked Nikki to read the poem aloud. I again thought we needed a full encounter with it.

The reading was followed by James muttering in a low voice that it still didn't make any sense. I repeated that, questioning, and he responded more forcefully, "No, I mean, the way I explained it before, that's how I think of it now." I think that he had moved on during this reading, noticing more in the poem that puzzled him. He was then drawn back by my question to what had so far made sense to him. I asked what it was that he had thought before, wanting to see how he described his ideas now, but as he started to answer, Nildo interrupted. Turning to me, he demanded, "What do *you* think it means?" The question was seconded by almost everyone: "Yeah!" "She knows what it means?" "Yeah. What's *your* opinion, anyway?"

I didn't want to lose James's response, but I had to address their questions. I did not want them to think that I was privy to some secret "right" answer that I was manipulating them into finding. The work then would cease to be theirs, and they would become angered over wasting their time with something that could just as easily be told to them in a sentence.

But how to answer them? Several major questions had already been raised thus far in our work with the poem: How does the last section fit with the first two? Is the woman described at the end of the poem an earlier version of the same woman described at the beginning? Are there two (or more) different women being described? And then there were the deeper questions: What, to use Nildo's words, is this poet *doing*? Why does the poem "exaggerate" so much? What is the relationship between this poem and more familiar forms of language?

They were asking all this at once, under the heading of the question "What does this poem mean?" I offered them some of my thoughts. I said that I thought they were asking big questions, impossible to answer in a sentence. (I was worried because there was no way for them to know this, to see that a poem could not be summarized. That would take a lot of entering into poems. It is in fact a way to say what my ultimate goal was for them in this work: the knowledge that a poem escapes any summary.) I also said that I did have some opinions about different parts of the poem, but I'd rather wait to talk about my ideas because I was afraid that they would be too powerful now, that the students would take them as "right," as "what the poem means" rather than as my opinions. I said that I thought they needed more time with the poem to form their own firm opinions.

Marco murmured something that sounded like "They don't give you a book . . ." and was drowned out by James: "They give you clues about what it means." I guessed that Marco was facing with surprise the idea that I didn't have a teacher's guide or some document to tell me "what it means." At the same moment, James speculated that the poem itself gives us "clues" about its meaning. Marco continued the discussion:

Marco: She wrote it for a purpose.
Nildo: Yeah, you don't see the *purpose* here.

James: She ain't lifting that person up. I mean, she ain't lifting
that person up. A little bit. I mean, she's *trying* to lift them up,
but . . .
Nildo: It's not working.
James: [Finishing his sentence] But I wouldn't be encouraged.
Marco: Yeah.

I had the feeling that this was a new idea for James, that he was building it out loud with the help of Nildo and Marco, both of whom seemed to
have an implicit understanding of what he was trying to say. I asked if the
rest of the group agreed that "she was trying to lift the person up," hoping
to encourage the discussion.

Nildo: I agree with that one, yeah.
Marco: No [forcefully].
Juana: Yeah.
Maddie: Yes.
Nildo: Because at the end . . .
James: [Interrupting, responding to Marco's "no"] She's trying, but
she ain't. I mean, I can see that she's trying, but she ain't.
LS: Where can you see that she's trying?
James: Right around the end, where she's saying, "stand up" and all
that. The whole last paragraph.
Nildo: "I stand up / through your destruction / I stand up."
Juana: Yeah.
Nildo: See, she'll be beside you if you have any problems, you
know, something like that.

I looked at Nikki, who was shaking her head in disagreement with
James's idea.

Nikki: Every time I read it it's making more sense. 'Cause here it's
saying, "wrapped up like garbage" and here it's saying, "in
your old man's shoes." I think they're telling you how beautiful
she is. [Marco moaned comically. His continual teasing, rather
than silencing Nikki, seemed to have the effect of drawing her
out.]
LS: How beautiful she is?
Nikki: I think they're telling you how beautiful that woman was.
Like a Georgia Rose.
LS: And that's the connection between those three parts?
Nikki: [Nodding] Mmhmm.

Nikki here attempts another reconciliation of those conflicting descriptions. By focusing on the images in the poem that have to do with clothing—"wrapped up," "old man's shoes"—she decides that the thrust of the description is on the "beautiful" appearance of the woman described. She here speaks about the person described as one woman; she seems to have moved, with this new attempt at reconciliation, beyond her previous idea that the different descriptions refer to different people.

Her idea is striking in its exclusion of much of the poem, notably the "garbage" imagery that she had tried to take into account before. But in this exclusion, her current idea is only the most dramatic example of the same feature of most of the ideas the students have voiced thus far. The outstanding shape that the poem has taken for them is that of two very general descriptions (a woman who "looks like garbage" and one who is beautiful) held in a kind of tension. The students have attempted various ways of resolving the tension, or at least explaining it, but their views of the poem are still defined by this gross distinction. They fit the specifics of the poem into this shape, and, therefore, much of the poem is still as yet unexplored.

What followed was an interesting period of Nikki's vacillating back and forth between the two poles of the conflict, seeing the whole poem as consisting of either one description or the other. It was as if she was acting out the conflict rather than standing apart and observing it, as the other students were doing.

In the same conversation, however, there was also a new element: a growing interest in the last three lines and the question, raised a little earlier with James's idea of "lifting her up," of who is standing up, and why. (James's description of "lifting her up" is an entry, it seems to me, into more of the specific or subtle workings of the poem, a movement beyond the blanket categories that they had been working with. Perhaps conceived to explain or resolve the tension between the two descriptions, it introduces into the discussion the speaker of the poem. The speaker's presence had been noted by Maddie and then Nildo early on. Now the group seems ready to take it on explicitly.)

> *Nikki:* I think everyone is standing up for her because she's beautiful.
> *James:* No, she's garbage.
> *Nildo:* Oh. Maybe she's poor. And they're standing up for her.
> *James:* This is too confusing.
> *Juana:* Yeah, too confusing. We should talk about this one week before the end.
> *James:* Later on when we master it, I mean when we get better at this.

Juana: It's too hard to start with.
Nildo: [Laughter in his voice] We should start with "Roses are red, violets are blue."

Everyone laughed at that. Their confusion here also seemed to signal the deepening of focus—their movement toward exploring more of the subtleties of the poem. This shift in focus had two forms that I could see. One was a beginning study of the speaker in the poem and the relationship between the speaker and the person being described. This is evident in James's "lifting her up" idea and is extended by other students in the dialogue above. The pronouns that they use to indicate the speaker are most often vague ("everyone" and "they"), but their growing recognition of the speaker's presence in the poem is nevertheless evident.

The other indication of a shift in focus immediately followed their recognition of the speaker. The students, now attempting to understand the place of the speaker in the poem, began to focus on more of the poem's text. They brought into the discussion more of the specifics of the poem: words, phrases, facets of the poem's language that they had not, previous to this point, noticed or taken into account. An example is the dialogue that follows.

Immediately after a reading aloud of the poem by Marco, the group again focused on the final three lines. This began with several students repeating these lines after Marco, almost before the sound of his voice had died away: "I stand up / Through your destruction / I stand up."

Nildo: I stand up to [*sic*] your destruction [puzzled voice].
James: It's what I said before about lifting her up.
Maddie: Yeah, but that doesn't make any sense.
Nildo: Wait a minute! I got something. I got something. Like this person, he did something to him- or herself . . .
Juana: [Interrupting] That's a girl.
Nildo: [Continuing] If the person, the author, right, is talking about somebody he knows, or she knows, right? They did something wrong to it.
LS: In what way?
Nildo: Something is wrong with them, because, "waiting for your mind / like next week's grocery" or something like that, like he did something wrong to himself or, either, herself [pause] and now he's standing up for her destruction or her mistake, something like that.

Nildo's switching of pronouns in his last statement ("he," "she," "them," "it") indicates his struggle with the speaker's presence and attitude toward the person described. But his focus on this presence is now explicit, and as he struggles with it he highlights a new part of the poem ("waiting for her mind . . ." [lines 9–10]) for the group's study. Some of the students continue to puzzle over that phrase (one suggests that we call "this Lucille" [the poet] for an explanation), but then they are quickly brought up short by Marco's statement, "It doesn't have to be a woman or a man, it could be the destruction of our forests or something. Something torn down. Or a farm or something." Nildo, still absorbed in his own idea and not fully hearing Marco, responded, "Hmm, yeah, that's what I say, it's a destruction——he or she is standing up for." The other students, meanwhile, had paused and turned to stare at Marco. Thus began one of the loudest and most animated discussions of this poem, a discussion that often consisted of escalating voices as several students talked at once.

> *Juana:* Yeah, but she didn't say "farm" or anything.
> *Marco:* She says "potato peels."
> *Juana:* No, because right here it says . . .
> *Nildo:* [Now understanding what Marco is saying] It's a woman!
> *Marco:* It doesn't *have* to be a woman!
> *Juana:* Yeah, Marco says it could be forests or something.

Nildo and Juana, speaking at the same time, refer emphatically to the poem in order to persuade Marco that his idea couldn't hold true:

> *Nildo:* It couldn't because when it says, "When I watch *you* . . . ,"
> you can't refer to a forest as like that, as if it would be a person.
> That's too much exaggeration.
> *Juana:* [Laughing] They're "watching" the trees? And it says
> "waiting for *your* mind."
> *Maddie:* [Referring to Nildo's statement about "too much exaggeration"] I know.
> *Marco:* No!
> *LS:* Go ahead. "No" what?
> *Marco:* It still doesn't have to be a woman, man!

In the preceding dialogue, as the other students challenge his idea, Marco stands behind it all the more firmly. Succeeding the earlier conflict of the two different descriptions in the poem, this new conflict now takes center stage in the sense that it claims the whole group's focus (my image is that it moved to the middle of the table around which we sat) and compels the students back into the poem's text to find support for their points of view. For example, in the preceding dialogue, Juana points out the absence of textual reference to a farm, which Marco counters by highlighting line 4 ("She says 'potato peels'"). Juana is about to point out something else in the text when she is interrupted (or drowned out) by Nildo, who a few seconds later highlights the phrase "When I watch you" (emphasis on the "you") to counter Marco's idea. Juana joins Nildo by emphasizing the "your" in "waiting for your mind."

Marco, however, as is clear with his half-shouted "No!" holds firm to his idea. I was confused about what he was trying to put forth, and also perhaps by his very steadfastness, which seemed much more than stubbornness or an arbitrary holding on. I wondered what had given rise to this "It doesn't have to be a woman" idea in the first place. His tone when he first broached it was more tentative, though not very. It was experimental. There was something that he was thinking through. Not yet being able to articulate what that was, his "No!" seemed a kind of placeholder, a barreling forth, in the face of the others' arguments, of something as yet inarticulate. He was asserting an idea that he did not yet have words to fully convey.

I was mightily curious about what that might be. And then something occurred to me. In one of the frequent split-second decisions about whether to speak or keep silent that accompanied me throughout this work, I turned to Marco.

> *LS:* When I try to write a poem, say, for example, about the ocean, and I can talk *to* the ocean—is that what you're trying to say?
> *Marco:* Yeah! It's talking to a man or a woman but it doesn't have to *be* a man or a woman.

He was working with the idea that the poem is personifying some kind of land. He continued to experiment in this way ("It could be an animal"), and Juana again countered his idea with another reference to the text: "Uh uh. It couldn't be what Marco was talking about. It says, 'When I watch You / You *wet brown bag of a woman*.' It couldn't be forests or an animal." Marco, however, had now found words, and he also referred to the text as he continued to develop his idea.

> About the grocery part [line 10], it could be a farm or something they don't get to and the potatoes. It's not gonna be used anymore so it's garbage . . . and the groceries, yeah, it's like this, this, this [pause] garbage, whatever it was that was the groceries, the potatoes were growing from it, it could be torn up and they call it garbage and it's destructing. And it's like, going to waste. So now it's garbage, whatever it was, the potato peels and the groceries and stuff is garbage.

He constructs the poem's images into a scene that stays true to the feeling of decay that the poem gives him. The other students listened to this in silence. James made an "Mhmm" noise that seemed to indicate understanding, and Juana nodded. Nildo responded most forcefully: "I see what he's saying. He's making it more——ah——simple now."

At this point Nikki reached for the dictionary, saying that she was looking for the word *gal*, which confused her. Juana joined her with the Spanish-English dictionary. They both concluded that *gal* meant "girl" ("The best looking 'girl' in Georgia"), and I wondered how Marco would take this. He seemed unperturbed. Nildo also, despite this definition, was still taken with Marco's explanation. He seemed to be trying it out.

> *Nildo:* It's like Marco says. It could be some type of vegetable they're talking about.
> *Maddie:* Really, Marco, "the best looking vegetable!" [laughing].
> *Marco:* You could call it a "girl."
> *Nildo:* I'm serious, because you could be exaggerating in a poem.

Maddie paused in her protests to speculate half jokingly that "You could call a girl a vegetable" (like "you potato-head") as an insult. This was an interesting reversal of Marco's idea about the poem, in which a vegetable or farm was being called a girl. Simultaneously, Marco was responding to Nildo's comment about exaggerating in a poem: "Yeah! It *could* be *anything*."

It took this last statement, with its emphatic "could," to make me realize the enormity of the question that Marco was raising. On the one hand, to say that the "you" of the poem could be anything is absurd; if it meant anything, it would really mean nothing. But Marco is not saying that the "you" in this poem does mean anything; he's saying that it *could*. The question is that of the boundaries of language. He's focusing on the nature of figurative language, in which the possibilities of meaning are exponentially increased by the movement beyond the boundaries of the literal. His assertions about the "you" in the poem are as much assertions about the figurative possibilities that he knows language to contain. (That may have been part of the reason for the force of his earlier denial of the others' arguments.) These possibilities, named "exaggeration" by the students in our first moments together, are implicit in all of our work with the poem. It must be so, since the poem embodies them. But Marco has forced an explicit study of them, because he needs these possibilities to make sense of the poem in front of us. As he and the other students struggle with his ideas, he making statements that the others then counter, each with reference to the text, they are exploring, even dramatizing, the very boundaries that secure the poem's meaning, that make it mean something rather than anything. I interpreted Marco's main question as follows: Once language moves beyond the boundaries of direct referring, once it becomes figurative, how do we secure its meaning? If it *could* mean anything, since it is no longer bound by the rules of ordinary prose, how do we determine what it *does* mean?

Into the fray of discussion about girls being called vegetables, along with some playing with the word "gal" ("I'm the best looking gal in Boston"), James interjected a firm statement.

> *James:* I think it's what I said before.
> *LS:* Say it again.
> *James:* It's an old lady that used to be—it ain't an old lady, I mean a
>   poor person—who used to look good and the woman is trying
>   to encourage, I mean, *get her up*, you know, so she could look
>   like she did before, I mean, that's what it means [emphatically].
>   Who agrees?

Here Nildo again shifts his allegiance. "I agree, I agree. I think he's trying to say, like, the woman is getting *rotten*, you know, it's talking about vegetables, something like that."

Nildo, at first reacting to Marco's idea about the farm with forceful disagreement ("It's a woman!"), began to see the sense within Marco's idea as Marco explained its two main facets: (1) the figurative possibilities of the "you" and (2) the way the poem's images fit into a portrait of a decaying farm. Nildo then subscribed to Marco's idea as he tried it out. In a way, he climbed inside of it. With James's preceding statement, which serves as a reminder of other aspects of the poem, Nildo seems to gain perspective on Marco's idea, to see it in a larger context. The poem's description resolves for him, the woman becoming the subject of the description rather than its vehicle ("The woman is getting *rotten*"). The images of decay, in other words, condense into the idea of "rotten." They become descriptive, and at some points figurative, rather than being the subject of the poem's description. Instead, the central presence is the woman. Nildo has in effect reconstructed the poem's description from the inside out. In his agreement with James (in the above dialogue), he takes facets of Marco's decaying-farm idea and gives them their place (the idea of rotten) within the explanation that James puts forth.

It is as if we journeyed into the heart of the poem's description in following Marco's idea; the vehicles of the metaphors became, for a while, part of the poem's literal landscape. We all had more familiarity with the poem's images as a result. As Nildo emerged from this journey, I wondered where it had left the others. The confusions highlighted by Marco were not his alone. Most of the students' comments thus far have pointed to some confusion between the vehicles and subjects of the poem's metaphors as well as confusion about who or what was the main subject of the description. I was curious about what effect Marco's focused study of these issues and of the poem's images might have had on the others.

James responded to Nildo's statement about the woman "getting rotten."

James: No, no, no, she's poor. She used to look good and now she's poor.
Nildo: That's what I'm saying, getting rotten, *herself.*
James: Rotten is getting old. She ain't old, you know, she just lost her job maybe. And now she's out on the streets.

James seems to have incorporated the same images that Marco was working with into his sense of the woman as poor and "on the streets." For Nikki, however, these images had somehow straightened out the time element in the poem. This is probably because Marco's work highlighted the idea of decay. It now made sense to her that the woman described at the end of the poem (lines 14–15) was an earlier version of the woman described in lines 1–13. Her focus, however, was still on the beauty of the woman described. She integrated the time element in an interesting way:

Nikki: I think she was beautiful, and like Miss U.S.A., and then it was over and they had to get someone else.
LS: What was over? Say that again, I missed it.
Nikki: Like she was "the best looking gal in Georgia" and she was like Miss U.S. or something and they had to replace her by somebody else.
LS: And that was her destruction?
Nikki: Uh huh.

Juana, also as a result of the focus on images of decay, now believed that the person described was old. She debated this hotly with James, who flatly disagreed ("She's not old, she's *poor*"), while Marco went into an explanation that made it clear that he was still occupied with his idea of a destroyed piece of land:

Marco: They could be saying the rose [pause] the Georgia Rose, this place was in Georgia and it was beautiful like a rose, and now it's no good, so this person stands up to the destruction because it was so lovely. [Firmly, in response to the other students' giggles at the word *lovely*, repeats] It *was* lovely.

LS: So what would the "standing up" be then?
Marco: Because it was being destroyed.
LS: So you mean standing up is in protest?
Marco: No. Oh, that's a good idea, though.

Nildo joined in here.

> Nildo: No, no. Standing up to her destruction is like when you did
> something wrong, you admit it, you tell her or she admits
> herself that she did something wrong and her destruction is
> [pause] *herself* in some sort of way, like——she messed up her
> whole life.
> LS: So who's standing up here?
> Nildo: Umm, the author! I say the author is standing up.

Nikki responded to this with a new idea, perhaps to some extent building
on what Nildo had just said.

> Nikki: She "used to be the best looking gal in Georgia," she "[u]sed
> to be called the Georgia Rose" and now she's standing up for
> herself.
> LS: So when it says here, "Through your destruction," who's the
> "your"?
> Nikki: The girl.
> LS: So the "I" is the girl and the "your" is the girl?
> Nikki: I think so.

I asked the others what they thought about this, in effect moving Nikki's
idea to the center of the table. Marco did not agree, because "it could be
something different besides a girl." James indicated his agreement with
Nikki, but said he also agreed with Marco. When Nildo protested that he
"couldn't agree with everybody," James insisted that he could, because
"they all agree with my points." He then added, "I'm right."

Maddie (probably responding to Nikki's idea) joined the discussion
with the statement, "She wants to be like somebody, but she can't. 'When
I watch *you* . . .'" She paused, then read lines 6–10 of the poem aloud.

> Maddie: [Repeating what she had just said] I think she wants to be
> like somebody, but she can't.
> LS: Somebody? You mean like a particular person? Or she wants to
> *be somebody*?
> James: Maybe she's a runaway.

Nildo: All I know is that the destruction is supposed to stand for her life.

Maddie: [Renewed interest in her voice] I think she wrote this, but she's talking about *herself* [pause] but she doesn't want people to think that it's her.

James: Yeah, that's exactly the same thing I was trying to say.

Maddie: "When I *watch* you," "When I watch *you*" [pause]. She wants to be like somebody, you know, somebody who dresses up nice [pause] or maybe she had a problem or something and she's describing about herself, and she wants to be like somebody.

Maddie here wrestles with the relationship between the "I" and the "you" of the poem, trying out various possibilities. She seems to be experimenting with the tone of the poem to some degree, paying attention to the speaker's attitude toward the person addressed. She tries out different emphases ("When I *watch* you," "When I watch *you*"), listening for the subtleties of this phrase.

We were ready, I thought, to hear the poem aloud again. We were near the session's end at this point, and I wanted them to have another chance to apprehend the poem whole before we stopped for the day. Juana and James, the two students who had not yet read aloud, each read the poem, one right after the other. The fortuitous result of this was that we had two different readings side by side to compare to each other. The students remarked on this, but there was no time for discussion. I thought that just as well right then. Let the readings stand.

I determined between sessions to pose a question that focused even more explicitly on the "I"s and the "you"s of the poem. I was somewhat confused, because of the sometimes rampant mixing of pronouns in our previous discussions as well as the students' tendency to refer to both the speaker and the subject of the description as "she," about how some of them were construing these words. I wanted a question that had the potential to acknowledge and draw into one discussion the varying ideas about the "I"/ "you" relationship that had ended the last session: (1) that a woman is talking about herself, (2) that one woman is talking to another, and (3) that the "you" is a piece of land and the "I" of the poem is chronicling its destruction. I was unsure whether anyone was still entertaining a fourth possibility: the idea, central to our earlier discussion, that there are two or more people being addressed.

James was absent from the next session. At the beginning of it, after noting his absence and briefly strategizing about when we would study a poem that Juana had brought in (written by a friend of hers), Juana read "miss rosie" aloud to start us off. After some seconds of silence, I posed the question of who is talking in the poem and who, or what (keeping Marco's idea in mind), was being addressed as "you."

"That name there, 'Lucille Clifton,' is the author, right?" Maddie asked. As I nodded she continued, "She's talking about somebody named Miss Rosie, I think." To Juana's speculation that "it's her boyfriend" (I determined that the "her" meant Miss Rosie), there were protests that "Lucille Clifton" is a woman. Nildo said firmly that the "I" is the author, seconded by Maddie: "The 'I' is Lucille Clifton and the 'you' is Miss Rosie."

Maddie seemed no longer to be considering her previous idea that the author was talking about herself. I wondered about Nikki, who had first raised this possibility, and asked her if she was still considering it. "I don't know," she said quietly. "I don't think so." She looked confused. Marco took this moment to agree that the "I" of the poem "could be the author." But there he departed, returning to his now familiar statement, "The 'you' could be anything." Maddie responded.

> *Maddie:* [Pointing to the title] It says right there "Miss Rosie."
> *LS:* [To Marco] It *could* be anything, but do you see clues in the
>   poem about what it's likely to be?
> *Marco:* Maybe it's an animal that's getting killed.
> *LS:* The "you," you mean?
> *Marco:* Yeah.

I said the first line aloud, "When I watch you," and Marco responded with "yeah," again. On an impulse, I continued, reading the entire poem aloud to them. I think I sensed that the students were not fully engaged, that the poem, on this day, had not yet come into the room. Possibly my "I"/"you" question was premature. I felt that they needed more of the full poem, in all of its facets—its sounds and building rhythm heard as a whole piece of work. Or perhaps it was I who was not fully engaged, and this need was my own. It may have been all of us; I had been noting with surprise since we had begun this work that the students' interest or engagement in the poem seemed to rise and fall as a group. That group included me.

Nildo's question followed immediately upon my finishing the reading: "What does she mean? Do you know what does she mean by 'You . . . brown bag of a woman?'" I said I thought it was a good question.

> *Nildo:* Maybe she's dark-skinned?
> *Juana:* She's brown-skinned? And she's poor.
> *Nildo:* [Referring to the date below the author's name] Nineteen
>   sixty-seven was the year of the civil rights movement.

Juana: Oh boy, he's changing to civil rights.

LS: Do you think he's changing the subject? Because I think he's saying that has to do with the poem.

Nildo: 'Cause it's the destruction or something like that [pause] 'cause there was a lot of violence and stuff [pause] or maybe she's a White person criticizing a Black person.

LS: Who's "she"?

Nildo: The author is criticizing the other woman.

LS: The author is African American. She's Black.

Nildo: Oh, she is?

Maddie joined in here. "I think she's writing a letter to her or something, 'cause it says, 'Miss Rosie When I watch you / wrapped up like garbage...'" I was confused by this and then realized that her point concerned the "Miss Rosie," that she was using the title of the poem as the salutation in a letter. She repeated the idea with more conviction: "She's writing a letter to her."

This gave Marco an idea. "Oh. Maybe she's in jail." This idea seemed to me to include both Nildo's reference to the civil rights movement and Maddie's view of the poem as a letter. To a background of protests, Nildo supported Marco's idea: "It could be, it could be, she could be." There was some speculation about "death row" and the idea that "maybe she's out in California" (where there was currently some controversy about the death sentence), justified by the poem's reference to "your destruction."

Maddie disagreed, reading the poem aloud through line 8. Then Marco and Maddie spoke simultaneously:

Marco: She could be poor.

Maddie: Maybe she's poor.

Nildo continued.

Nildo: Or maybe she could be, you know, she's not fighting for her rights or something and she's losing her dignity and stuff and she's destructing *herself*?

LS: Who's "she"? The "you" or the "I"?

Nildo: OK. She is the, um, she is the "you."

LS: OK.

Nildo: OK. Maybe she's not fighting for her rights and she's losing her self-respect, you know, she's like a bag lady or something like that, all right? And she's poor and everything, and she can't, she doesn't know what to do with her life. You know? The "you" I'm talking about now.

LS: Mmhmm.

Nildo: And this "I" person, the author, is probably telling her, you know, trying to bring her up——to stop——you know, to do something with her life, or something like that.

The other students were listening carefully to Nildo. After a brief pause, I asked whether there were any particular lines or words in the poem that he was concentrating on, trying to encourage him to continue. In response, Nildo read the first four lines of the poem aloud. "She's around a lot of garbage. And then there's her old shoes and stuff like that, you know?" He was about to continue reading when Marco interrupted to speculate that the "too" in line 4 could mean "two"—"two old potato peels." He seemed to be experimenting, playing with the possibilities of the words. Almost at the same time, Juana began to try out Marco's previous idea about the "you" of the poem: "It could be an animal too." Marco then continued with another idea: "Maybe she's talking about homeless people. Some people are homeless." To my "What in the poem would suggest that?" he replied, looking back at the text, "Wrapped up like garbage." Maddie joined in here.

Maddie: She's probably talking to Rosie. She was writing a letter. Or they don't talk to each other. She might be away.

LS: Oh, so you think she knows her.

Maddie: Yeah.

LS: That's interesting.

Maddie: And they don't get along, so she's writing this letter to her.

As Nildo responded, Maddie's "letter" idea took its place at the center of the table:

Nildo: I don't understand how can that be a letter.

Maddie: I mean, it could be a letter, it could be a poem, it could be anything. 'Cause it don't rhyme anyway, so why should it be a poem?

LS: Why should it be a poem.

Maddie: 'Cause it don't rhyme, it don't make no sense, 'cause . . .

Marco: [Finishing Maddie's sentence] Nobody knows why she wrote it for.

Maddie: Mmhmm.

LS: [To Marco] But you're the one who said yesterday that she wrote it for a purpose, right?

Nildo: Yeah.

Marco: But we don't *know* the purpose.

I was captivated by this discussion, again silently urging it on. I remember my feeling that they had *arrived* somewhere, under their own steam, though I could not articulate just where it was that I believed they had come to.

I continued with a question about whether they had more of an idea of the purpose than they did initially. I think I intended the question to keep the discussion going, but they needed no encouragement at this point. The question was an intrusion. Thankfully, it was ignored by the students. Maddie continued the discussion.

> *Maddie:* And right here it says, "Who used to be the best looking gal in Georgia / Used to be called the Georgia Rose. . . ." Now "Miss Rosie," they're calling her "Rosie."
> *Nildo:* This is what I . . .
> *Juana:* That's what I say.
> *LS:* What do you say?
> *Juana:* What Maddie says right now.
> *LS:* Could you repeat the part you agree with?
> *Juana:* The part that she said she wrote Rosie a letter. It could be like that.
> *Nildo:* I disagree completely.
> *Maddie:* 'Cause it say, "the best looking gal in Georgia / Used to be called the Georgia Rose. . . ." And now from "Rose" you could take out "Rosie."

This was a new idea for Maddie—the matching of "Rose" in line 15 with "Rosie." There were murmurs from some of the others—I am not sure exactly from whom, though Nikki was one—suggesting that it was a new connection for them also. Maddie, however, was not making an isolated point here. She was using this connection as evidence for her argument that this poem is in fact a letter addressed and written to Miss Rosie. She tried again to explain how she was seeing the poem: "'Cause, you see, look at: 'Miss Rosie.'" Maddie stopped here to make clear what she was about to do: "I could read it like a letter." She continued, "'Miss Rosie' [spoken as an address], 'When I watch you / wrapped up like garbage. . . .'" She proceeded to read the poem through to the end. Nildo responded.

> *Nildo:* I don't get your point.
> *Maddie:* [Somewhat impatient now] I'm saying that Miss Lucille Clifton is writing a letter to Miss Rosie. You know what I'm saying?
> *Nildo:* But this doesn't go like a, it doesn't sound like, it doesn't sound like . . .

Marco and Maddie interrupted, talking at the same time:

> *Marco:* It doesn't have to be a poem.
> *Maddie:* But to be a poem, it has to rhyme . . .
> *Nildo:* [Responding to Maddie] It doesn't have to rhyme.
> *Maddie:* [Amending] To make sense. A poem make sense.
> *Marco:* Mmhmm.
> *Maddie:* And a poem rhyme too.
> *Marco:* Mmhmm.
> *Maddie:* But this is like a letter.
> *Nildo:* A letter is supposed to make sense too. It has to has a point.
> *Marco:* Yeah.
> *Nildo:* What's the point in this? If it's a letter?
> *Maddie:* Well, for me it make a point because it seem like she's
>   talking to her about something that she don't like or something
>   or she's prejudiced or something. I don't know.
> *Nildo:* [Laughing in sympathy] See? I don't get this.

Maddie's "letter" idea is another step in a building question about the
poem's purpose. It is a step that takes brilliant account of the speaker of
the poem—of the form of address in which the poem is written.

The students continued the dialogue about the letter with a consideration of the "point" that Nildo had pressed Maddie into articulating ("What's
the point in this, if it's a letter?"). Maddie explained:

> She's prejudiced against Rosie, or something. [Pause] Oh! I think
> she, Lucille Clifton, is better than Rosie and Rosie is turning into a
> bum or something—'cause she's saying that she used to be the best-
> looking girl in Georgia . . .

Nildo interrupted with "That's my point, that's my point" as Marco simultaneously said something (mostly inaudible on the tape) about Miss Rosie
being "homeless." Nildo seemed to be asserting that this idea also fit with
what Maddie was saying. Maddie then continued her statement.

> *Maddie:* And now she's saying right now [pause] that she's not.
> *LS:* So that she's changed.
> *Nildo:* Yeah. She's changed now.

Maddie's reframing of the poem into a letter seems to allow her to
further explore the speaker's attitude. Her ongoing confusion between what
seemed to her the speaker's admiration of Miss Rosie on the one hand ("the

best looking gal in Georgia") and contempt for her on the other ("You wet
brown bag of a woman") begins to resolve here. In Maddie's previous work,
each of these attitudes excludes the other and becomes for her the whole
of the poem. In her preceding statement, her emphasis shifts to the time
element in the poem ("and now she's saying *right now*" [emphasis mine]),
thus allowing her to incorporate both attitudes into one interpretation. It
is this emphasis that secures Nildo's and Marco's agreement.

I would have liked to know how Maddie would now respond to the
last three lines of the poem, but Nikki had been silent for a while, and I
turned instead to her, asking if there was anything she wanted to add.

> *Nikki:* I think——they're still talking about two persons, and one of
> them is a woman, the other might be a man.
> *Maggie:* "*Rosie*" is a man?
> *Nikki:* No, I know. The other one.
> *Nildo:* Oh, yeah, maybe she's talking about, maybe the "I" might be
> a man.

Nildo and I together (he might have been half teasing me about my now
predictable responses) commented, "That's interesting."

I was not sure that Nikki was in fact talking about the "I" of the poem;
she could have been indicating that there were two "you"s, one being Rosie
and the other a man. The reference to "old man's shoes" may have suggested this, as well as the repetitions of "When I watch you," which makes
it possible to attribute the poem's descriptions to different people. Several
students had entertained this idea of different people early in our work. I
had thought the matter pretty well settled by now, especially with Maddie
connecting "Georgia Rose" with "Miss Rosie." It became clear, however,
that Nikki was not reopening the question of the conflicting descriptions
(a beautiful woman and a person decaying). She understood the present/
past ("used to be the best looking . . .") connection in the poem. What she
was now wondering was whether there was yet another person in addition to this one, a person described in lines 1–10 (before the description is
broken by the words "I say" in line 11). Lines 12 through to the end she
saw as describing the past and present Miss Rosie.

What struck me about this idea was how *possible* it was, given the
poem's grammatical structure, and at the same time how far it was from
my own. (Thinking it through after the session, I concluded that it was only
the title and the later, connecting reference to "Georgia Rose" [and, perhaps more significantly, my familiarity with the repetition within the
structures of lyric poetry] that kept me convinced that one person is being
described.)

I was admiring Nikki's ability to keep this question open, to keep it at the center of the table in the face of the others' disagreements. I had been afraid that, soft-spoken as she was, she might allow it to close prematurely, before it was given its due—before it was considered in light of the text of the poem. She did not. In fact, she went on to show the others how the poem could be describing *two* people in addition to Miss Rosie, one in lines 1–4 and the other in lines 6–10.

This was received with some confusion. Again confronted with multiple possibilities (as Nildo said, "We have too much ideas for this"), several students followed Nildo into a repetition of "I don't get this," "It doesn't make sense," "Let's do another poem." The tone of these remarks, however, held more self-mockery than it had the last time they had taken up this refrain. Each time they took it up, there seemed to be more amusement accompanying the frustration, more exaggeration of their own comments. Here they were mocking the comments even as they were making them.

This was the end of the session. I realized afterward that my place in the work had changed. Much of my previous role—of supporting questions, holding them open, using them as paths back into the poem's text—was taken up by the students. The debate that arose between Maddie and Nildo about whether the poem was really a letter, for example, during which they were guided by the poem's text, was like a current, with full capacity to carry them on its own.

Another way of saying this is that they were now giving their faith to the poem, allowing themselves to be guided by it. The evidence for this is the growing frequency of their references to the text, their spontaneous readings of it, their experiments with its words and tone, their growing ability to use it as a support for or a challenge to their interpretations. They were demanding more and more from it. These dynamics between the students and the text had been building, growing more and more evident to me throughout our work. They solidified for me during this session into that feeling of arrival.

James returned for the next session. He expressed his surprise that we were "still on this poem." After some comments about several poems in the school literary magazine, which some of the students had taken home with them, we focused, at my initiation, again on "Miss Rosie." The students were reluctant. I decided to see how it went; if there wasn't a building of energy, I resolved, we would move on to another poem.

Nildo read the poem aloud. There was a silence, and after a moment, I asked if they remembered some of their thoughts from the previous day.

Nildo: Yeah. "You wet brown bag of a woman." She's dark-skinned. She's Black, dark-skinned.

LS: Who's "she"?

Nildo: The "you." And, and I think the "you" is a reflection of the "I." They're the same one.

LS: You think the "I" and the "you" are the same person?

Nildo: Yeah. And, you know, she's dark-skinned, and she's going through maybe pain or [pause] confusion. And she says, "I'll stand up / to [*sic*] your destruction" as like when you say like this, "My life is going bad right now but I'll face it," you know? Like you have to face the music.

Maddie: You have to face the facts.

Nildo: Yeah.

I pointed out here that the poem did not say "to your destruction," but "through your destruction." Nildo, particularly, had been reading that line throughout our work with the word "to." (This was not surprising. My own inclination when reading the poem is also to substitute "to" for "through." My sense is that the poet, by implying the common phrase "stand up *to*," is purposefully juxtaposing those two words.) As Nildo looked back at the text, James spoke up.

James: That don't make no sense. What he was saying, I mean. About her being Black. "Brown bag?" It's Black, you know.

Nildo: But . . .

James: If they wanna say that she's Black, they're just gonna write "Black." That'll be a clue, if it was Black. [He had said in the first session that a poet gives clues about meaning.] But brown——

Nildo: But James, but they're exaggerating right now.

LS: [Trying now to get him to be more explicit about this term] What do you mean by exaggerating?

Nildo: They're *exaggerating*. "You wet bag of a brown lady."

James: No. They're just saying right there that she's, she's a bum. [Marco laughed at this, and James continued] Yeah, you know. Like she's dirty, almost.

LS: So do they need the word "brown" in there to say that?

James and Nildo responded simultaneously,

James: Nah. You know. They're just talking about the bag.

Nildo: Yeah. What do you think "brown" is supposed to stand for?

There was a slight pause before James answered Nildo.

James: It's the wet brown bag, like they're saying.

Nildo: [Picking up on James's hesitation] You see?

James: That's what it stands for, but they're just saying that, you
know [pause].

LS: You're saying that "brown" is describing "bag"?

James: Nah. I mean, kind of like "the brown bag," the whole thing.
You know, "you wet brown bag." It's kind of a diss [disrespect,
an insult], so it's like she's dirty or something.

LS: Not necessarily that her skin is brown.

James: Nah. It ain't that.

The close study of this metaphor, begun by Nildo the day before, along
with Maddie's explication, also in the previous session, of the metaphor in
lines 9–10 signaled to me a deepening of focus. Or perhaps *tightening* is a
better word. The students had earlier been content with looser connections
between the poem's words and images. They were more likely to isolate
words from their contexts and string them together into a somewhat
impressionistic interpretation. Marco's description of the farm in the first
session is a dramatic example of this, as is the initial categorizing of the
poem into two very general, conflicting descriptions. Most of the early ideas
exemplify this stringing together to some degree. Here, in contrast, the
students study the words within their context and thus apprehend and
explore more fully the figurative weight that they bear.

Maddie joined in here to recapture her focus on the relationship of the
speaker and Miss Rosie.

Maddie: I think, I don't know. I think she's writing this story to
Rosie. A girl named Rosie. It could be anybody, an old lady, a
young lady, whatever. She's the jealous type. She wanted to be
like Miss Rosie, but she can't, so she talks bad about her. That's
what the "wet brown bag" is.

Marco: It's saying that she's old and [pause] *used*. Something bad.

LS: Who's the "she"? [I asked this because of his previous idea that
the "you" was not necessarily a woman.]

Marco: Oh, the "you." [Pause] It could be anything, but [pause] . . .

When it became fairly clear that he was not going to continue, I took this
opportunity to probe, playfully, the reaches of this idea, to test my feeling
that he was asserting the freedom of figurative language.

LS: When you say the "you" could be anything, do you really mean
anything?

Marco: Yup.
LS: Like a scissors?
Marco: Mmhmm.
LS: Or the wind?
Marco: Yeah.
LS: Or a leaf?
Marco: It could be anything.
LS: Okay. It *could* be anything. But do the words in the poem
     narrow it down [Marco starts nodding here] to what it's more
     likely to——
Marco: [Interrupting. It was clear that he had already thought this
     out.] Yeah. It's most likely to be a woman.

James joined in here to give support to Marco's point, which he clearly had fully understood: "Some sailors, they call ships 'shoes.'" Nildo responded, "Oh yeah."

By this point, Juana had asserted that Miss Rosie is "an old woman" and Maddie was beginning to pursue her ideas about lines 9–10. After reading the lines aloud, Maddie began to articulate her thoughts and then paused. James responded to the lines with the statement, "She's lazy."

LS: Who? Miss Rosie?
James: Yeah. I mean, I mean, it could be anybody. I mean, lazy, you
     know. I mean, don't work good. I mean, tired, beat up, some-
     thing like that.

James and Maddie here begin to speak at the same time.

James: You know.
Maddie: You know that part right here, James? James—
James: That's being lazy, you know, I mean, you know.
Nildo: I don't think so.
Maddie: James, you know that part that say, OK, "waiting for your
     mind / like next week's grocery," right? It's like when you're
     sitting down and you be like, I be like, you be *thinking,* you be
     sitting down, you be *thinking,* and I'll be like, "You hurry up."
     It's like telling you.
Nildo: It's not because you're *lazy.*
Maddie: [Agreeing] Yeah.
James: Yeah, lazy.
Maddie: No.
James: Yeah, it is.

Nildo: Can't be lazy.
Maddie: I'll be like "waiting 'til tomorrow" or something.

James said something unintelligible at this point. (They were all talking almost on top of each other.) Nildo continued.

Nildo: Just because, just because somebody, you know, if they take
    a long time to think about something doesn't mean they're
    lazy.
Maddie: Yeah. It sounds like, 'cause see, OK, I'm waiting here, and
    I'm thinking, and I'm going out with like, somebody like you
    [looking at James] to another class. You be like, "Hurry up,
    Maddie, you gonna wait until tomorrow?" or something. It's
    like you're being lazy, or *thinking*. [Pause] Them two are wrong
    [indicating Nildo and James, apparently forgetting that Nildo
    had been agreeing with her]. I'm right [emphatically].

I asked her what in the poem indicated to her that this person is thinking.

Maddie: Because it say, "waiting for your *mind*/ like next week's
    grocery." She's waiting for her mind to set up or something.
LS: To set up?
Maddie: Like to wake up.
James: She's being lazy.
Maddie: No, it's not lazy. "[W]aiting for your mind" to, to *decide*. To
    go or whatever, to go to the grocery or whatever.
James: That's lazy.
Nildo: "[W]aiting for your mind"——waiting for your decision?
Maddie: Mmhmm.
Nildo: Uh, yeah, that's a good idea though, but—
James: Or maybe she's confused.

Here Maddie and James began to speak simultaneously, their tones of voice, interestingly, both changing to become more experimental.

Maddie: She don't know where to *go*, she got a lot of things on her
    mind——
James: She ain't got nothin' to *do*, and when you just lay around
    that's being lazy.

Maddie here moved into further speculation about the relationship of speaker and person described, speculation that highlights the close connection between her ongoing concern with this relationship and her other ongoing concern: that of the purpose of the poem—the question of why it was written.

> *Maddie:* Or Lucille Clifton saw this *girl* walking down the street, and then she met her and she knew about her and everything, and she's like kind of weird, so she maybe stopped being friends with her and she started writing this about her.
> *LS:* What makes you think she's kind of weird?
> *Maddie:* Who, Clifton or Rosie?
> *LS:* No, yeah, Rosie.
> *Maddie*: Kind of weird? Because, like Lucille Clifton's talking about her. Look at the way she's talking about her.
> *LS:* What about the way she's talking about her would make her seem weird if you met her on the street?

James and Maddie again talked at the same time as they answered this.

> *James:* She wouldn't be weird. She'd be poor.
> *Maddie:* Like, I don't know. Okay, I'd be walking down the street and I meet you [James], right? He acts stupid, I mean, he's ignorant, of course I'm going to write a story about him.

Her focus is still on why the poem was written—on what moved the poet to write it. It becomes clear in the dialogue above that this question is at root the *same* question for Maddie as that of the relationship between speaker and person described, since she sees the speaker as the author of the poem.

The discussion of lines 9–10 had thus far concentrated much more closely on line 9 ("waiting for her mind"), and I therefore highlighted the other half of the metaphor (line 10) with a question about its purpose. Nildo immediately expressed his interest in this line ("Yeah" [stated firmly]). He then continued, "It's lo-o-n-ng" [stretching out the sound of the word to illustrate his point]. It later became clear that he was referring here to "next week's grocery," to the amount of time it takes to get groceries, connecting that to the "waiting" that is central to this metaphor. James was next in responding to my question:

> *James:* Waiting for food, lazy, expecting somebody to help her out.
> *Nildo:* No, it's not waiting for food. It doesn't have to do, it doesn't have to do . . .

Perhaps Nildo is struggling here to articulate his sense that "next week's grocery" is the vehicle of the metaphor, not its subject; I imagine his sentence (the preceding) completed as follows: "It (the grocery) doesn't have to do with real food." Maddie interrupts here.

> *Maddie:* Like if you're lazy, you expect me to give you everything in
>   your hand.
> *Juana:* Right.
> *Nildo:* No! I think it means . . .

Maddie misinterpreted Nildo's emphatic tone, hearing more the disagreement than the fact that he was trying to articulate an idea. She impatiently told him to "sit right down here and explain everything" if he knew "all about the story." At the same time, Marco was describing an idea that caught everyone's attention:

> *Marco:* She could be hungry to know something. She's wanting to
>   know.
> *LS:* And that's what the connection with "mind" is?
> *Marco:* Yeah. She's waiting to know.
> *James:* [Teasing] "Hungry to know something," Marco?
> *Juana:* I want to see this girl who wrote this poem.
> *James:* [Still teasing] You've been hanging out with Mr. [a teacher]
>   too long.
> *Marco:* [Unperturbed] She wanted to know so bad that she's, she's,
>   it's like she's comparing the hungry or groceries to wanting to
>   know [pause] what he's thinking or what's going on.
> *Nildo:* Yeah! [The emphasis on the comparison may have been what
>   he was trying to articulate earlier.]
> *Marco:* [Continuing] But he's not telling, he's holding out, so she *has*
>   to wait, like she has to wait for next week's groceries.

Marco's use of "he" here is confusing. James continued by acknowledging Marco's idea as possible:

> *James:* *Could* be. Or it could be waiting for next week's welfare
>   check. That could, that could be a welfare check.
> *LS:* What could be a welfare check?
> *James:* The grocery. I mean, you know, waiting. Could be. Put it all
>   together, you know. All the other things. She's poor. Away
>   from work.

I would have liked to have slowed the discussion here, to highlight these interpretations. But we were too near the end of the session at this point. It would probably be our final session with "Miss Rosie," and I wanted the students to have time to again experience the poem whole.

Nildo, at the end of his comments about the metaphor just discussed, tacked on the statement, "*And* I think the 'you' is a reflection of the 'I.' It's the same person." Good-natured groans greeted this now familiar statement. The threads of several ideas from our previous work had come forth again during the current session, to be either woven into the emerging fabric, held in abeyance, or discarded. I asked Nildo what had convinced him of this. He could not explain. "It just fits," he replied. I think perhaps he also simply liked the idea; it was clear from his expression that at least he liked to say it.

As we neared the end of the class period, I asked the students to read the poem aloud again, but with a difference. "This time," I said, "read it to someone else as if you were the 'I' and the other person was the 'you.' Or," I added, in light of Nildo's final statement (but not sure how they would accomplish this), "you can read it as if you are both the 'I' and the 'you.'" It took a little more explaining to get this clear. Maddie thought I meant that they should go and read it to someone else in the school (who was not in our group). I told her that I liked that idea too, but for our present purposes we should read it to one another.

Maddie started things off, reading to James. There was laughter and some coaching from the group ("Look at him when you talk," "Don't forget to make face expressions"). Other pairs then took the stage. Nildo read looking into Juana's mirror. The readings were different from our many other out-loud readings in a way that is hard to describe. They were more feelingful, somehow. I attribute this somewhat to the partnering, but more to the fact that the poem now carried for us the weight of all of our work. Even within the group's playfulness, there was a marked seriousness to each reader's voice as, one by one, we spoke the poem to each other: "I stand up / through your destruction / I stand up."

A Final Note

I have attempted, in the present chapter, to portray the fully organic and growing quality of the dynamic that arose between students and a poem. I have attempted this as an answer to the prevailing structure of curriculum, which presents subject matter (poetry, in this case) by paraphrase, translating it into a predetermined logic. In this way, a list of questions about poetic techniques replaces the vitality of a direct and extended meeting between reader and poem. In the present work, poetic features *were* isolated, in a way, as they were explored, but it was the students who initiated this, and it was done within the context of their developing intimacy with the poem as a whole. Such isolations were moments, not endpoints, and served (were subservient to) the students' own developing apprehensions of the poems. The students, in other words, as they isolated features of the text, moved under the guidance of their own feelings and ideas. The poem did not become an example of "metaphor"; the metaphor became a vital and functioning organ of the poem.

I suggested, in setting forth the background for this work, that the frequent disengagement of the students from school curricula is a response to curriculum as paraphrase rather than as a real encounter with a facet of the world. The students' disengagement expresses the profound resistance of the human mind to being reduced, pulled out of shape—torn away from its own integrity. In this work, I have tried to show what happens when students meet a poem with the full integrity of their own minds. That portrait is my hope for the written document. What is my hope for the six students who lent themselves so fully to the work? Perhaps it is that they will now seek out poetry. But that is really just a fraction of it. My larger hope, and the potential of the work, is that each of them has come to know more incontrovertibly his or her intelligence; and this to the point that an encounter with a poem or with some other intriguing facet of the world will arrest them, that they will find it, and by extension their own viewpoints, worthy of a second look.

References

Clifton, L. (1987). miss rosie. *Good woman: Poems and a memoir 1969–1980*. Rochester, NY: BOA Editions.

Duckworth, E. (1996). *The having of wonderful ideas* (2nd ed.). New York: Teachers College Press.

Rosenblatt, L. (1978). *The reader, the text, the poem*. Carbondale and Edwardsville: Southern Illinois University Press.

3

Journal Journeys:
An Exploration with Young Writers

Hallie Cirino

February 8: First Day

"The pig is getting married. The husband is giving a Valentine's card." Four-year-old Anne smiled as she "read" her picture to June, James, and me.

"I like your picture, Anne," commented June, who is 6.

"I'm making a pig, too," piped James, drawing. "Oops! I guess it looks more like a turtle." Five-year-old James then wrote "TAEL" (turtle) directly underneath his rendition.

"What is your turtle doing?" I asked casually.

"I guess it's walking on the letters," was James's literal response. He wrote next to "TAEL" "WCE LD" (James did not leave spaces between these words) and read aloud, "A turtle is walking on the letters."

"That's funny!" giggled June, who was writing beside her illustration of a cat. She had written, "thIs Is MI MAT AND BKSITH IT HAS a caT IS BKSITH THe SIB AV MY MTA Is caT" and then rhythmically chanted, "This is my mat and because it has a cat is because the symbol of my mat is cat!"

Anne, James, and June were 3 of about 15 students in a prekinder-garten/day care class in Cambridge, Massachusetts. The children were from well-educated families that put value on academics. I was one of three teachers, working part-time in the mornings.

To learn more about how young children write, I decided to observe closely, listen to, and work with three children, a manageable number to my mind. I chose students who represented the broadest chronological and developmental range in my class. This allowed me to see a variety of different writing abilities, as well as to observe how their interactions played a part in their learning.

In this first February class, Anne was not yet writing words. She drew pictures and told stories about them. She exhibited a great deal of confidence in doing so. James was moving from using a single word to writing a simple phrase. He had relatively poor fine-motor control (Oops! His pig became a turtle!), but was able to compensate quickly by changing his topic. When James read his writing, he did it from memory (rather than looking at the words he wrote), simultaneously adding words as he spoke, to make the reading fluent. In a similar way, his stories unfolded as he saw what he was drawing. June, on the other hand, was a bit more sophisticated with her writing. She used some spelling conventions, explanatory language, rhyming words, and a mixture of capital and lowercase letters. When June read her writing, she pointed to the words and truly read them. She left spaces between her words. On this day, June wrote autobiographically; and she continued to exhibit a tendency for doing so.

Anne, James, and June had so many "wonderful ideas" that I knew they must write about, think about, and discuss them often. I also knew that I, too, must do the same. Therefore, the recording and analysis of writing sessions with the children was key to my research. Putting pen to paper allowed me to move beyond the classroom "basics" of teaching, listening, and observing. I was able to analyze more completely what the children already knew, as well as develop a clearer idea of what they were currently learning and where they might go with this new knowledge.

I met with Anne, James, and June every Tuesday morning for about 30–45 minutes in an empty room adjacent to our main classroom. This room was set up as an open space for physical play, so when we met as writers, we had to improvise a bit. There were no tables or chairs, so the children spread their things out on the floor to work. Although we met weekly, I have selected here those sessions that seemed best to tell the story of their development as writers.

On the first day, February 8, each student was presented with a handmade journal consisting of about 30 blank sheets of heavy paper that I had painstakingly sewn together myself. The journals had cardboard covers with wallpaper glued to them. I held up the journals and flipped through the blank pages and then asked the children what they thought these were. They said they were books. I asked them what they thought was missing from the books. They replied that the books were missing pictures and words. Next I introduced pencils, markers, crayons, and colored pencils and told them that their job as writers would be to use these tools to fill their books with pictures and words. All of this "official" writing equipment was apparently very appealing to the children, as they eagerly dug in and began work on this first day.

As the weeks passed, the children looked forward to our Tuesday mornings writing together. Anne continued to draw pictures and tell us about them. She always wore an enthusiastic smile while focusing on her work. She seemed interested in seeing the letters that James and June wrote in their journals. Frequently, when James was trying to sound out letters to write, June would interrupt and tell James the letters he needed. Each time June did this, James's look of concentration, with his brown eyes rolled skyward, would fall. He'd shrug and write the letter that June said. Meanwhile, June continued on writing.

April 10: Anne Writes Words and James Writes Sentences

Anne and James were present during this week's writing time; June was absent. Anne opened her writing book and announced, "I'm going to make a jungle!"

Curious about whether Anne had a story line in her mind or simply a topic idea, I asked, "What is going to happen in your jungle?"

Anne replied, "I'm not telling you; I just want to write it," and she began drawing a tree. Then Anne said, "Guess what I'm writing?"

"I thought you said you were writing about a jungle?" Anne nodded in the affirmative.

James, watching and listening to Anne, said, "I know a monkey named Curious George. He comes from a jungle in Africa." Anne nodded and continued to illustrate trees, and James started to draw a tree as well.

"I like your tree," I commented to James. Anne looked at his illustration and asked, "Is it a tree from a jungle?" "No," answered James. Anne said, "Well, I think it's great!"

Both children drew quietly for a while. Then Anne said, "Hallie, I really like this school." I asked her what she liked about it. While continuing to draw she said, "I like activities, I like writing, I like dressing up, and I like outside time."

"Seems like she likes everything about school," said James, and the two continued drawing quietly.

At this moment it occurred to me that this was the most relaxed writing time we'd had together. I thought about the group dynamic: June was not there. She had a fairly powerful presence sometimes because she wanted to tell the other children what letters to write. She would hear them sounding out words and she would blurt out the letter before Anne or James could think of it themselves. June could also offer supportive comments, such as "I like your picture" or "You really wrote a lot of words this time." Anne and James would not necessarily have noticed the amount they had written. Yet her simple presence seemed to give them something to strive for.

Anne looked up from her writing and said, "Everything June writes she knows." (I wondered if Anne was reading my mind!)

"What do you mean?" I asked.

"June always knows all the letters for everything."

"Well, June is a little older than you," I told Anne. "She has a little more experience with writing than you do and she tries to be helpful. The more times that you write a word, the easier it is to remember how to write it the next time. Think about your name, Anne. Do you need to sound out the letters of your name every time you write it?"

Anne laughed, "No!" She then started to write about her illustration with the words "this is." Anne always wrote the word *this* with the single letter z. As she wrote her z she said, "I never have to think about how to write the word *this* because I know it's a letter z." It is likely that Anne was comparing her writing ability to June's: knowing letters without having to think about them.

"Adults write the word *this* differently," I mentioned to Anne, "But I know what you mean when you write the letter z." This was the first time Anne called her z a z; in the past, she always called it a "zig-zag."

Anne stopped writing and said, "I want to draw more on my picture before I write anymore." Did Anne need to develop ideas through her drawing before she could write?

James finished his illustration, and I asked him what he had drawn next to his tree. He pointed to a long rectangle and said, "This is a piece of wood." He pointed to a second, similar rectangle and said, "And this is a ladder." James then wrote, "ZANS iS WWDN AD A REN." He read aloud, "This is wood and a tree."

"Why is there wood and a tree?" I asked.

In answer, James wrote, "BKNZ G T B AA REN HOS," and read, "Because it's going to be a tree house." In the first sentence, when James was writing, and he came to the word *tree*, he sounded it out aloud. He was stuck on the *tr* blend and eventually wrote an R. When he came to writing *tree* the second time, he started sounding aloud again, then turned to me and asked, "How do you write *tree*?"

"You've already written it once, James," I prompted, to see if he could find the word and apply it.

"Oh, yeah." James read through his piece, pointing at each word as he read, until he came to the word tree. He kept his finger on it and wrote it down again.

Anne was still busily drawing while James put away his things. Thirty-five minutes had passed and I couldn't spend that much more time with her. I said, "You need to finish your drawing in one more minute. Then you can write about your picture."

"OK," Anne replied in a very annoyed tone of voice.

I then remembered what Anne had said earlier about wanting to *finish* drawing before writing. I said, "You can finish drawing on your own; I need to help out in the other room. Please call me over when you are ready to write."

About 10 minutes later Anne came to me with a beautifully detailed picture. "Hallie, I'm ready to write now," she said with a smile. Anne began by crossing out her original *z*. Then she said aloud, "This," and wrote a new *z*. In the past, she had written a *z* for *is*, too, but this time she wrote "AC." In all, Anne wrote, "Z AC A GL W A LI PP" and read aloud, "This is a jungle with a lion peeking out of a tree." This was also the first time Anne did not use a *Q* for a *W* sound. Anne had missed 2 weeks, and I was amazed by how much she had grown in her writing and illustrating over that period. She was learning about new letters and sounds each week. I was delighted by her ability to apply this new knowledge so readily.

When Anne finished reading, she said quite seriously, "My Papa is very pleased with my writing."

I smiled, gave her a hug, and said, "I am, too."

In this session, Anne seems to have picked up the strategy of writing words to go with her drawings, as June and James have done. Her drawings were still the most important part of her writing; she would feel the need to finish drawing before she could write. Her drawings were her text, and the words she now wrote were there to support her text.

James began *really reading* during this session. For the first time he pointed to the words he had written and read them. For the first time he decided how to write a word by seeing how it had been written before (admittedly, by himself). And for the first time he started writing in complete sentences and leaving spaces between his words. He connected Anne's writing to literature via his comment about knowing Curious George, a monkey who lives in a jungle. James seemed to exhibit more enthusiasm about his writing than he had been showing. He was usually more subdued, but became quite bubbly when something piqued his interest.

April 25: Anne Finds Letters, James Spells on His Own, and June Reveals Several Surprises

In the previous session, the children built desks out of large, hollow, wooden blocks that were stored in this room. The desks were about a foot high and the children sat on the floor with their journals upon them. On this day, when the children and I entered the room, June asked if they could build desks again. I said sure, and the three built very elaborate desks, much higher than last time—so high, in fact, that they needed to fetch chairs from the other room in order to reach them. They then built a fourth desk for the writing tools and placed that in the middle, with their desks encircling it.

June sat at her desk and said, "Hallie, I don't know what to write about."

I smiled and asked, "Do you know you tell me that each and every writing session?"

June laughed, "Yes!" I asked her if she knew what my response would be, since I always responded in the same manner. She said, "You'd tell us that authors always write about things that they know about."

I said, "See? You already know exactly what I'd say."

Then June said, "I hate writing at home because my Mom and Dad always tell me what letters to write." I told her that that is probably the way her parents learned to write when they were her age. I mentioned that that was the way my teachers taught me to write and that even today, many teachers teach kids to write that way.

Anne, who was listening carefully, half shouted, "That's not fair! That's not fair! Kids need to learn by thinking for themselves!" I agreed with her but told her that many people don't like teaching in that way. Anne sat frowning and thinking for a while. Then she said, "I know what to write! I'll write about the garden I'm going to plant this summer with my Grandpa!"

James, who had not said a word up to this point, was illustrating very quickly. He then turned to me and said, "I don't know what to write about my picture."

I looked at his journal and asked, "Can you tell me about your picture?"

"It's another tree house."

"Why did you decide to draw another tree house?"

"Because I love them! Can I write that?" I said of course and he began by writing, "I LVOEZ" and then stopped. He said, thinking aloud, "Let's see . . . now how did I spell *tree*?" and he started flipping through his writing book to find the other story he had written about tree houses. He found the page and read carefully until he came to the word *tree*. He said, "R,E,N. Hallie, is that how you spell *tree*?"

"That looks like the way you wrote it the last time," I offered. He flipped back to his new illustration and wrote while saying the letters aloud, "REN." He read, "I love tree . . ." then he wrote "HOS." I told him that now I understood why he chose to write about tree houses more than once. I joked with him and asked him if he had a tree house in his apartment. "No!"

he laughed, then added seriously, "But I do have some small plants grow-ing there." James shut his book and left.

Anne picked up the black marker that James had used for his writing and said, "I've waited for this marker for so long." I noticed she hadn't written or drawn anything yet. She began drawing her garden and said, "Hallie, I love you very much."

"I love you and all the children, too," I responded. June, who was busy writing, smiled up at me. "June," I asked, "Can you read what you've written to me?"

June put her book in front of me and said, "You read it." She had written, "I DO WRETING WITH HALLIE." I told her that I knew that she writes with me and that maybe she could tell me more about it. She con-tinued, "I CID OF TING EIS BORING BOT I OSO CID E LEC IT" (I kind of think it's boring but I also kind of like it).

"June, what do you feel is boring about writing? It is important for me to know because I am going to be teaching writing for many years. I want to be the best writing teacher I can be."

"Well, it's boring to sound out letters."

"I'm surprised you think that's boring, June. Just before you told me you hate it when your parents tell you what letters to write, and don't give you a chance to sound them out." I was genuinely confused.

"Well, you sort of like it, but you don't. Like a dilemma," responded June.

Once again, I was surprised; surprised that June knew and understood the word *dilemma*. I told her that many times, when I am writing, I feel the same way. I went on to say that writing is still a very important skill to learn because everyone needs to do it throughout his or her life. June nod-ded and sat thinking.

Anne said, "Hallie, can you help me write?"

"What do you want to say about your picture?" I asked.

"I want to say, 'This is a garden me and my grandpa are going to plant.'"

I asked her how she would start writing that. She began sounding out, slowly saying the words she wanted to write, then writing the letters she felt corresponded to those sounds. For each letter sound that she made for which she did not know how the corresponding letter looked, she would look it up on the alphabet strip. Rather than ask me to show her where the letter was on the strip (as she had done up to then), Anne began by placing her finger on the letter *A* and saying aloud, while pointing to each letter, "A,B,C,D," and so on until she came to the letter she was looking for. She would then hold her finger on it and copy it onto her paper. I loved her strategy and total independence. When she finished, she had written, "Z S

A GRD ME A M GRI R G T PT." She read, "This is a garden me and my grandpa are going to plant." I told her that I loved the way she figured out what the letters looked like on the alphabet strip. She asked, "Can I go outside now?" I said, of course, and off she went.

June was still there, but had not done any additional writing. She said, "I want to make one of those lists you told me about." (She was referring to my suggestion that she create a list of possible topics to write about. She could look at this list if she ever felt stuck for an idea to write about). I said OK and she turned to a fresh page and wrote "LIST" at the top.

"Do you have any topic ideas to put on the list?" I asked. She wrote a number 1 and wrote "DANIEL" next to it (Daniel is her baby brother). Then she put a number 2 and wrote "HAWS" (house). She closed her book and I asked, "Are you done with the list?"

"That should keep me busy for the next two writing times," smiled June as she left.

There seemed to be evidence of a certain degree of ritual during this writing session. The children could not settle into writing until they had built their desks. June could not write until she had reiterated her weekly conversation concerning not knowing what to write about. Anne couldn't write until she had a specific marker to use, a behavior she had exhibited in the past. James told me he didn't know what to write about his picture. He frequently seemed to need to talk about his drawings first, prior to writing anything. Don't most adult writers rely on similar rituals?

In moving away from ritual, June was full of surprises during this particular session. Her expression of dislike concerning parental interference was particularly interesting when it was coupled with her conflicting thoughts on writing—June's dilemma! June was ready to use the topic-list strategy this writing time, but, again, she surprised me. She knew how to organize a list by both labeling and numbering it. June took ownership of the idea by letting me know she wanted to make one, and by simply doing it herself.

During this session, James preplanned his drawing; he knew he wanted to write about tree houses again. In the past, his topics seemed to unfold as he drew. James's independent strategy for looking up how he had previously written "tree" was wonderful. Whereas last time James needed prompting from me to find the word *tree*, this time he did it entirely on his own. He was exhibiting more and more confidence in himself through his writing.

While James has become independent in word finding, Anne has become independent in letter finding. She initiated a terrific strategy for finding out on her own what letters look like. It astounded me that she knew that a certain named letter made a specific sound, yet did not know what that letter looked like. Also, this time Anne knew what she would write about before she put pen to paper; she had well-formed ideas for her writing.

May 15: Anne Grows by Leaps and Bounds, James's Unprecedented Decision, and June Relaxes

When the children entered the room, they immediately began building desks again; this time without asking my permission. Rather than build a fourth desk for the markers, this time they created, from the blocks, a triangular-shaped track for sliding, or passing, the markers along. Their desks encircled the track, so that each point of the triangle met the front of one desk. It was really quite elaborate.

With the desk construction out of the way, the three children sat down, and I handed them their journals. June asked, "When will the last writing time be?"

"Mmm, probably next week."

June got a worried look on her face. "Does that mean we can no longer write at school?" she frowned.

"June, of course you can write whenever you want. You have many more pages left in your journal. And don't forget you also have your other writing book in the other room."

"I'm worried that I'll forget about writing and I'll miss writing with Anne and James," she trembled. "Can we still write on Tuesday mornings together?"

"Yes," I conceded. "But James's Mom doesn't like having to get up early to get James here in time for writing. I can't ask her to continue doing that for us. I promised her the last time would be next week."

June nodded, smiled, and said, "Guess what? I don't know what to write about!" I reminded her that she had previously made a list of possible topics for writing and suggested she look at it for an idea.

Anne opened her journal to the page where "Z S A GRD ME A M GRI R G T PT" was written. Anne pointed to each word she had written and carefully sounded out (read) the entire sentence, "This is the garden me and my grandpa are going to plant." This was the first time Anne had actually read something that she had written earlier. I was very excited and tried to ask calmly, "Do you realize this is the first time you really read your own writing?" Anne shrugged her shoulders (why wasn't it exciting for her?) and told me she would like to continue her story. I told her that I thought that was a great idea and she began to draw on the facing page.

June was leaning her chin on her hand and lamented, "I still don't know what to write; I don't feel like using any of these ideas [gesturing to her list]." But suddenly she began to write. She quickly wrote, "I all OMOST 6 Ye OLD" in large, heavy black letters. Then she picked up a purple crayon and colored in some of the letters. I never before saw June using a "playful" approach to her writing. I was pleased she was not being so rigid and told her that I liked the way her letters looked, colored in.

James was once again drawing some trees (the fourth week in a row). This time he had drawn three trees and what looked like some kind of animal. Out of curiosity, I asked him where he had got his idea from (it somehow looked familiar). He said seriously, "I got my idea from Anne, but I'm not copying."

Anne looked at James's drawing and reassured him, "I know you're not."

Then I knew; a month or so ago Anne had drawn three trees (a jungle) and a lion. I assured James that I knew he was not "copying," and I told him I thought it was really neat that he could get ideas from friends. I said that that was one of the reasons why I thought it was important for children to write together rather than alone.

June looked up from her writing and asked, "Do I have to draw a picture?"

"Only if you want to; if you think it's important for your story," I said, then continued, "Some children need to draw a picture before they can write anything."

Anne looked at June and egocentrically added, "Most kids need to draw a picture first."

June said, "Well, I'm drawing a patchwork quilt," and she proceeded to make squares of color next to each other.

"I have a book about patchwork quilts," mentioned Anne.

"I know. So do I," said June.

"Does yours have a milkman and a cat?" asked Anne.

"No, I have a different one," answered June.

James was saying aloud, to no one in particular, "I don't really know what to write."

"What do you feel is important for people to know about your picture?" I asked.

"Well, the lion's [it was a lion, like Anne's] sniffing around for meat," said James.

"I didn't know that by looking at your picture, James. Do you think you could write about that?" I asked.

"The lion is also sniffing around for his friend," continued James. I suggested that he write whatever he felt was the most important to know about his picture. He then drew a person in the trees, behind the lion. I asked him who it was. "It's me. I'm sneaking up to pull the lion's tail to catch him before he catches me." I said that I thought that the story was getting very exciting.

James then flipped back several pages in his book till he came to an illustration of himself talking to the sun. He said, "This is me walking towards the woods." (He turned the page to a picture of trees.) "Now I'm getting deeper" (turned page to more trees), "deeper" (turned page to the next set of trees), "and deeper into the woods." (He turned the page to today's illustration.) "Now I'm walking towards the lion!" Then James paused for a moment and said, "I still don't know what I should write. I have so many ideas [points to his head], I don't want to get mixed up."

"Well, James, what is the first thing you would want a person to know if they are looking at this drawing?" I asked.

James wrote in response, "S S ME W TORS Z LIN" (this is me walking towards the lion). I asked him if he'd like to show his multiple-page story idea to June and Anne. He said, "Sure!" and "read" it to them in the same manner.

"That's great, James," commented Anne.

"You wrote all those pages today?" inquired June.

"No," answered James. "Only the last one."

"What's going to happen next in your story?" I asked.

"I told you. I'm going to capture the lion before he catches me!" I asked him to pretend I didn't know he said that. I told him that if another person were to read his story, they wouldn't know that part because it wasn't written down. James sighed, "Well I'll write about that next time." (He seemed exhausted after all that hard work.) He closed his book and left.

In the meantime, June had closed her journal and left, too. Anne told me she had crossed out the page she had started earlier because she didn't like it. "Anne, that's great you feel you can cross out something you don't like. Whenever I make a mistake or I write something I don't like, I just cross it out, too," I commented. (The last time Anne didn't like something she had drawn, the only way she could cope with it was by covering the page by gluing a blank sheet of white paper over it entirely).

Anne was drawing a flower. She said, "Hallie, do you know what I didn't like this morning? I was writing and my mummy told me the last letter."

"Oh? What word were you writing?"

"Food. I wrote F, O, O and then she told me 'D.'"

"Anne, you can tell your mother you don't like that. You can tell her you like thinking about letters yourself."

"OK," said Anne. "Hallie, do I have to write about my picture?"

"I would like you to," I answered.

"Why do we have to write?" she asked.

"Well, of course you don't have to write," I said. "But I'm interested in learning about how children learn to write. If children don't write anything, then I can't learn anything about how they write."

Anne then sounded out and wrote independently, without help from me or an alphabet strip, "Z I A FOWR" (this is a flower). She closed her book and said she was finished.

During this session, Anne, too, began to really read. Her independence from both the alphabet strip and me was a marvel. This progress combined with her feelings of disgruntlement with her mom's spelling interference was indicative of Anne's newly felt empowerment. Four-year-old Anne was now both a writer and a reader, and she felt very good about what she knew.

James had begun rehearsing prior to writing; he was attempting to sort out story ideas and sequence before writing. He demonstrated a great deal of both creativity and flexibility in his multiple-page story idea. James had developed strategies for topic ideas, spellings, and story line, while simultaneously growing in his self-confidence.

June had "lightened up" her approach to writing through illustration (in the past, her written words were much more significant than her pictures). June still did require the extra strokes of reassurance prior to writing. Her world seemed to be rigid and rule-bound—reflected in her worry about whether she would ever be writing again.

Thoughts and Reflections

Through my exploratory journey with these children, I became both learner and teacher. Reading the interesting research on early writing (Butler & Turbill, 1987; Dyson, 1997; Ernst, 1995; Gibson, 1989; Graves, 1983; Hansen, 1987; Lane, 1993) further stimulates my quest for knowledge. I am always looking for ways to integrate new learning into my classroom.

This study has helped me appreciate that children can and will happily produce writing at a very young age when provided with both the opportunity and appropriate tools. I never really told the children anything about writing. I gave them "books" and asked them to add what they thought was missing—pictures and words, or "writing." I refrained from being critical of the children's work, thereby allowing them to feel free to explore any and all ideas in their journals. I also refrained from telling them things that might then remove a productive struggle for them. When the students asked me questions, I would usually respond with a question, or point them to available resources for answers they could find on their own—often their own writing.

The study also helped me appreciate the significance of the children's pictures to their writing. The pictures often carried more importance than the words—and indeed were very often the source of the words. As pictures are said to provide contextual clues for reading, we might say that the children's drawings provide contextual clues for their own writing.

I found that placing the children in a setting where they could interact enabled them to share a great deal about writing. They shared ideas for pictures, topics, how to figure out which letter is needed and where, if necessary, to find it. They also gave each other encouragement, both by their simple presence and with explicit praise.

This writing seemed like an integral, natural way to foster children's development. Social skills, phonetic concepts, confidence, and a sense of empowerment all seemed to grow during this process. They seemed to feel very good about what they were able to accomplish. As new skills were acquired, they were readily built upon, in tandem with the child's confidence.

Since this study, I have always introduced writing journals in this same way to whole classes of young students on the first day of school. We start off the school year with writing because I want them to know that writing is important, a priority. The children never fail to produce some sort of writing on this first day, and they look forward to future writing times where they can expand and build upon what they are learning, just like Anne, James, and June.

In addition, I found that I continue to be able to make added connections to students' development and learning by writing about what I see them do and hear them say. Since this study, I have kept a journal where I record conversations and actions of pupils, and write reflections about them. I add my own sketches and drawings. Somehow, illustrating students at work helps me learn and remember more about them.

Along my own journey as a teacher, I carry these insights carefully with me. While I am more thoughtful, reflective, and aware, my eyes and ears are more acutely open to my students. Anne's words in particular will forever resonate within: "Kids need to learn by thinking for themselves!"

References

Butler, A., & Turbill, J. (1987). *Towards a reading-writing classroom*. Portsmouth, NH: Heinemann.
Duckworth, E. (1996). *The having of wonderful ideas* (2nd ed.). New York: Teachers College Press.

Dyson, A. (1997). *Writing superheroes: Contemporary childhood, popular culture, and classroom literacy.* New York: Teachers College Press.

Ernst, K. (1995). *Picturing learning.* Portsmouth, NH: Heinemann.

Ferreiro, E. (1986). The interplay between information and assimilation in beginning literacy. In W. Teale, (Ed.), *Emergent literacy.* Norwood, NJ: Ablex Publishing Corp.

Gibson, L. (1989). *Literacy learning in the early years.* New York: Teachers College Press.

Graves, D. (1983). *Writing: Teachers and children at work.* Portsmouth, NH.: Heinemann.

Hansen, J. (1987). *When writers read.* Portsmouth, NH: Heinemann.

Lane, B. (1993). *After the end.* Portsmouth, NH: Heinemann.

4

Children Map Their Neighborhoods

Ileana M. Quintero

How do children come to know their geographical environment? My interest in this question, and in geography as it is taught in school, arose from various personal experiences as both a student and a teacher, as well as from interviews and observations I carried out in Boston and Puerto Rico. First, looking at 4th- and 5th-grade social studies curriculum in Puerto Rico, I found that conceptions of social reality were presented throughout the curriculum in a fragmented and undynamic way. Social studies material was presented as a set of unconnected facts not to be questioned. The main activity required was memorization. As a student of Paolo Freire's work, I felt that this type of teaching gave the learner a static, nonproblematic conception of social reality. Furthermore, the concepts introduced were presented without exploration of the learner's understanding of them.

In addition to analyzing the written curriculum, I interviewed teachers and students. They voiced a major complaint: As a school subject, social studies was irrelevant to the students' understanding of their social problems; students usually were bored and did not enjoy the course.

I also wanted to explore what happens during classroom interactions and the way teachers include, or fail to include, the learners' everyday experience in the teaching-learning process. To pursue this inquiry, I studied a group of 12 Puerto Rican children at an elementary school in Boston. They were in a 2nd-grade bilingual classroom, using Spanish, for most of them did not know English. The teacher was also Puerto Rican. Some of the children were U.S. born, and most of them traveled back and forth between Puerto Rico and the United States.

School reports prepared by teachers, psychologists, and social workers described one of the major problems affecting these children as "a lack of attention span." These evaluations puzzled me, since I found the children very attentive and engaged during certain activities, but not during others.

93

In the staff's evaluation of the children's weaknesses and strengths, the children were described as being weak in academic skills such as reading, writing, and mathematical problem solving, whereas their strengths were considered to lie in dancing, cooking, and social relations. It seemed, from this evaluation, that the children were more interested in "nonacademic activities." This raised some questions: What underlies this division between formal and nonformal learning? Is this separation the result of a lack of connection between school life and everyday experience? Why does the school fail to engage these children in formal learning activities? Are there some formal activities that attract them? Which? How? Why? Although it was not my intention to try to answer all these questions within these earlier studies, they were present during my observations.

My observations showed that the students were, in fact, engaged by science activities. This was particularly true when they were inquiring about familiar animals and fruits. In addition, they were engaged when involved in activities concerning their families. They were inattentive, however, during reading lessons in which they had to repeat and memorize words that did not have any meaning for them. Their texts were designed for use in Mexican American communities and thus included words from the Mexican dialect of Spanish, with which Puerto Rican children are unfamiliar. When the stories they were required to read were aimed at younger children, they became inattentive and bored and began to talk among themselves. When the teacher asked a question, they tended to guess and make up the answers, using their own stories. It is interesting to note that the stories they made up on these occasions were related to their daily lives. However, rather than talking about the personal, everyday concerns underlying these stories, the teacher responded by reprimanding them.

These initial observations revealed that the problem I had perceived in the social studies classes transcended subject matter. The origin of the problem seemed to lie in general conceptions about the teaching and learning processes on which curriculum development is based. When the learner is regarded as a passive recipient, ready to receive knowledge from teachers, the subject matter will be correspondingly full of predetermined ideas not necessarily related in any way to the learners' concerns. In this kind of educational model, a child is successful when he or she memorizes and repeats the information. Failure, by contrast, as in the case of most of the Puerto Rican children I observed in Boston, implies being unable—or perhaps unwilling—to attain that goal.

I believe, to the contrary, that when the learner is seen as an active being, constantly discovering and inquiring, both teacher and learner are involved in a process of inquiry about the subject matter in question. The teacher's inquiry will focus on, among other things, how to integrate the content of the subject matter and the relevant aspects of the learner's every-day life.

With this perspective in mind, when confronted with the problem of attempting to build a curriculum, I decided to take a different approach and develop a different kind of curriculum for geography—one based on the children's own experiences—which could open to them parts of the world they might not have previously thought about. Through understanding the concepts that children have developed about the spatial organization of their immediate neighborhood, I could lead them to examine one another's spatial ideas, thereby facilitating connections that would help them gain a broader sense of the spatial organization of their environment.

Description of the Setting

My research took place in 1996 at the Abraham Lincoln Elementary School in Old San Juan. The students in the school come from three of the four areas on the San Juan islet: La Perla, Old San Juan, and Puerta de Tierra (see Figure 4.1). I selected this school for several reasons. First, the school was examining ways to change the curriculum. This opened the door to my discussing possible changes with the social studies teacher. Second, the three areas have a rich variety of geographical features. Third, La Perla and Puerta de Tierra are both areas that have profound social problems, such as a high level of drug addiction, unemployment, and students dropping out of school. (The police had made raids in both communities, creating more or less a state of siege. This government operation was known as the "mano dura contra el crimen" [get tough with crime] program.) Given the circumstances, it was particularly interesting to explore different alternatives for these children's learning.

Old San Juan. Old San Juan is a walled Spanish-colonial city founded in the sixteenth century and used very early on as a military bastion. The city wall served to mark the limits of the city, separating and distinguishing the territory within from that outside the walls.

Old San Juan is now a residential and commercial area. The old structures have been largely restored.

La Perla. La Perla took its name from a small fort that had stood there. La Perla, whose development began at the beginning of the twentieth century, is located in the northern part of San Juan on the side of a steep hill that drops down to the sea (see Figure 4.1, upper left). Separated from the rest of Old San Juan by the city wall, La Perla was settled by people who

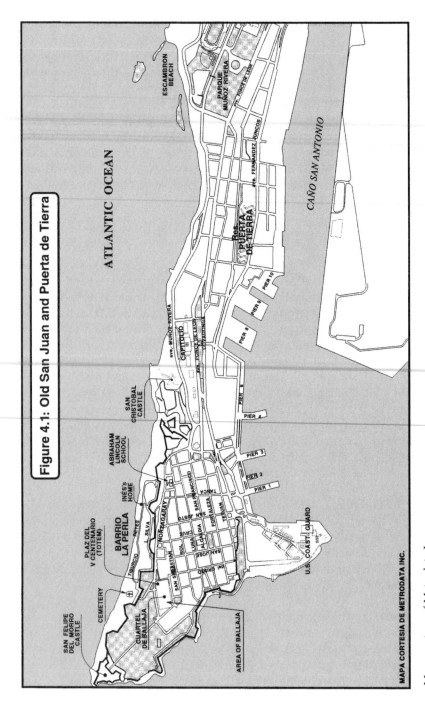

Figure 4.1: Old San Juan and Puerta de Tierra

ATLANTIC OCEAN

CAÑO SAN ANTONIO

SAN FELIPE
DEL MORRO
CASTLE

CEMETERY

CUARTEL
DE BALLAJÁ

PLAZ DEL
V CENTENARIO
(TOTEM)

BARRIO
LA PERLA

AREA OF BALLAJÁ

INÉS's
HOME

ABRAHAM
LINCOLN
SCHOOL

SAN
CRISTÓBAL
CASTLE

U.S. COAST GUARD

PIER 1

PIER 2

PIER 3

PIER 4

PIER 6

PIER 8

PIER 10

CAPITOLIO

AVE. MUÑOZ RIVERA

AVE. PONCE DE LEON

AVE. FERNÁNDEZ JUNCOS

Bo.
PUERTA
DE TIERRA

PARQUE
MUÑOZ RIVERA

ESCAMBRÓN
BEACH

TIBURCIO
REYES
SILVA
NORZAGARAY
SOL
CRUZ
LUNA
SAN SEBASTIÁN
SAN JOSÉ
CRISTO
SAN JUSTO
SAN FRANCISCO
TANCA
FORTALEZA
ALCALDIA
TETUÁN

MAPA CORTESÍA DE METRODATA INC.

Map courtesy of Metrodata Inc.

came from the countryside to work in the city. At present it is a very poor neighborhood, though superficially it has the attractive appearance of a country town. La Perla has two or three main streets wide enough for vehicular traffic, and it is full of small footpaths. At the time I carried out the project, no official map included La Perla. I had found a map of the San Juan islet that included Old San Juan and Puerta de Tierra, but not La Perla, which appeared only as an area of sand. After a month of calling fruitlessly from office to office, including that of the Highway Authority, I assumed that there was no map with La Perla on it. Much later I found a map, more a sketch, of La Perla at the Instituto de Cultura Puertorriqueña. Still later a map was produced (Metrodata, 2000) which is included with this chapter as Figure 4.2. This version was adapted from the original in order to highlight landmarks identified by Inés, a student in my study, whose work is described in this chapter.

Puerta de Tierra. Puerta de Tierra got its name from a former door made of sand at the eastern edge of Old San Juan. The area was settled by people from the coast who came to work at the wharf. At that time 61% of the population was Black or Mulatto, and that has not significantly changed. Puerta de Tierra has always been a mostly working-class neighborhood. Living conditions have always been very poor, and the housing of the inhabitants was illegal for a long time because there were no deeds for the land on which it was constructed. Some areas of Puerta de Tierra were mangrove swamps filled with waste and sand.

As a result of the need for housing for the labor force near the workplace, land speculation grew and made the urban development of Puerta de Tierra a very peculiar one. The area is not laid out in any specific order nor does it follow a particular plan.

At present there is considerable exchange of people between La Perla and Puerta de Tierra.

Profiles of the Children

I worked with a group of six 3rd-grade children. I selected that grade because it is at that level that children are introduced to certain basic concepts of geography, such as cardinal points, oceans, islands, and continents.

I had the teacher select the children for me. I asked her for a group that would include girls and boys, children from all three areas, and academic diversity. She chose two children from each of the three areas, but she had difficulty with the other two criteria. She pointed out that they were all of similar academic level, one that she characterized as "very low." As

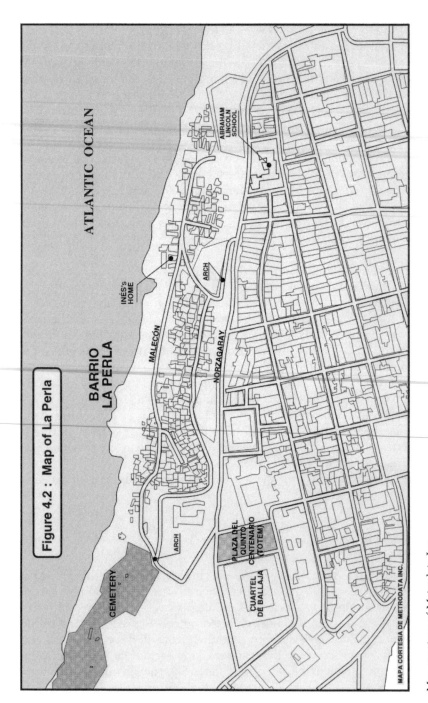

Figure 4.2 : Map of La Perla

Map courtesy of Metrodata Inc.

for difference in gender, that posed a problem, since there were only four girls in the class of 26 children. (This was unusual for most Puerto Rican classrooms.) Two girls were from La Perla, one from Puerta de Tierra, and one from Old San Juan. The teacher, not wanting me to take all the girls in the classroom, allowed me to take the two from La Perla. In addition to them, the final work group included two boys each from Old San Juan and Puerta de Tierra.

Julián. Julián was from Old San Juan, and at 10 years old was the oldest in the group. He repeatedly claimed that he was "dumb," having failed once in school. Julián was very active and loved to roller-skate. He showed concern for the other children and was popular with them. Julián loved rap, and he and César commonly finished the activities by rapping out a song.

Julián lived in Old San Juan and walked to school every morning. He enjoyed exploring, both by himself and with friends of the same age, walking around Old San Juan, La Perla, and El Escambrón, a beach located in Puerta de Tierra. He also roller-skated around Old San Juan.

From the beginning, Julián was interested in the work we were doing. It was the first time that he had thought about his area as an object of study, and he was delighted. He liked to think about and give order to his area based on his daily explorations. After our meetings, he would continue with his drawings and observations.

César. César also lived in Old San Juan. Nine-year-old César was a very open, vivacious child who defended his ideas vigorously. He loved rap music, and he would sometimes describe routes by rapping about them.

He often explored the area with Julián, as well as walking alone in San Juan. His aunt lived in La Perla, and he spent the afternoons at her home. He walked to El Escambrón, so he had gone through Puerta de Tierra. In contrast to the other children, early on in the study César developed confidence in his mapping of the area and became very involved in our work.

During our research his house was raided by the police. His father went to jail, and his mother moved with him to another town, Carolina, a 50-minute drive from Old San Juan, although he continued at Lincoln School. His mother drove him to school, but he was frequently absent, and I considered removing him from the group. Because of his interest, however, I let him stay. In fact, the teacher used to say that I should tell him when I would be working with him because that would motivate him and he would insist that his mother bring him to school.

César and Julián were best friends, and both were leaders of the class.

Javier. Javier, 9 years old, was from Puerta de Tierra. He was very shy when working alone with me but participated actively when other children were present. His ideas were best expressed when he worked with Inés or Armando. Since Javier would always ask to work with other children, I rarely worked with him alone. He never became completely involved in the activities. He liked to work, but he was never as excited as César, Julián, or Inés.

Javier almost never explored his neighborhood alone. His mother picked him up at school, and they returned to Puerta de Tierra by bus. He loved to play basketball, and there was a basketball court in front of his house.

Armando. Armando was from Puerta de Tierra. At 8 years old, Armando was the youngest one in the group. He was a very open, extroverted child. He was the student who most enjoyed activities such as the field trips. If he did not like an activity, he would say, "What we did today was awful." His father was in jail, and he mentioned this frequently. Although Armando was easily distracted, there were two activities that interested him enough to keep him working: the drawing of Fort San Cristóbal and making the cardboard model. Going to El San Cristóbal was his idea. He liked to go outside the classroom and be with his friends, although he was not very engaged in mapping the area. I was not always sure of when he was paying attention to his work and when he was just doing it as a requirement to get outside the classroom. Nevertheless, he did the work.

Armando explored alone somewhat more than Javier. He went alone to the docks in Puerta de Tierra. Like Javier's mother, his mother picked him up after school, and they returned to Puerta de Tierra by bus. Javier's and Armando's mothers always traveled together from Puerta de Tierra to school and back.

Elena. Ten-year-old Elena was from La Perla. Born in the Dominican Republic, she had come to Puerto Rico 4 years earlier and had lived only in La Perla. Elena did not know the Island of Puerto Rico well, but was very familiar with La Perla. She loved to include details in her drawings and remembered her friends' houses and little stores.

Elena took strong stands with the other children and even defended them by fighting. The teacher referred to her as "stubborn." During the research, she had a violent fight with a girl who was not in the group. As punishment, the teacher wanted to take Elena out of the research group, but I thought that that would be helpful neither to Elena nor to the other girl. I spoke to the teacher about it, and Elena remained in the group. However, she was frequently absent, including for the entire last month of the work.

Inés. Inés, 9 years old and from La Perla, was very shy and had a sweet disposition. She seldom spoke; when she did, her voice was very soft. She loved to draw, and she produced brightly colored maps. When Inés was small, her biological mother had gone to jail. One of her older brothers took care of her, and since then she had lived with her brother's family. She seldom explored the area alone, sometimes moved around La Perla with girlfriends and brothers (nephews). She walked to Old San Juan with her mother (her brother's wife) and traveled farther away from Old San Juan with her mother or father (older brother).

Although she did not verbally express that she wanted to work with me, she indicated it with a big smile every time I called her. Sometimes when I went to work with other children, and I saw her, bored in the classroom, I would call her too. She sat quietly beside me, drawing her path from home to school.

The Project

In the process of trying to understand the children's spatial thinking, I involved them in a number of geography-related activities, described in the following account. The purpose of these exercises was to engage the children in learning about their geographical space and, once they were engaged, to uncover their ideas about how they perceive and come to know their geographical environment. Throughout these activities, I repeatedly asked questions in order to reach a clear understanding of the children's thinking and their conclusions. Most of the activities involved drawing, or building models of, their home areas and other areas of the San Juan islet. I worked with the six children of the study in different-sized groups. Most of the time, I worked with them individually or in pairs. However, during five sessions, I had all six children with me, and on three occasions I took the whole 3rd grade, because the other children asked to work on the geographical activities with me.

The six children were among the least disciplined in the class. After one of the lessons, during which they were out of the classroom working with me, the teacher said, "Today was so calm! For once I was able to cover the whole lesson." My group was small, but lively.

In addition to the formal activities, I also observed the children informally in the classroom and at play, and I interviewed the teacher about the social studies class. On several occasions I went alone to the areas where the children lived. I observed and mapped the surroundings and the routes from home to school to understand their map work. When I stayed late at school, I would pick up the two boys from Puerta de Tierra, along with their mothers, at the bus stop near the school and give them a ride back to their homes. During those trips I spoke informally with the two mothers. At first, the mothers did not want me to go to their housing projects, but they relented once they were accustomed to seeing me with the children. All these additional sources of information gave me a better understanding of the children and their home areas.

At the beginning of the research project, the children were surprised and confused by the tasks; they did not quite understand what I was asking them to do. As the activities developed, they understood better and consequently became engaged.

The Abraham Lincoln School is located on the top of a hill in Old San Juan. We worked in a second-floor corridor with a balcony overlooking a portion of Old San Juan, La Perla, and the Fort of San Cristóbal. The sea was in the background. Sometimes they also looked through the classroom windows, which overlooked Sol Street and another portion of Old San Juan (see Figure 4.3). The balcony and the possibility of looking through the classroom windows allowed the children to observe the areas and develop and check hypotheses.

When the children were drawing, they sat at different positions in the corridor, sometimes facing one way and sometimes another, so that they were in different relationships to their neighborhoods. In their descriptions they referred to places as being in front of them when they were facing the locality, in the back when the places where located behind them, and to the side when they were to their right or left side.

Most of the drawings were made on 4' × 5' remnants of newsprint rolls. For purposes of analysis and presentation of the drawings, I worked with Maritza Maymí to reproduce them on the computer. Maritza did not want to work directly from the children's maps, because she had not been involved with the children. Instead, the reproductions were created as follows: I first made a drawing of the children's maps on a piece of paper. In order to do that, I observed the children's drawings carefully and redrew them. Once that was done I used my field notes to reflect on the children's logic and understanding of the area. After I shared my interpretation with Maritza, she and I checked my drawing against the children's maps for accuracy. Finally she drew my maps on the computer. This process was very helpful in allowing me to understand the ways the children were perceiving and organizing the geographical area.

In some of the reproductions (Figures 4.7, 4.8, 4.10, 4.11, 4.13), I have added a symbol of a small person to indicate the children's positions.

(Words in Spanish were put by the children. Words in English were put by me.)

FIGURE 4.3. View from school's balcony windows (Ileana)

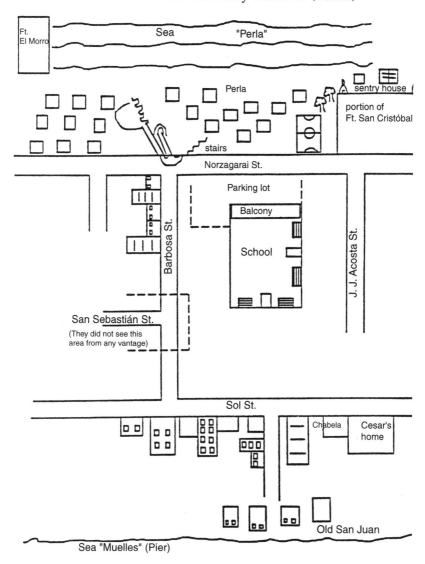

In this chapter I will follow the development of the work of one child. I chose Inés, even though she was a quiet student who seldom spoke as she worked, because I found that she was very engaged in the tasks and tried very hard to express her ideas in a way that enabled others to understand them. I observed her frequently looking over the balcony, and she called me whenever she found a place she wanted me to look at. When analyzing the data, I realized that Inés worked with me almost every time I was at the school, even if it was not her turn.

Inés's home area, La Perla, is very complex to map. The drawings of Inés and Elena seldom included streets, and I did not understand why until I went to La Perla and discovered the great number of tortuous footpaths that existed there. The area has two or three main streets and many pedestrian paths connected to these main streets (see Figures 4.2 and 4.4).

First Drawings of the Area

The first time I asked the children to draw their home area I gave each of them an 8" × 11" piece of paper, crayons, magic markers, and pencils. Inés did two different houses: her home and her grandfather's home (see Figure 4.5). She used two pieces of paper for each drawing.

When I then asked her to draw the route from home to school, Inés reacted, "¡Diache, que largo!" (Wow, that's long!) That day we were working in the school library in front of a big window from where we could observe La Perla. Inés sat in front of the window, and she kept looking through it the entire time she was drawing. Finally she drew her house, one straight road, the arch (that according to Inés indicated the entrance to La Perla), and the school (see Figure 4.6). There are two main entrances to La Perla, and both have an arch. One entrance is near the school, to the left as one looks from the school. The other is near the fort at El Morro and the cemetery (refer to Figure 4.2). In her drawing, Inés located places next to one another in a horizontal line, although they were in fact far from one another. In addition, she was not concerned with showing how they related to one another; it was as if she were drawing a series of independent pictures. When she explained her map to me, she said, "This is my house, then you pass by the arch, and then you get to school." She drew the places in the same order in which she traverses them enroute from home to school. According to her first drawing, her house was connected to the school by a straight line. When I asked her if she went home in a straight line from school, her response was that she did not have enough paper to make her drawing complete.

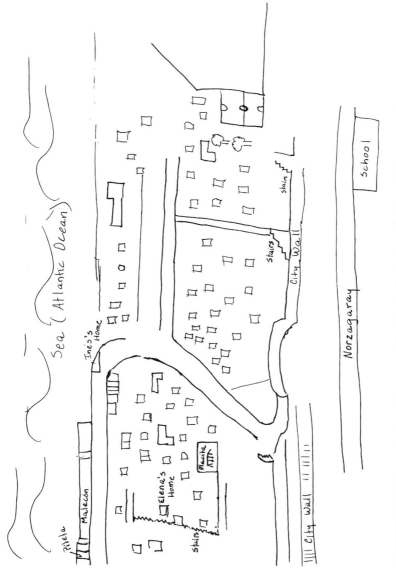

FIGURE 4.4. Ileana's sketch map of La Perla (Inés's and Elena's home area)

FIGURE 4.5. Inés's first drawing: Home Area

a) Inés's home

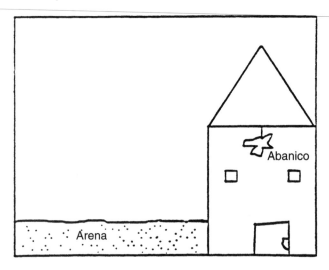

b) Inés's grandfather's home

FIGURE 4.6. Inés drawing of the route from home to school

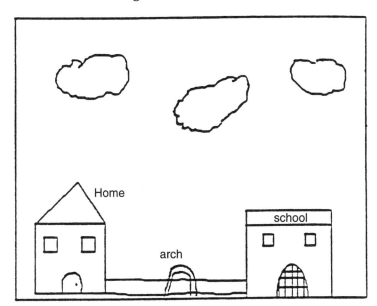

Unlike Julián and César, Inés had limited experience exploring her area; she constantly struggled with her idea of it. So she had a dual problem: understanding the area and coordinating a picture in order to translate this understanding into a map.

After the first drawings, I had the children build a model of their home areas on a 2' × 3' piece of cardboard. The children worked in pairs. I brought them pieces of foam and wood, toy cars, and magic markers of different colors. With the foam and wood they constructed houses and buildings and they used the magic markers to draw the roads and streets. Inés and Elena also used the magic markers to draw some landmarks in which they wanted to include more details. Inés enjoyed this project very much because it was big enough to allow her to include many places.

For this activity Elena and Inés went to the balcony. They looked at and spoke about the places they could see in front of them and included the ones they remembered seeing. Elena drew the road; Inés constructed the buildings and drew the notable places, employing many details and colors. Inés located the places next to one another, following the order in which she and Elena had seen them from the balcony of the school: first the benches at the entrance of La Perla, then the arch, Elena's house, the park with swings, and her house. She described it while she made the figures and placed the landmarks (see Figure 4.7). She located the places, although most of them she

FIGURE 4.7. Inés and Elena's cardboard model

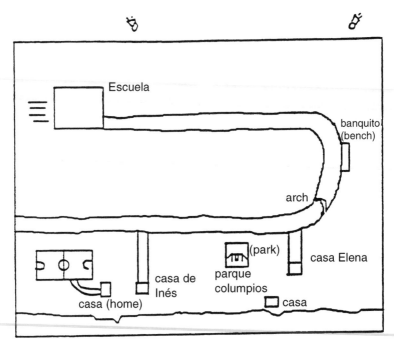

did not connect to any particular road. I did not intervene much during this particular project, because I had not yet visited La Perla and I didn't have a clear understanding of what they were doing.

A Large Drawing

The next activity was drawing the area on newsprint measuring 4' × 5'. Inés again liked the fact that the paper was bigger and she could include a lot of details. This activity also was done in pairs, and again Inés and Elena went to the balcony, looked, and then went back to work on the paper. As they sat, they were facing La Perla (refer to Figures 4.2 and 4.8).

> *Inés:* Over here [she pointed straight ahead to the middle of the paper] we should put the swings. They were there [she pointed straight ahead of her, across the balcony].
>
> *Elena:* No, they have to be over here [on the right side of the paper].
>
> *Inés:* Should we put Maritza's store here? [On the right side on the paper].

After discussing where they should locate various places, Elena and Inés began to draw. Elena drew the main entrance to La Perla (the arch). This entrance also appears in the cardboard model (refer to Figure 4.7). In this drawing Inés located a number of places in La Perla with their correct spatial relations. She drew them from the perspective of the balcony, so Elena's house is closer than hers and the basketball courtyard is also closer, toward the right. Although she included these places and gave them a certain order, she did not connect them to any particular route. After this first attempt to organize the places, she continued to draw, adding and including places, even if they didn't have any particular order. Inés preferred simply to include places rather than give them a certain order (see Figure 4.8). For example, while she was drawing, I asked about the church:

IQ: Do you think that the church is near the sea?
Inés: No, it is not there, but I don't have space in the paper to include it. [She described it as being very far away and she

FIGURE 4.8. Drawing of the area on end roll paper (Inés and Elena)

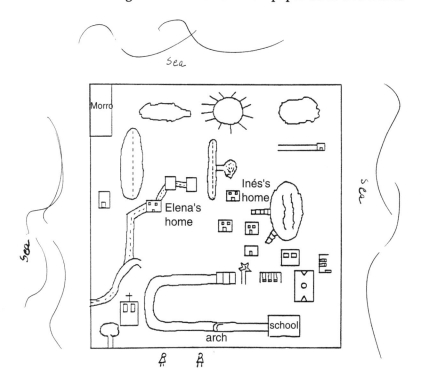

> thought she could not fit it into her drawing in its proper
> place.]

She liked to include all the details of the houses, flowers, and plants. She also included birds, cars, and people. Her drawing included the area from the school to El Morro; this is almost the entire area of La Perla. Inés located El Morro Fort by standing up, looking across the balcony, coming back, and then drawing it in the upper left section of the sheet of paper. Inés always went to the balcony to look at the places in La Perla, also calling me to look at them. She wanted to represent her area in a way that would allow me and the other children to find the places, but she did not always succeed. When she was making the drawing a boy from La Perla came by and asked:

> *Boy:* Where is my house?
> *Inés:* Over there. [She indicated it on the paper near Elena's house.]
> *Boy:* Oh, no! My house is beside the sea.

Another time she asked me if I understood her drawing, and I proceeded to affirm my understanding of it with her. We stood together on the balcony to find corresponding places in the drawing and in real space. Some coincided with the organization of places in her map and others not. After doing this she remained at the balcony for a while observing La Perla and her drawing which was lying on the floor just inside the classroom.

The representation of real space in conventional maps has a certain logic and rules of organization that do not necessarily coincide with an individual's position in space. Inés, however, was following her own logic: She was trying to draw the area using the position of her own body as a guide. So far, she had two ways of representing what she was seeing in real space. One was to use what I call picture landmarks. Often, children remember churches, friends' houses, or buildings of some significance or other and draw them on a map in the order in which they encounter them as they walk from home to school. Inés, however, drew them as isolated pictures without streets or connecting routes, perhaps because she could see things from the balcony. Therefore, it was difficult to follow and identify locations in her map.

The other way she had of representing what she was seeing in real space developed because she wanted other people to understand her maps. She began to establish connections between places and to locate landmarks, one next to the other. Whereas her first drawings reflected what she remembered from her walks, now she used her body to figure out where the object was located in real space. That is, "in front," "behind," "beside" coincided with the relationship to the real position of her body in space.

While drawing she put on the left of the paper what was on her left in real space; she put on the right of the paper what was the right, and so on. Most of the time she was sitting facing the locality she was drawing, so locations, such as right/left, closer/farther, and in front, coincided with the real position of her body in space. However, whenever she moved around the table she was drawing on, in order to reach another place on the paper, she faced a different angle. The added locations were drawn from that new position, again with her using her body, but this new configuration of places was not connected with the previous one. In addition, if she remembered something she wanted to include in the map, she would simply add it as an isolated picture. At the end, there were some sectors that were in the correct location and others that were not. When she compared her view from the balcony with her drawing, she did not say much, although she noticed there were differences. She remained silently at the balcony looking at the locality and at her map.

Fort San Cristóbal and the Aerial Photograph

For the fourth activity, we took a walk around Old San Juan. The children decided where to go and how to get there. They chose Fort San Cristóbal (refer to Figure 4.1), and some of them (Inés was not among them) drew the route before setting out. At Fort San Cristóbal, the guard, whom they knew, took us through all the tunnels and out to "La Garita del Diablo" (the Devil's Sentry Box—its legend well known and loved by the children). But the children were fearful in the tunnels and did not put them in their drawings.

From a hill inside the area of the fort, on the side of the Devil's Sentry Box, we could see La Perla, Old San Juan, and Puerta de Tierra, and we discussed the relationships between the three areas. Javier and Armando were very pleased, since it was the first time they had seen their houses during the activities. Inés showed more interest in the story of the Devil's Sentry Box than in looking out over the city or observing the area.

Back at the school, however, Inés was very impressed and surprised when she observed the aerial photograph, with an approximate scale of 1:3,000, of La Perla and Old San Juan. At first she could not find her bearings. Then I pointed to the basketball court.

> *Inés:* Is that the basketball court from La Perla?
> *IQ:* Yes.
> *Inés:* Is it really?
> *IQ:* Yes. Where do you think the school is?

Inés: Is the school here in this photograph?
IQ: Where do you think it is?

After I pointed out the basketball court, she began to recognize places. She went to the window to look for places and then located them with her finger on the photo. She called me to show me the places she had found. She stayed there for a while looking at the aerial photograph and looking at La Perla. She took the photo home and two days later told me that she had found her house in it; I could see that she was really happy.

From then on, Inés started working with me almost every time I went to the school. She sat quietly beside me, and during four consecutive sessions she made the same drawing—her route from home to school (refer to Figure 4.6). Inés located the house or the school on the left or right side of the paper, depending on where she was sitting. If she was facing La Perla from the school, she drew her house on the left side of the paper and the school on the right side of the paper. If she was sitting with her back to La Perla, she drew her house on the right side of the paper and the school on the left. Sometimes she made the path shorter, sometimes longer, but the subject was always the same—home, arch, school.

Last Drawings

At this time the children began to work on making maps that extended beyond their three neighborhoods. To observe this extended area from different perspectives, we drove around the San Juan islet, riding in a station wagon. On the whole, the children did the guiding. Periodically, when we were about to turn a corner or crest a hill, I asked them to predict whether we would see the sea. On a number of occasions they were surprised to see it in places where they were not expecting it. For example, when we turned off Norzagary Street, we left the sea behind. I asked them where they expected to see it again. They said: at El Escambrón (the beach). But at the top of one of the hills we were facing the south part of Old San Juan (the docks), and they were surprised when they saw the sea again in front of them.

We proceeded to Javier and Armando's neighborhood, where they showed us the areas that were significant in their lives—their homes, some friends' homes, some shops, fighting roosters, and the place where drug transactions occur. Following this, we drove over the bridge that links the San Juan islet to the main island, then went into the Capitolio (capitol) for an interview with David Noriega, representative-at-large in the Puerto Rican House of Representatives.

Afterward we visited the neighborhood of Inés and Elena. They, too, showed us homes, shops, an ostrich (!), and, again, the place where drugs are sold. Finally we drove past Julián's house in Old San Juan, before returning to school. "Oh, no!" the children shouted. "Back to school again!"

The first time Inés mapped anything outside of La Perla and the school was in a drawing of the trip around the islet. Before she made the drawing, she asked me to review the trip. I mentioned the places we visited, but I did not describe the route to her, nor did I refer to the sailing ship we had seen; but while reviewing the field notes, I remembered that Inés had been very impressed by the sailing ship, and in fact it was she who had called our attention to it. We were near the Capitolio when we saw it. In her drawing, she began with the school building, followed immediately by La Perla, even though that was the last place we had visited. She used six different sheets to draw the trip, with four of the six pictures representing La Perla. Those pictures followed the sequence of our visit. The last two [5: "La casa de los Amigos" (friends' house at Puerta de Tierra); and 6: "El Capitolio y el barco"] were separate images, like different stamps (see Figure 4.9).

During our twelfth meeting, we looked at an aerial photograph of the San Juan islet, this one with an approximate scale of 1:11,000. It occurred to me to ask Inés to draw the route from school to the area of Puerta de Tierra. I wanted to explore whether she could make a different drawing of a route—different from the ones she had been making of the course she took from home to school. She said it was impossible:

FIGURE 4.9. Inés's drawing of San Juan islet field trip

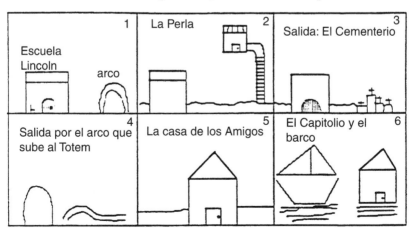

IQ: Can you draw the area of Puerta de Tierra?

Inés: No, I can't.

IQ: Can you try?

Inés: No, I don't remember.

IQ: And do you remember the route from Puerta de Tierra to La
      Perla?

Inés: No.

IQ: Do you know the route from La Perla to El Escambrón?

Inés: I don't know any route. I always travel with my father and my
       mother.

IQ: Which route are you sure of knowing?

Inés: None.

IQ: But you have described the route from home to school several
      times.

Inés: Oh yes, that one I remember. And I also know how to get to
       Fort San Cristóbal.

With great effort, Inés drew the route from her home to Fort San Cristóbal
(see Figure 4.10). It was the same drawing she had been practicing of her
home area, but she extended a sequence of landmarks in linear fashion;
that is, one beside the other connected to a particular path. She was beginning to connect places independently of her body. She was facing San
Cristóbal as she drew.

The first linear segment, as she described it, was first her house, then
another house (there are not too many houses between her house and the
hill that takes one up to the school); after that she said she crossed under
the arch and got to the school. In a different horizontal plane designated
by a line, she drew Fort San Cristóbal. According to Inés, San Cristóbal came
after the school as she walked. Before finishing her drawing she asked a
question:

Inés: Should I draw both forts or just one?

IQ: Draw it as you want.

At that moment I was surprised by her question and did not understand it. However, when I left the school I understood: The fort has two
different and separate entrances, separated by a large wall. One of the
entrances is on Norzagaray Street and the other on Muñoz Rivera Street.
One could easily think there are two different buildings. One of the entrances is at the north end of the fort, at the same level as Lincoln School;
the other is at the south end and at a lower level.

FIGURE 4.10. Drawing of Inés's route from La Perla to San Cristóbal

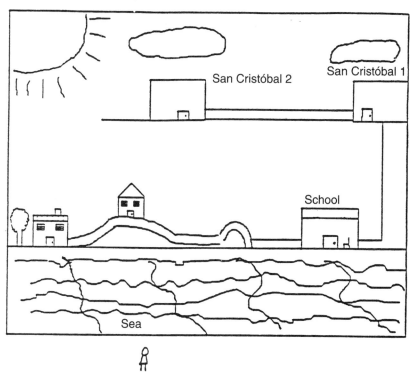

During a later session, she and Javier made a map of the San Juan islet (see Figure 4.11). It was interesting for me to observe the way in which she organized the area of San Juan with Javier: First they asked me to show them the aerial photograph of the San Juan islet again. Then Javier drew the sea and a fish at the bottom of their sheet of paper. Inés did most of the rest of the drawing. Again, she drew horizontal planes indicating the order of the sectors as one finds them when walking from La Perla to El Morro. It should be said that, in fact, as one walks, La Perla extends on the right all the way to El Morro. She drew the way from the school to El Morro via Norzagaray Street (see Figures 4.1 and 4.2). That's why La Perla and/or the sea appears on three sides.

Inés was on the balcony facing El Morro as she did this map. She first wrote the names of the areas: Puerta de Tierra on the left side and La Perla on the right side. She then began to work on the right side, placing La Perla on the lower edge of the drawing. Above La Perla she located the school and the arch marking the entrance to La Perla.

FIGURE 4.11. Javier and Inés's drawing of the San Juan islet

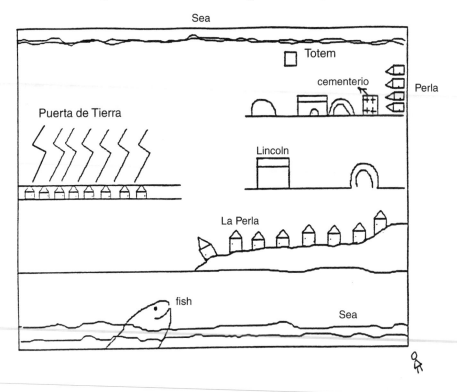

Working on the area on the other side of the school from La Perla (a section of Old San Juan known as Ballajá, refer to Figure 4.2, left side) was a difficult challenge. She drew a line above the one where she had drawn the school and the arch near it. Then she drew El Totem (a statue in the middle of a square, where the children skate on roller blades). In the middle of the upper line, she drew a second arch, the other entrance to La Perla, and to the left of the arch, she placed the building that marks the entrance. To the left of that again another arch indicates the other end of that tunnel. To the right of all this, she set the cemetery and then drew La Perla again on the right side of the paper. Although the arches are similar in structure (small tunnels used for fortification by the Spanish), the one near the Morro is longer and is curved. From one end, the other end of the tunnel is not visible, so Inés has drawn both ends. By contrast, the arch entrance beside the school is shorter and straight so one can easily see the end from the beginning.

Inés then started on Puerta de Tierra. She made an aerial representation of the buildings of the housing project, based on her observations of the aerial photograph. She was impressed with the shape of the buildings as they appeared in this photograph. Then she added the small houses of the area, below the housing project. The image in her drawing is similar to that in the aerial photograph.

In this ambitious piece of work, Inés again followed a linear sequence, the same pattern of spatial organization that she used for her own area, La Perla. Again she located places as they came: first La Perla; next, the school and then Ballajá. She then selected some particular landmarks belonging to the sectors established by her divisions, and she organized places within the sectors. For very limited areas, she used small perpendicular segments. For areas that were too "big," too extended, she used the horizontal levels. A large extension for Inés meant at least the distance from home to school.

After she'd finished this map of the San Juan islet, I asked her to draw her home area again. She said in reply: "I will try to do it because I have been observing La Perla and the route from home to school." She used two pieces of paper. On one, she drew the school and next to it the basketball court. Then, instead of the arch, she used the stairs. Next to the stairs, on the second piece of paper, she drew a house and then her home (see Figure 4.12).

The following day, she came to work with me again. In preparation for her last drawing of the area, she went to the balcony and looked over to La Perla. She called me to where she was and indicated the places for me.

FIGURE 4.12. Inés's home area: First final drawing

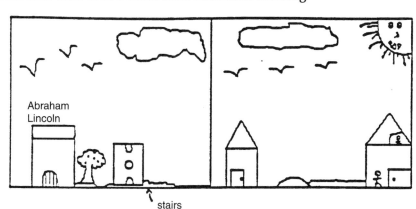

Inés: You see, Ileana, down there is La Pileta [the remaining foundation of a collapsed house, which waves fill with water at
high tide; the children used it as a swimming pool], then
Elena's house and other houses next to hers. [From the balcony,
Elena's house seems closer to the sea than it really is.] Then you
go up and behind Elena's house is the store and the cultural
center. Then, up is my house and the house next to mine, then
up the stairs there are more houses, the bench and the school.

IQ: Can you draw all that for me?

Inés: I will try, I will try.

She spent 45 minutes drawing the area. She went back and forth between
the paper and the balcony. Her last drawing of the area included what she
called "the entire" La Perla area and the school (see Figure 4.13). She was
very happy and proud of her drawing. I also liked it very much, and for me
it revealed her great effort to understand and translate the area into a drawing. I was so impressed with the drawing that I showed it to several people.
Two of the people who looked at the drawing suggested that it could be La
Perla seen from walking along the *malecón,* and then from Inés's house to
the school. While reproducing the drawing, I realized that each of the lines
had a slight inclination indicating the climb from La Perla to Lincoln School.
Reading from the lowest level to the uppermost, the map reader needs to go
from left to right on the first, bottom, level, from right to left on the second,
left to right on the third, and right to left at the top, ending at the school. This
inclination is not rendered in the computer version.

In order to include the entire area of La Perla, Inés drew four horizontal planes beginning with more distant (from the school balcony) areas at
the bottom of the paper and ending with the closer areas at the top of the
paper (see Figure 4.14). The Ballajá area was clearly problematic. It's near
the school, and it's also around the coast (more or less). In Figure 4.11, she
ended up putting the sea on three sides of the school, as she tried to work
in Ballajá (upper right). In Figure 4.13, she changed her approach, and
started her "walk" with Ballajá, now at lower left. In this way she located
the Ballajá area (indicated by cars, the arch, and the building) at the left
end of the lowest horizontal plane. Even though the totem is not in the same
horizontal plane as other landmarks in the lowest box, she uses the Ballajá
area to indicate the location of the arch that is near the cemetery. She located the school at the left end of the uppermost horizontal plane. Between
these two planes she drew two more planes representing the areas in between, doing this in order, from bottom to top and back and forth side to
side. She continued this pattern until she had included a large portion of
La Perla. She uses the arch which is near the cemetery, as a landmark to

FIGURE 4.13. Inés's home area: Final drawing

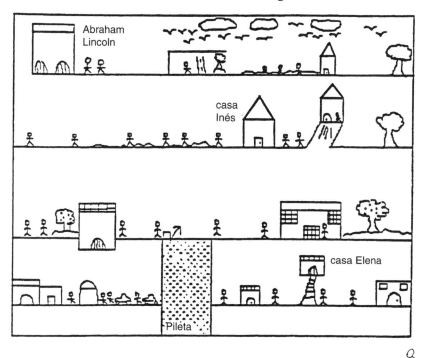

indicate the transition to La Perla from Ballajá. It seems as if she was trying in her drawing to show a walk, starting from the totem, going down
past the cemetery to Malecón, and on up to the school.

In her last cardboard model, Inés extended the map to include Calle
del Sol in Old San Juan. I found this a great achievement (see Figure 4.15).

Commentary

Although from the outset most of the children had some idea of the area
where they lived, none of them had thought about it as an object of study.
They were surprised that someone else could be interested in their knowledge of the area. They now had to think about it in a different way. They
needed to organize and document their ideas to be able to explain them to
me and to the other children. After working with me for a time, some were
delighted with the idea of exploring the area from different perspectives
and did not want to stop. For example, Julián was constantly drawing the

FIGURE 4.14. Ileana's analysis of Inés's final drawing

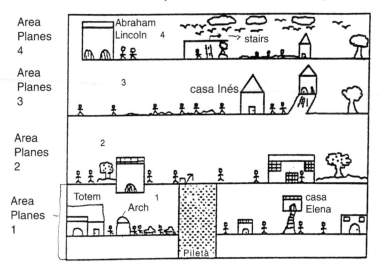

area, asking me questions, and coming up with new ideas and hypotheses and changing them. Inés, although not as talkative as Julián, continually practiced drawing her routes, extending the area a little bit at a time until she obtained a whole picture of her home area.

In carrying out their activities, the children worked with two main geographical problems: scale reduction and the spatial arrangement of places in their neighborhoods.

I did not work directly with the issue of scale reduction. But during the first two activities, we worked with 11" × 8½" sheets of paper, and the children expressed their difficulties with the scale reduction mostly by saying that the area was too big to be drawn on such small pieces of paper. After the second activity, and from then through to the end, drawings were done on 2' × 3' pieces of cardboard and 4' × 5' sheets of newsprint. They felt more comfortable with those large areas to work on. Then they began to express their difficulties with the organization and translation of a mental image into a map.

All the children approached these difficulties differently. They persevered in developing strategies in order to organize a congruent image of the area. When the pattern of organization was not complex enough for the ideas they wanted to express, they sought other ways of organizing them. Each child developed a set of strategies to explain to herself or himself where places were located and how they were related to one another in space, and each child moved from one strategy to another in her or his own way.

Both Inés and Julián practiced the patterns they already knew several times before they incorporated new ways of organizing the area. When they understood that the pattern was not complex enough, they gradually began to introduce small changes into their drawings. Inés added segments and sometimes made the route longer and then shorter again. She frequently added segments of streets to the route she already knew.

Inés made her most intricate maps in three different but integrated stages. First she located landmarks as she remembered them, following the routes she took. At the beginning of the work she remembered and located isolated places, connected neither to each other nor to a particular route. After several explorations, she began to locate places next to one another as they were arranged in a particular linear path. This was the basis of her organization. Then, to some of the landmarks located along that original route, she added places before, after, and to the sides. Then she added to her drawing not just landmarks, but entire areas, such as the area of Ballajá, and various different sectors of La Perla. She added those areas as horizontal planes, one above the other. She developed a very complex and specific way of organizing and representing the area (refer to Figures 4.10, 4.11, 4.13, and 4.15).

During the project the children developed their ideas through a variety of activities different from those normally realized in a regular classroom. During the initial exercises with the children, I was torn between their enthusiasm for the work they were doing and my own doubts about its relevance to the official social studies curriculum. But very soon I began to alter my vision of what was important for them to learn. The truth is

FIGURE 4.15. Inés's second cardboard of the route from home to school

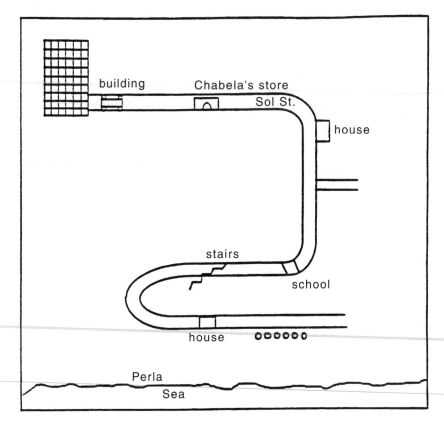

that they were bored in the classroom, memorizing facts and not understanding the complexities of geography. By contrast, they were power-
fully involved while mapping and trying to understand and develop their
knowledge of their geographical area. What they were learning was real
and full of meaning for them. They were learning about their familiar geographical space, about the places they liked, the streets where they enjoyed
playing, their homes and their relatives' and friends' homes, the places
where important events in their lives had taken place.

In Inés's classroom, I noticed that the students were studying a conventional world map, identifying and using rules such as scales, perspectives, and coordinates to locate positions and look at the sizes of continents.
After locating the positions of continents on the map, they memorized the
names and all the locations. Because I noticed that Inés rarely spoke and

seemed shy and intimidated, I asked her to show me in a drawing what she had understood from her teacher's explanation. What she drew is shown in Figure 4.16. Inés thought of the world in a way very different from that of her teacher. She saw it as formed of two pieces of land separated by a large sea. This makes sense if we consider that she was thinking about it from her experience standing at La Perla, observing the ocean and knowing that there was land other than where she was, far away. Instead of acknowledging this understanding and using it as a point of departure, the teacher discarded it. Inés learned that she was wrong, and another way was presented to her. Even so, it did not change the way she thought about it.

I concluded that in trying to be faithful to the curriculum, a teacher can hamper learning when she or he isolates it from the child's experience, explorations, discoveries, and thinking process. Without realizing it, the teacher is also discarding what the child does know. In our mapping study, for example, Inés was bringing complexity to the understanding of mapping. Her drawing awakens interesting reflections about maps: that they are drawn from a particular perspective, that they represent places and visions of places. Without knowing it, Inés was deepening the simplicity of the official curriculum.

During this research project, children developed their ideas through a variety of activities that were different from those carried out in the regular classroom. I explored their understanding about the organization of space and mapping, taking as a base their own ideas. They had the opportunity to explore, think, and compare their views with those of other children. They were able to observe and investigate, to pose questions, and to rethink and reformulate their ideas. Through this experience children expanded and deepened their knowledge of the area where they lived. In fact, as they worked, their maps became more complex and more representative of their particular areas. This process engaged and excited them. It gave them confidence in their capacity to observe, to think, and to express their

FIGURE 4.16. Inés's drawing of the world

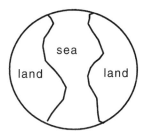

own ideas. As the children worked together, the perspectives and interpretations of each others' projects allowed for the expansion of their own
maps and their understanding of the area.

Learning became an exploration and a research process. Doing fieldwork in the community, observing and exploring, are essential elements
not only in learning geography, but also in integrating classroom experiences with community experiences.

At the conclusion of our project, teachers at the school were so moved
by these children's engagement in our geographical activities that I was
asked to continue my collaboration there. This classroom collaboration has
reaffirmed my view that this approach can take place in regular classrooms.

Now as a team, Inés's teacher and I lead the class in exploring the community that furnishes both the children and ourselves with the geographical questions that intrigue us. Based on my previous experiences with the
children, we are creating an environment and trying to develop activities
that enhance their passion to explore and to learn.

Acknowledgments. I want to acknowledge my debt to Maritza Maymí for reproducing the drawings electronically. I would also like to thank Carlos Marazzi,
Christian García Rivera, and Héctor Meléndez from Metrodata, for the maps of
Old San Juan and La Perla that they generously adapted and gave to me for inclusion in this chapter.

Related Readings

Carbonell, J., & Sepúlveda, A. (1990). *San Juan extramuros*. San Juan: Carimar.

Freire, P. (1993). *Pedagogy of the oppressed*. New York: Continuum.

Hart, R. (1971). *Aerial Geography: An experiment in elementary education*. Worcester,
    MA: Graduate School of Geography, Clark University, Place Perception,
    Report 6.

Hart, R. (1979). *Children's experience of place*. New York: Irvington.

Hart, R. (1986). *The changing city of childhood: Implications for play and learning*. The
    1986 Catherine Molony Memorial Lecture, The City College Workshop Cen-
    ter, New York.

Hart, R., & Moore, G. T. (1971). *The development of spatial cognition: A review*. Worces-
    ter, MA: Graduate School of Geography, Clark University, Place Perception,
    Report 7.

5

Understanding the Presidency

Mary Kay Delaney

Teaching social studies requires attention to and consideration of creative tensions. An engaged social studies teacher choreographs materials and questions to challenge students to make connections—between the past and the present, between stasis and movement, between textbook dryness and soap opera interesting, between objective distance and subjective closeness, between institutions and people, and between particular issues or events and more general considerations.

As a social studies teacher, I managed these tensions, in part, by always relating history, government, and economics to discussions of current events. While particular current issues changed from year to year, general issues and questions persisted: What is effective leadership? What is a democracy? How can citizens act to promote democracy? The particular events of the day interested students and were relevant to their lives. Discussion of current events provided entry to discussion of more general institutional and political concerns. Moreover, as students began to understand institutions, political processes, and the details of particular issues, they would begin to engage in questions of political philosophy and ideology.

I began the following account in 1986, when Ronald Reagan was president. The Union of Soviet Socialist Republics, now Russia and independent republics, was an intact Communist regime headed by Mikhail Gorbachev. Libya was in the news as its president, Muammar al-Qaddafi, challenged the United States to cross the "line of death." The Congress of the United States, the president, and the public engaged in debate about "contra aid," funding for the opponents of the Sandinista government in Nicaragua. In addition, the presidency as executed by Reagan was a focal point for discussion. Reagan was an adroit user of media. His staff openly thought of the management of his image as its job. For the first time, the White House staff and the media used the terms *spin, spin control*, and *spin doctors*.

Although the particulars are different now, the general issues raised in conversations that I had with two high school students during the Reagan administration remain startlingly current. Of the issues raised in our sessions, United States–Russia relations continue to be enigmatic; the relationship between Islamic nations in the Middle East and North Africa continue to present a challenge; and questions about the appropriate role of the United States in the affairs of Central American nations have endured since the Monroe Doctrine. Perhaps most immutable are the issues raised about the institution of the presidency itself. For example, an issue of great importance in the sessions—image management in the presidency—is a recurring theme in public discussions as pundits and former officials weigh its effects on civic life and democratic traditions.

Thus, as Mark and Tim (then high school students) and I (then a social studies teacher, now a teacher of teachers) sought to understand particular social issues and phenomena associated with the Reagan presidency, we encountered larger questions of value and of epistemology. As Tim and Mark reveal, seeking to understand current events can lead to critical participation in democracy. Understanding how students understand government and politics can guide teaching and curriculum-making because it can provide insights into how and under what conditions students develop new ideas and how these ideas support or hinder their critical participation in democracy.

Prelude

This journey begins with a social studies teacher's fascination with high school students' ideas about the presidency of the United States. Just how do high school students and adults understand the presidency? One question leads to many more: What kinds of questions capture students' interest and prompt them to think more deeply? What questions and problems challenge students to read between the lines of a news report? What facts about the presidency, if any, do students know? How do these facts affect their opinions of the person in office? What do they think about how the office works and how effectively? How does the person holding the office affect its execution? What understandings promote or inhibit comprehension of democracy and politics within a democracy?

Turn on the news or open a newspaper, and you can find at least one story about the president of the United States. Like the moon in the night sky, the president in the media is a highly visible focal point. And like the moon, the president and the presidency are familiar. We are aware of ascendencies and phases, temporary disappearances and momentary glimpses of grandeur, in both. Too seldom do we have time to stop to probe, to assemble data, to analyze ideas. Besides, we often *think* we understand how the presidency works until we stop to question.

Mark (age 15) and Tim (age 16) attended a large urban boy's high school where a colleague of mine taught. I asked each of them to keep a "president journal," in which they wrote one observation about the president per day (ideally), indicating the source of the observation (TV, radio, newspaper, and so on).

I had intended to meet regularly with both of the students together; however, except for the first session, we did not manage to find shared time. Instead, after the first session, I met with Mark and Tim individually.

In the Eyes of What It's Supposed to Be

Mark, Tim, and I had worked together briefly before—on a project about how adolescents understand the law. Our first meeting, therefore, began with a discussion of the purposes of laws and evolved into a discussion of the relationships between nations. I knew I would eventually introduce the idea of studying the presidency during this meeting; but at the beginning, I wanted to encourage a habit of talking about current issues when we were together. I thought I could do this best by simply listening.

In explaining the difference between U.S.-Soviet relations and U.S.-Canadian relations, both Mark and Tim agreed that while the United States and Canada have been friends for a long time, the Soviet Union and the United States have not. Tim compared U.S.-Canadian relations to a situation with one of his lifelong friends and the friend's girlfriend. Between the United States and the Soviet Union, Mark explained, "there's not enough there." When I asked Mark to explain this, he continued that U.S.-Soviet disagreements will not turn into armed confrontation because "there has been enough there so we each know who or what we're going to do. There's a relationship."

Neither Mark nor Tim seemed to draw on specific knowledge about the nations involved. Rather, they drew on ideas from their own experiences. Moreover, Mark did not seem uncomfortable with conflicting ideas. When I asked him to explain his last two statements about the United States and the Soviet Union, he simply reiterated each statement. Their approaches confused me. How could I set up questions, I wondered, that would start from Mark and Tim's experience, but then move to other considerations? Because I could not solve this problem, I decided to find out what they knew about the presidency. I introduced this topic by asking them what the president does.

Tim replied, "In the eyes of what it's supposed to be, the president is equal to us and he's just a representative to do what we want. . . . he's not supposed to think he's better than us."

Tim further explained that "you gotta break it down—every town has a representative that goes to the Senate or whatever—the House of Reps. If everyone in the United States voted on every issue—there'd be voting on ballots every day."

In this way, Tim showed that he knew one reason why we elect people and that he had a notion of the layers of representation. Still I fell unsure about this. He had started his passage with "In the eyes of what it's supposed to be," indicating some observation of his own that things do not always work that way. I pressed him about "in the eyes of what's supposed to be." Does the president always represent all the people?

Tim responded, "Not always. 'Cause he's not a computer. He uses his own opinion. He has to make decisions, like with, the hostages . . . not enough time to get all the representatives together."

Mark, who had been listening, added, "Like someone attacking us. He does what he thinks is best for the people, not just for himself. If you have some kind of war, you need the best decisions fast."

The confidence that these two had in the president and in the system overwhelmed me. I thought that these issues were so important that I had to think about them before challenging Mark and Tim's views. I decided that I would come back to some of the questions implicit in their statements in a later session. For this session, I continued with finding out more about what they thought the president does.

This confidence in the president came into play again. Mark suggested that the president vetoes bad bills and signs good bills. I asked, "How does the president decide which laws are good and which are bad?"

Without hesitation, Mark replied, "On his own opinion. He wouldn't [have to] choose because he has the same views as the people that voted for him."

I pointed out to Mark that many people who voted for the president disagree with him on some issues. Surprisingly, to me, Mark was not the least bit distressed by this information. He explained, "Um, a lot of people like him because he's charismatic. . . . [G]enerally, he knows what he's doing. He talks about defense. He's more commercial." (I understood Mark's use of *commercial* to mean media savvy.)

Before I could respond, Tim jumped in with his explanation: People wanted to give the guy another chance because it seems fruitless to elect a new president every 4 years. Tim goes on, "Yeah, it's not something that just happens. BANG, right in the middle of the newspaper, 'Reagan fixes U.S.' It's something that happens over a period of time."

Mark followed, "So people won't get scared of it, of things, won't get really confused on the subject of what we're going to do. They want gradual change."

I thought we were really getting somewhere, but I wanted to be sure. The words seemed somehow too familiar for this social studies teacher, echoes of lessons past. I wondered how deeply Mark and Tim had incorporated these ideas into their own thinking. I asked Mark and Tim to explain what "it" and "things" were.

Mark replied, "War."

"Any other things?" I asked.

Mark, "He just sits there."

This last comment by Mark was not meant to make sense. This kind of signal, I was to learn, was Mark's way of saying not to push anymore. I shifted focus. We discussed how one would go about learning about the president. This conversation lasted about one minute before I heard: Why would we want to? We're just kids.

Although I panicked when I heard this, I also thought it was a fair question. I suggested the president journal. They agreed to go along with me. When I left them, I was nervous. They were so confident about their understanding of the presidency and so confident in the president. What were they going to learn from this project?

Through the Camera's Eye

To prepare for this session, I collected photos of the president and the presidency-in-action from newsmagazines and newspapers. I had been thinking about David Hawkins and "Messing about in Science" (1974). Hawkins writes of the importance of providing learners with time and space to explore science materials and equipment before beginning more focused investigations. In putting together the photo file, I sought the social studies equivalent of science materials for science. I wanted Mark and Tim to be able to touch the stuff of the presidency—to be able to turn it, pick it up, look at it, ponder, play. It is very difficult for students initially to have concrete experiences with social studies—so many concepts and processes are abstract. Yet real people carry out real ideas in real life and the easiest, most accessible records of this were newsmagazines and newspaper photos. I did not know how the photos would guide our sessions, or even if they would have any effect at all. I only knew that if Mark and Tim did not bring an issue to the session then we would look at the photos together. We were at the beginning of our discussions, and "messing about" was, I (as teacher) thought, crucial for building a base for further discussions and questions.

When I arrived, I learned that Tim had forgotten his journal and that Mark was absent. Tim and I started this session, as we had the first, by talking about current events. As Tim spoke, I started pulling out pictures of Reagan and a few other world leaders. I spread them around the table. We looked at Qaddafi's photo, and then at a photo of Reagan and Gorbachev. Our eyes came naturally to this photo because it was large.

Tim could not identify Gorbachev, but when he read that the president was sitting with Gorbachev of the Soviet Union, he said: "Oh, this is their meeting? This is where they meet, by this cozy fire? . . . [The photograph] makes it look like they're coming closer together or something. It's not like they're at a table or something with people all around them. They're just like sitting in the chair, the rug, they're relaxed . . . just makes it look like . . ."

Tim's repeated use of "makes it look like" prompted me to ask if the photo was planned. This proved to be our theme for the day—wondering whether the photo could have been set up. Initially Tim wanted to know more about the scene: What did meetings usually look like? Like this? Were there other people in the room? Are Reagan and Gorbachev just "sitting there talking and shooting the breeze?" We used other photos in the collection to try to find answers.

Tim decided that at least *part* of some meeting would have looked as the Reagan-Gorbachev photo looked, but that most of the time many more people surrounded the leaders during a meeting.

After answering questions about the logistics and physical setup of the meeting, I asked Tim again if he thought the photo was planned. He had mentioned that the photo was not a typical "meeting" picture. He responded: "Planned for what? To take a picture of this? Uh, well, I guess it just worked out that they took the picture. Do you mean, did they actually plan to have these people meet in this room so they could take a picture?"

This was exactly what I had meant. Near the end of the interview, however, I realized that I did not know who "they" were to Tim. I was thinking of Reagan/Gorbachev/staff. Tim may have been thinking of the photographers. He continued: "I think they probably just did it."

I took this comment to mean that the photograph was candid, taken while Reagan and Gorbachev met.

Throughout this time, Tim interspersed his observations and answers with "I don't know much about these things," so I decided that we needed more data. I asked Tim simply to state his observations about the photo. This is what Tim saw:

Room in a house you might have, if you lived in a nice house.
Fire makes it homey, not like a meeting
Two men in comfortable chairs

Men seem relaxed
Reagan has his leg up
Very close, could kick each other if they wanted to
Nice, Oriental rug
Not real bright [Again, Tim told me, it's not like a meeting; meetings
    have lights above a table.]
Might be going over the same thing—like a proposal about arms

In the middle of his observations, Tim said: "The photo is not planned. They wouldn't sit and look like that, just pose for a picture. The last thing on their minds is their picture. Reagan may be explaining something to Gorbachev. Gorbachev is just sitting and listening. Reagan may be thinking about what to say."

I asked Tim why he had said that Reagan was explaining. I'm not sure how his answer is related to the question, but it certainly reveals what I think is a conflict in his thinking:

"They're here for a different reason from the photo. . . . They want to show friendship *or at least make it look like it.* . . . They didn't come all the way to Switzerland to sit in a room." (Emphasis added.)

Right now I wonder why I did not ask about "or at least make it look like it." If I remember correctly, Tim's observations continued rapidly. These observations seemed to center on image:

"They're wearing suits. . . . They're leaders of countries, can't just come in, crack a few brews and sit around in shorts. . . . [T]hey're serious. . . . Gorbachev looks more serious than Reagan."

When photographs are taken at summits, leaders go to great lengths to ensure that no one leader appears more powerful than the other. Looking at the photo and thinking of this, I asked Tim to fold the photo in half. He did this and said: "[It's] equally split right down the fire. The chairs are *set up perfectly* around the fire." (Emphasis added.) I had not noticed this symmetry until Tim started observing the photo.

Tim's words again prompted me to ask if he thought that maybe someone thought about dividing the photo perfectly. He thought not.

We went on to talk about the photographer—David Hume Kennerly. When I asked Tim what he would like to know about Kennerly, he replied, "Where he's from—Russia, the U.S., Switzerland. If he's neutral. Because if he wanted he could've caught them in a different atmosphere . . . looking aggressive or like negative toward Mr. Reagan, or Reagan could've been laughing. . . . They're both in an equal state [in this photo]—not one looking better than the other or worse than the other."

This comment was key because it demonstrated that Tim thought about the intention of the photographer and that this intention was linked to Reagan and Gorbachev being portrayed "in an equal state." This was Tim's first observation of the "equality" character of the photo. Later on he described the photo as "mutual."

Tim then used the collection of photos to show how different moods can be captured. As he looked over all the folders on the table, he quickly generated three categories: private and social life, professional life with "human" qualities, and professional life. Not knowing myself what we would find, I asked Tim to look at the photo credits in each group. Of the nine photos in the personal and "human qualities" groups, seven carried White House credits.

In a discussion of why these photos might come from the White House, Tim seemed confused about who the "White House" was and what its relationship to the president was. I asked, "Who took this photo?"

Tim answered, "A White House person, they want to make it look like . . ."

He paused, so I pressed, "Who is 'they'?"

"The people who are interested in his public words—the public's view of him. No one from the White House would want him looking like *that*," Tim replied while pointing to an uncomplimentary photo.

"So does the president have people working for him who try to make him look good?"

"No, that's not the reason they're working for him. They're not working directly for him either. They're working for the White House."

He explained that the White House doesn't "want the wrong pictures getting around. . . . They want to show him [the president] as a pretty down-to-earth guy."

I asked again who "they" were, who the White House people were. He decided that "the White House" probably consisted of staff people who (1) were photographers, (2) were concerned with the president's image, and (3) cleared photos for publication.

At the end of our session, Tim looked at the photo and said that *Time*, Kennerly, Reagan, and Gorbachev did not plan the photo. (He did not mention any White House staff.)

I asked, "You don't think that Reagan and Gorbachev could've thought about the photographs?"

Tim replied, "Right. I mean, they think about what they look like to the public—they wear makeup and they have these people do their hair, but their main—Reagan seems to lead us in the right direction. He's not going to be thinking about the picture-taking. He's going to be thinking about the right comments to say. His mind's going to be on whatever those two pieces of paper are."

Tim's last comment was illuminating for me. I think that his thinking went like this:

1. Reagan leads us in the right direction.
2. To lead, one focuses on the issues.
3. Being involved in or part of the media/public relations process is not focusing on the issues.
4. Therefore, Reagan does not think about the media/public relations.

Part of this reasoning related to his distinction between the White House and Reagan. He recognized that the White House has an interest in how the president appears to the public. However, this recognition did not seem to include an understanding of the kinds of maneuvering by *both* the president and his staff that must occur in order to create/project an image. These maneuverings would include photo-opportunity sessions.

Tim seemed to be on the verge of recognizing the public relations or political aspects of the presidency. He seemed to resist it. The public relations nature of the office was not included in his conception of leadership.

The concept of "the White House" appeared to be fuzzy; it was a phrase referring to the president's house and the president. He did not think about White House *staff* members and their purposes and functions.

Negative Photos and Loyalty

Mark and I had not met for 3 weeks. He wanted to know all about the sessions with Tim. Tim had told Mark that our last session had been "intense." Thus, we also started with the photo of Reagan and Gorbachev by the fireplace.

Starting from Tim's concern in the last session, I asked, Is the photograph planned? Did Reagan, Gorbachev, or both, or the photographer or someone else plan how this photograph would look?

Mark replied, "That's interesting. I've often thought about that, but I can't answer it."

"What have you thought about it?"

"I'm not sure."

Because he seemed unwilling, rather than unable, to articulate his thoughts at this point, I suggested that he just make some straightforward observations about the photo. His observations about file photo included

It looks fake in a way.
They're both sitting like statues.

They look like they were put there.

On the other hand, since they're reading something they could be just reading.

Two world leaders

Dressed similarly ("I think that's kind of funny," he said pausing to look longer.)

Bright fire

Same kind of shoes

Look involved in what they're reading

Nice rug—looks pretty expensive

Maybe there's a person standing there [on the right side where there is a dark form resembling a pants leg], I don't know.

I can notice the age difference: the almost frailty of Reagan's bone [of his hands]; and the huskiness of Gorbachev's. You can't see the bones.

Reagan looks pale. His face is kind of messed up. It's all wrinkled. He doesn't look as diplomatic as he does doing TV speeches.

Gorbachev looks pretty confident. His face is flushed—good-looking.

Earlier, Mark had picked up another photo of Reagan and Gorbachev. I asked him to fold the second photo in half.

"Are there any similarities?" I asked.

"It seems like they're trying to copy each other. Here [first photo] they're both reading. Here [second photo] they're both trying the same, the same type of look. [In the second photo,] each has a bodyguard. [Both] photos have the same type of background . . . darkness around them."

I asked Mark if the darkness affected the photo. He replied that in the first photo the darkness contrasted with the fire and gave the photo a warm feeling. He added that Reagan and Gorbachev seemed distant and friendly —as if they were saying,"Yeah, yeah, yeah, [let's get on with it]."

"When they went to the summit, there was all that hype—publicity stunt. Nothing got accomplished."

I asked, "What about it made it a publicity stunt?"

"All the press. I know it's a big event, the coming together of two nations [like the meetings at Camp David]. . . . I don't know, they're there for business."

I still did not fully understand what he meant. I asked Mark *who* made it a publicity stunt. His response, I think, reflected a combination of responses—attention to my question and to his own:

"As far as Reagan goes, I think that he doesn't take what he's doing seriously. He's doing it [publicity] to get people to believe him, to get the American people going."

From his response, I thought that much more was in Mark's head than my questions were eliciting. I wondered how to unravel all these ideas. His response seemed to indicate that he had some notion of how the president might use the media.

"What does the president gain from the 'publicity stunts'?"

"Support for whatever he wants. If you get the American people to believe you, you can do whatever you want. Like with contra aid, pleading for people to believe him because then Congress will have trouble not passing [the contra aid].

"On my sheet [journal], I have a lot of talk, most of it of Reagan commenting on contra aid. I heard this guy on a talk show. He said, look at what Reagan's doing. First he shuts off economical aid to Nicaragua and then forces them to go to Russia, which gives us a reason to go in."

I asked if he had ever heard that idea before.

He replied, "I never thought of it before. It made sense to me. I didn't know about the cutting of economic funds to Nicaragua. I do agree with him [the talk show person]. What really starts the economy going and brings the country together is war. I think that's part of what he's [Reagan] trying to do."

It had been 3 weeks since we had had a session, and Mark had obviously been watching and thinking. I wondered what else was in his head. In response to any encouragement, Mark usually went on, and he did:

"Yes, [it's interesting] because it's hard to decide which side to be on. Like last night on *60 Minutes*, did you see it? [I had, thank goodness.] Dean Smith [an American singer who lived in East Berlin and was a popular entertainer within the Eastern bloc] talked about how much people in other parts of the world hate us. Why can't we let them run their own government? [He said] we were once proud to be revolutionaries; other people don't want to be colonies of the U.S."

One of themes of the *60 Minutes* piece had been whether the singer was disloyal to the United States. This theme coincided with one of Mark's earliest statements about the presidency: it's wrong to disagree with the president. Despite the digression from the original question, I asked Mark what he thought about the theme. "Do you think a person is disloyal to the country when he or she disagrees with the president?"

Without hesitation, Mark offered this explanation: "No. You have to distinguish between two things. A president is gonna base his decision on two things: either on what the majority of people like *or* on what he knows best. If he decides to rule by his feelings on a subject on which he knows more than the public, then you can't say those people are un-American, not every American knows in depth."

It seemed to me that Mark was saying that ignorance did not make a person disloyal. I asked him if it was possible for some people to know as much as the president. He said, yes, it was possible. "Well, are these people disloyal if they disagree?" I asked. To this he replied, "No, not everyone in the country voted for Reagan."

I felt that we had uncovered many hypotheses—and observations. I was not sure what to do with our few remaining minutes, so I decided to ask Mark what he wanted to do. He wanted to go back to the first photo. He could not decide whether it was planned. I read his observations to him. Still he could not decide. I asked him to view it from another angle. What evidence is there for the photo *not* being planned?

"They just look like they're looking over proposals about arms reductions. They're taking a break from discussing. If it was set up, who would think about how it would look?" Mark asked.

In response, I asked Mark to look at the credits. Photo 1, the photo of Reagan and Gorbachev sitting in front of a fireplace, is credited to David Hume Kennerly. Photo 2, showing Reagan and Gorbachev with "bodyguards," is credited to the White House. Observing the White House credit, Mark said, "How can the president have a photographer? . . . [T]hat's pretty absurd. [Why?] Because it's not natural. To show the public something's going on when it's not."

He then went on to say that he had thought about photos being planned before, because of press conferences: "When you flip the channels, it's always the same camera angle."

"In this picture [first photo], it looks like he's into this . . . [as if he were saying] 'Yeah, we're on the right track to nuclear disarmament.' It could help discourage negative photos."

"Negative photos?" I asked.

"The people don't want to see Reagan and Gorbachev fighting. He wants to keep people happy because people want to see them getting along, which is a form of censorship. . . . if the people are happy he gets support."

With this loaded statement, we had no time left.

This session raised countless questions for me. Among them was the notion of "negative photos." This idea came up with Tim also. I wondered how Mark and Tim thought that negative photos were kept from the public. I also wondered about their thinking regarding the American people, the public. In all of our sessions, both Tim and Mark had mentioned "the public." Their notions of the public seemed monolithic. Was a diversity of responses and opinions included in their notion of the public? How did they reconcile their visions of the public with their own differences of opinion and with their ideas that "everyone has a right to their opinion"? Did it occur to them that the public embodied these different opinions?

In our very first session together, Mark had been insistent about the notion that disagreeing with the president was disloyal to the country. In this session, he argued that it was not. However, I sensed a great deal of ambivalence about his position. I was not sure why he thought this. He insisted that we had to distinguish between two ways of making decisions: (1) the president bases his decisions on what the majority of the people think and (2) the president bases his decisions on his own feelings. I did not understand the connection he was making between these decision-making methods and loyalty. And what did "not everyone voted for Reagan" have to do with it? I suspected, without being sure, that a notion of right and wrong decisions underlay these connections.

On Nicaragua, ambivalence again emerged. Finding out that the United States had cut off aid to Nicaragua seemed to make Mark entertain a notion that he had not thought about before. He asserted that "it's hard to decide which side to be on." This kind of statement was unusual for Mark. In fact, it was the first time he had ever mentioned that deciding could be difficult. I wondered where this would lead him. He had believed that we should send troops into Nicaragua. Had this new information changed his position on Nicaragua? I was not sure.

Mark seemed to understand how the president's public appeals could affect Congress. But then again, is the public monolithic and malleable?

Both Mark and Tim seemed reluctant to view concern for public perception as part of the "business" of the summit.

There was an enormous amount of material to pursue, and I had a hard time keeping myself focused. What were Mark's ideas about how Reagan, for example, made sure that the people were happy? What did Reagan have to consider? How did he go about ensuring public happiness? What did people base their decision on? Mark left me with many questions. The next time I decided to return to his notion of the two ways of decision-making.

Breaking Through the Majority—Mark Alone

In our previous session, when I asked Mark if a person is disloyal to the country when he or she disagrees with the president, I did not understand his explanation. I asked Mark about it again now. I read to him what he had said. He said, "Yeah, I know you didn't really understand all that." I said, "I'm trying."

He explained, "People that do [know] as much as Reagan, they still disagree. Because of a particular subject, if they didn't agree . . . Now you got me stuck." Mark, the confident one, was stuck. I was delighted with his thinking and his admission. Laughing gently, I exclaimed, "Good," trying to communicate my pleasure in his thinking. Quickly, I then asked, "Can someone be loyal to the country if they have voted for Reagan and they disagree with him?"

"Yes. Everyone's different. Not everyone is going to have the same feelings in things. That's just common sense."

Mark was truly stuck. He was hesitant from "particular subject" on. He never liked being stuck. (His right leg would bounce at a rate of about 300 bounces per minute.) Often he just needed time to get his thoughts together. When I replied "good" to his "stuck" comment, we both laughed. I could see him relax somewhat. At that moment, I thought that we might do better if I diverted attention away from this question for a while. I asked, "Is there anything about the president that you just wonder about?"

"I wonder if Reagan is really competent enough to handle the presidency. Sometimes he seems dumb, absentminded, almost senile. When people do jokes it starts to seem that way. . . . I can see him in two ways. In his speeches I can start to see him in other ways."

This comment was expressed with genuine concern and puzzlement over being able to see the president "in other ways." I thought that because Mark seemed a little hesitant to talk, political cartoons might serve as a vehicle for understanding this comment. Alas, I did not have any. I had brought the wrong folder.

That the president might be incompetent seemed very unsettling for Mark. Maybe I was wrong, but I felt as if this was a vulnerable moment. I felt confused: on the one hand, I had wanted him to question his notions of the presidency; on the other hand, I felt as if this project had "robbed" him of certainty. In addition, given that we had only a short time to work together, I did not want to pursue this wondering about competence without careful thought. With his current notions of national government, I wondered, can he, in the short amount of time we have together, entertain the notion of incompetence without feeling disempowered?

With most of these thoughts in my head, I told Mark I needed to think about what he had said. He thought that that was okay.

I asked him to explain once again his notions of the two ways presidents can make decisions. He said, "Well, first it's not just the president. All politicians have that choice [to decide based on majority opinion or based on their own judgments]. It would be good if, well I shouldn't say 'good' because then you'll think . . . well, anyway, it would be good if politicians in order to get into office, tell people what they want to hear, but once they're in just do what they think is best. . . . [L]ots of politicians will say what you want to hear. Once they're in, they will do what's best for the city. That may go against what they said to be elected. But if what they're doing is right that's okay."

My mind went in two different, but related, directions: (1) What if what the politicians do is wrong? and (2) Who determines what is right and wrong and how do they determine right and wrong? For some time I had suspected that Mark's view of decision-making rested on an assumption that decisions could be classified into either right or wrong.

I asked him, "How do you determine if a decision is right?"

"What would benefit overall the people."

I pressed him to explain: "How do you decide what would benefit the people overall?"

"I'm not sure."

Mark needed a new avenue, and I tried to provide one: "Let's look at an example that we've talked about . . ."

"OK." Mark seemed relieved to shift focus.

"Contra aid. In the public opinion polls, the majority of the American people seem to oppose aid to the contras. Yet the president supports it. How does he decide that the majority is wrong and he is right?"

"How do we know," Mark asked carefully, "that the majority knows all the sides of the issue? You don't know that. The majority could be people who just don't like it. Some people know. Some don't."

From this statement, I realized that Mark probably thought of the "majority" as one huge chunk—a monolithic entity holding the same views for the same reasons. I didn't think that he linked his "everyone's different; not everyone is going to have the same feelings on things," to his understanding of majority. *Majority*, a noun representing a group of people as a single entity, obscures individual differences. He seemed to accept this single-entity noun as a single position.

I suggested that we make up a poll to look at. I drew this:

Contra Aid
1,200 People Interviewed

Against	For
52% (624)	48% (576)

I asked: "This 52% represents 624 individuals and this 48% represents 576 individuals. Had you thought of that? [Yes] OK, how do you know if these 624 individuals know or do not know about the contra aid issue?"

He responded: "I could say the majority don't know or I could say this minority don't know. You would have to do a very in-depth study."

"Knowing" to Mark seemed to be directly linked to "right," and "not knowing" to wrong. In this session and the previous, he used *right* and *knowing* interchangeably. To know is to be right. In reaction to his previous statement and this realization, I asked if it might be possible that some people in the majority know a lot, and some know very little. Also, can some people in the majority be misinformed and some informed?

"It's hard to say whether the majority can be . . . hard to say because some people just base it on what they saw in the news and not on what's real."

In this last statement, we have plenty of questions for another session: What's the difference between the news and "what's real"? Bypassing this for a moment, I decided to rephrase my question, using his terminology.

"Is it possible that some people in the majority base their decisions on the news and others on what's real?"

Silence. Mark was thinking—hard. I could practically hear his brain working when he suddenly said, "Wow. I never thought of that before."

"What?" I tried to conceal my excitement.

"That a majority could have different reasons why they're on that side."

Again, silence. I think we were both thinking about this new idea. I wondered how this new idea would apply to the contra aid issue. I also wondered about his thinking on the issue because in the last session I had sensed some ambivalence.

"What are some of the different reasons people would be against contra aid?"

"The money could be used for something else. We should leave them [Nicaraguans] alone because it's their country. And why bother at all? There's no logical reason to be there."

"Do you think some people support the Sandanistas?"

"No, because most people are aware of the trouble [that a government must have caused] for people to be fighting against that government."

We were nearing the end of the session. Therefore, this last comment was left unchallenged, as were others. I wanted to hear Mark's reasons in support of contra aid. These included:

To stop the spread of communism
To aid a former democracy in the Third World
To avoid using money for making missiles (to take money away from missile-building programs)
People would rather send money and weapons than send troops.

He finished with, "Now do you want to know what I think?"
"Yes."

"I think we should send troops down. First we cut off funding. Then Russia went in there. Now let's go down. Just go in like Grenada."

"What would we accomplish?"

"Probably nothing."

"Why risk it?"

"I don't think we'd lose much. If I were in the marines or the army, I would want to fight," Mark added.

With comments such as these, I always go through mental gyrations. From a personal perspective, I did not think we should fight Nicaragua. From a teacher's perspective, I did not think this comment should go unchallenged. But how could I challenge it without imposing my viewpoint, without risking silencing Mark's voice? In cases such as these, I often resort to what other people think (especially when time has run out). Therefore, I said, "Some of the soldiers that have been stationed in the Honduras have said that these people are so poor they need food, not military assistance. What do you think of that?"

"I don't know. I haven't been there."

With this last comment, our time together ended. At my suggestion, Mark set out to watch the week's news for examples of how people on the same side of an issue might agree for different reasons, and to gather more data on how the president decides.

As it turned out, Mark and I were not able to arrange another meeting time. Sports schedules and end-of-school-year activities made it impossible to arrange another session with either one of the boys.

Thinking about Thinking and the Implications for Teaching

Mark, Tim, and I developed new understandings and grappled with the issues of living in an imperfect democracy. Thinking about Mark and Tim's thinking became part of the process of deciding what to do in subsequent sessions. In this way, their thinking guided my curriculum making. Of particular interest are the resistance to entertaining new ideas that emerged in sessions about whether or not an official summit photograph was planned; Mark and Tim's understandings of collective nouns that could potentially pose a "critical barrier" to understanding democratic process; the bipolar thinking that underlay discussions of right and wrong in decision-making and discussions of the president's competence and incompetence.

Conflict and Resistance. Both Mark and Tim came very close to accepting the idea that a summit photo would be planned. Yet neither would commit himself to it. In discussions of whether the photos from the Reagan-Gorbachev summit were planned, Tim used the words "makes it look like" when describing the photo. He used this phrase throughout the session; yet he said he did not think the photograph was planned. His resistance to thinking that the photo was planned was linked to his conception of the responsibilities of the president and his staff. Both he and Mark thought the president and his staff had "more important things to do" than think about a photo session. Because they did not consider concerns with the president's image important to the job, they could not openly entertain the notion that a president might think about how he appeared to the public during a summit.

The emergent ideas inherent in Tim's language and Mark's questions, and resisted by both, indicate that these topics are exactly where to begin and to continue teaching. Further, teaching in these areas of conflicting ideas is exciting—for both student and teacher. Tim told Mark that the session was "intense." I often wondered if Tim's idea of the presidency later expanded to include the politics of image. Did Mark come to decide that the president's staff does plan photo sessions?

The examples of Mark and Tim reveal the importance of pursuing an understanding of the many political aspects of the president's responsibilities. A student who continues to resist or deny the interest of a president (or other public officeholders) in maintaining a positive, strong image is vulnerable because he or she is less prepared to evaluate critically any information about public issues.

Collective Nouns as Potential Critical Barriers. Part of U.S. public language consists of a variety of notions representing groups of people who share some or one characteristic: majority, minority, electorate, the people, the public, Democrats, Republicans, Americans, society, workers, staff, executives, Administration, Congress, the Supreme Court, the court, undecided, and so on. In teaching, I have often thought that these nouns constitute what David Hawkins calls "critical barriers" (Hawkins, 1978)—in this case a barrier to understanding the dynamics of politics and thus to understanding democratic principles. These nouns obscure individual differences inherent in any group of people. We toss these nouns around often—in conversing, in writing textbooks, and in teaching—without stopping to consider what we mean by them.

That is why I found Mark's realization that "a majority could have different reasons why they're on that side" so exciting. I had hoped this realization would challenge him to think anew about right and wrong decisions, and I had intended to pursue his conception of right and wrong decisions, in the next session. I also had intended to try to relate this conception to the issue of the president's competence.

Bipolar Thinking—Understanding of Right and Wrong in Decision-Making. Mark's notion of decision-making seemed to me to rest on a belief that absolutely right and absolutely wrong decisions were possible, and that part of the president's job was to identify the right decision. He had said in our first session, "It's wrong to change your opinion. You can't just change it like that." This seems a curious statement at first glance, and the juxtaposition of the statements seems even more curious. However, if you believe that your opinion is right, then both statements and their relationship begin to make sense: If you are right, then changing your opinion is wrong.

Mark's explanation of how politicians should act (1) to get elected and (2) to carry out their offices seemed to be based on a belief that absolutely wrong and absolutely right decisions can be identified. His explanation also showed an understanding of how people are elected ("tell people what they want to hear") and how the demands of political office may require that a politician act differently from how he or she intended. A *right* decision by a politician "would benefit overall the people." Yet Mark was unsure how to determine this "benefit," how to judge it. He did not seem to entertain the possibility that once in office, a politician might do something wrong. In later sessions, we could have investigated the description of the powers of the executive branch as outlined in the Constitution and compared them to Mark's conception of the responsibilities of the president. (A central premise of the Constitution is that people will eventually abuse power unless "checked.")

In part, I think that this question of a politician doing wrong might have been related to another notion of Mark's. When asked if some people might support the Sandanistas, Mark's negative answer implied that he assumed two ideas: (1) that the people fighting against a government are probably the "good guys" and (2) that there is widespread consensus about this. This assumption of consensus may be linked to his implicit trust of U.S. government officials and to his belief in "right" and "wrong" decisions. According to U.S. foreign policy under Reagan, the "good guys" were those fighting their governments—the contras in Nicaragua and the freedom fighters in Afghanistan. The language that Reagan habitually used and the way he framed these issues might well have made it appear that one decision is right and another wrong. The language of public officials and the reporting of issues may imply a consensus.

I need to mention that Mark was a football player whose hopes for college rested on an athletic scholarship. His alternative plan was to join the marines. The uncertainty of college measured against the certainty that he could become a marine might also have been linked to his assumptions and his trust. These aspirations might have been related to his thinking about Nicaragua. In the previous session, he brought up "new" information—that the United States had originally cut off funds to Nicaragua and that this had forced the Sandanistas to look for aid elsewhere. Since I knew that Mark originally supported the idea of contra aid, I wondered how this information would affect Mark's position. In this session, I found out. He had directly incorporated this information into his original position: "I think we should send troops down. First we cut off funding then Russia went in there. Now, let's go down. Just go in like Grenada." His position seemed to be based on the perceived success of the Grenada invasion. He did not consider the internal dynamics of Nicaragua. In fact, his viewpoint seemed to be based on an extension of self to country. "I don't think we'd lose much. If I were in the marines or the army, I would want to fight."

Bipolar Thinking—Competence and Incompetence. The issue of the president's competence raised at least two points: (1) the bipolarity of viewing the president as either competent or incompetent and (2) the role of the president in the national government.

This vision of bipolarity seemed to be at the heart of Mark's understanding. Why was he so disturbed by questioning the president's competence? If he viewed the president as an entity that is either competent or incompetent, then the prospect of an incompetent person in the office could be terrifying. Now to make the prospect even more disturbing, imagine that the workings of the federal government depended on this incompetent person.

Although I am not *sure* that Mark thought this way, I suspected that to some extent he did. In the following session (which, alas, never took place), I wanted to ask him to describe ways in which he thought the president was competent and ways in which he thought that the president was not.

A great deal of Reagan's competence was in political savvy, expressed publicly in his speeches and other public appeals. Neither Tim nor Mark, however, perceived Reagan's media relations, public relations, or speeches as part of his job as president. Perhaps this refusal to see politics as a dimension of presidential decision-making and policy-making prevented Mark from understanding this president as competent in some areas, but not in others. Mark could not draw on Reagan's political talents to develop an idea of a president having a constellation of responsibilities and competencies.

This resistance to accepting the politics of the president's image may have posed another critical barrier, a barrier that kept them from seeing the president as part of, not the sole leader of, the national government. I had feared that by focusing on the presidency, this project might reinforce the view that the functioning of the federal government depends only on the president. I had hoped that the question might be raised. I had not expected it to arise from discussions of competence and incompetence.

These sessions with Mark and Tim have continued to affect my teaching of social studies and my current teaching about teaching. For one thing; I learned to expect conflict and resistance from students and to view conflict/resistance as learning-in-progress. In making decisions about curriculum and instruction, I begin planning at points of conflict, resistance, or both. Areas of conflict and resistance reveal what students are thinking about, how they feel, and what questions are important to them. These areas also reveal what students might not know. As a teacher, then, by attending to students' reactions and questions, I have invaluable information.

In my planning now I also try to have concrete examples even of concepts that seem obvious to adults. For example, I have introduced the concept of the White House staff by showing photographs of major White House personnel and followed this with discussions of organization charts. I have asked students to imagine, based on the organizational chart, how many people might be employed as White House staff. My objective is to deepen the concept of White House staff and challenge the monolithic nature of collective nouns that I found might pose a critical barrier.

From Mark and Tim I learned that by listening to the reasoning of my students and by seeking an understanding of their perceptions and questions, I can ask questions that are relevant both to the students personally and to broader discussions about democratic life. In this way, students engage in public conversations that are personally relevant. In my classrooms, the next steps after these conversations have included students' writing letters to the editor, writing newspaper articles, taking photos of public events, or writing about an idea for new legislation.

As I brought these ways of listening and talking into classrooms, I have noticed that students are interested in one another's thinking; extended conversations with one or three students in a classroom can happen without my losing the rest of the class. This practice challenges some current notions about classroom engagement. Sometimes extended conversations with a few students can in fact engage everyone and push an entire class to think more deeply.

Finally, the sessions with Mark and Tim continue to remind me that if I want students to learn about government and politics, then helping them to connect with the real issues of the day, with real policy-makers and elected officials, with real materials (real drafts of legislation, for example), is crucial. I cannot predict how or which specific issues will engage students. However, by listening, asking questions, and providing materials and experiences that are personally and sociopolitically relevant, I can, as teacher, facilitate adolescents' entrance into public life.

References

Hawkins, D. (1974). "Messing about in science." In *The informed vision: Essays on learning and human nature*. New York: Agathon Press.

Hawkins, D. (1978, Autumn). "Critical barriers to science learning." *Outlook, 29,* 3–25.

6

Newborn Developments

Isabella Knox

As a neonatologist, I have taught many students in a neonatal intensive care unit (NICU) over the past 10 years. In this project, I spent eight sessions with Aral, a first-year medical student, so he could learn about premature babies. Usually when I teach students, in groups from three to ten, a major part of our time together consists of my telling them information about babies. In this project I decided to try to minimize the amount of telling. Instead, I would structure experiences for Aral to have with babies, from which he would learn about them. I chose to work with only one student so I could follow his thinking in detail.

The setting is the NICU at the University of Connecticut School of Medicine. At the time I had been on the faculty there for 8 years, caring for babies and teaching students and residents at the university hospital. Premature babies (or preemies), many as immature as 24 weeks gestation,[1] are delivered at the university hospital and often stay for months until they can go home to their families. The NICU is a busy place. Most of the babies are in plastic incubators, some with bright lights shining on them to treat their jaundice. Alarms sound frequently and staff members rush to the infant to make sure she or he is OK. I am at home in that environment, although it is a home that is not relaxed or contemplative. In most of my time there I have been on duty, when I must be prepared to deal with any emergency. During most of these sessions, on the other hand, I was there only to teach, which was a new experience.

Before each session, Aral met me at my office, and we walked together to the NICU. We put on cover gowns and scrubbed our hands, and then we went into the nursery to see the babies. Sometimes we looked at a baby through the walls of the incubator. Other times we were able to hold or feed a baby. Our conversation each session, and my reflections as I tried to understand his thinking and to design subsequent sessions that would allow him to take his ideas further, constitute the story. To each session I wore a portable microphone, and I taped our words. I kept a journal log of my experiences and reactions to each session.

My plan was that I would choose babies for us to observe, let Aral notice things about the babies, and allow our focus to emerge from what he noticed. My work during the sessions would be to try to understand how he was thinking about the subject. In my log I tried to imagine what things he might notice about a premature baby: "Thin, shiny skin; tiny features; extra hair; jerky and uncontrolled movements; breathing difficulties; connected to many tubes and wires." I speculated about some of the areas that we could pursue: "Breathing, . . . neurological development, . . . physical development, . . . cardiovascular functioning, . . . and feeding."

Session 1: February 25—Aral Notices Many Things about Dominic

I'd chosen Dominic for us to observe. He had been born at 26 weeks gestation, 14 weeks prematurely. When we arrived, he was sleeping quietly in an incubator, with oxygen and feeding tubes taped to his nose. He was tiny, only 3 pounds, with smooth pink skin. Aral and I stood at his bedside, looking through the plastic walls and talking about what we saw. Working through the incubator hand holes, I removed Dominic's blankets and clothing bit by bit, so that we could see him better. This activity also woke him up slowly, and he moved his arms, kicked, arched his back, and opened his eyes.

Aral immediately found the card taped to the incubator with Dominic's birth date and weight. He calculated that Dominic was six weeks old and had already gained more than a pound since his birth at 795 grams (1 pound, 12 ounces). He noticed Dominic's size: "very, very tiny. . . . I just can't get over the fact that he's so adorable; he's very tiny, and I want to pick him up and protect him almost"; his movements: "just very delicate movements; . . . he seems to have these little motions, like he's trying to move around a little, and I don't know whether they are involuntary or voluntary movements"; his prematurity and the effects that might have on the baby:

> I'm very curious about just being born that small. What are the problems that will happen internally, with his organs and stuff? . . . There's just a little bit there and you know that it's going to develop into something, but you don't know what it's going to be. . . . The idea that in the womb it's completely dependent on everything

from the mother, its eating, its oxygen, everything. . . . Then it
moves into that stage when it's still dependent on the mom or dad
or someone to feed it and to hold it, but yet it can breathe on its
own.

These were only a few of many ideas and observations, and at the time
I did not give them more weight than the others. However, looking back,
this is the start of what Aral eventually focused on: What processes occur
during the period in gestation that some infants, born prematurely, spend
in the NICU instead of in utero, and how does the change of environment
affect those processes?

At the end of this session, I asked him what else he would like to know
about Dominic or the other babies. He said:

Well, I'm definitely interested in their development, especially their
mental development. But then also how their body develops with
them. Especially how he's going to catch up, or whether he will
catch up. It seems that he should catch up, if he's going to . . . be a
normal-sized person.

During this first session, Aral was very willing to tell me what he was
thinking. I mostly asked him questions about what he said, to try to understand better what he had observed and what he thought about it. I made
an effort to wait for his observations, rather than jumping to interpreting
for him. For example, near the end when Dominic was lying on his back
wearing only a diaper, Aral said, "It seems like his chest is moving a lot. Is
that as a result of him moving, or is it his heart?" I was also watching
Dominic at that point, and I saw a breathing pattern that is very typical for
infants, one that would be useful for someone interested in babies to know
about. However, instead of explaining the pattern (as I would have in my
usual teaching), I said, "Oh. When you see what you mean, tell me," and
we watched some more. Aral said, "I guess it's from his stomach up to his
thoracic cavity. There's a lot of movement in that area." There were several movements during this time, so when Dominic was doing the breathing movement that I considered so classic, I said, "Do you mean now?"
Aral said, "Yeah." I tried to focus us on what we were seeing, but I didn't
point us to an interpretation, even though I had one all ready.

In my journal reflections on the session, I wrote, "The baby was wonderful. So many things to see. I realized how wonderful it is to spend time
with a baby."

This first session accomplished several things. First, we had a common experience, which could be the basis for further explorations. Second,

Aral observed many, many details about the baby, which gave him an idea of the range of possible aspects to the study of babies. From that he could choose what interested him most. Third, in his observations I could begin to see possibilities that connected what I knew to what he noticed. This enabled me to start thinking of other experiences that would connect to and enrich his ideas.

Session 2: March 8—We Observe and Hold Christian, and Aral Compares Him with Dominic

For this session we spent time with Christian, a term baby with a brain abnormality. Aral, showing again his ability to make detailed observations, noticed many things about Christian. He particularly noticed Christian's movements, which he described as quick, short, and not as complex as Dominic's. We were able to take Christian out of his incubator, and Aral held him for a few minutes.

The most interesting part of the session occurred after we had left Christian and went over to see Dominic. Aral immediately began to talk about Christian's movements in comparison to those of Dominic. He said that Christian just kept doing his movements over and over, whereas Dominic seemed to be moving around to get comfortable. I tried a couple of times to get Aral to describe what was different. He attributed a purpose to Dominic's movements—to get comfortable—whereas he thought Christian was doing more writhing, expressing his "anguish." We did not go further with this discussion, but we came back to it the next week.

I told Aral I had chosen a baby with a brain problem "since I know that you're interested in development." While writing about the session later I realized that brain problems and development might not be connected for him the way they are for me. I had initially thought that I might go further into this baby's brain problems and show Aral the X rays of Christian's brain. However, the development of normal infants seemed sufficiently complex, so I didn't pursue it.

Session 3: March 18—Aral Compares Two Preemies and Begins to Wonder How to Think about Age and Development

On our way to see the new baby I had picked out for us to observe, we stopped to visit Dominic. Aral noticed that Dominic looked bigger (he'd gained a pound in the 3 weeks since we'd first met him), and he commented, "He looks more alive just in terms of his whole look and action and size and everything. He's even looking around more. . . . Seeing him these 3 weeks, I definitely notice a progression."

I asked Aral, "How old do you think [Dominic] is? How do you conceive of his age?" and he said, "Maybe this is my bias or something, but I think of his age as how far developed he is, not necessarily size, because he's starting off at a different point, but in terms of what he does physically, or what he may be noticing." This is a fascinating answer to my question about age. Aral did not refer to time at all. Rather, he talked about development—what can the baby do, physically or mentally?

We went over to see JJ, just 2 days old, who was 27 weeks gestation. He lay on his left side, with a breathing tube[2] in his mouth, his right arm curled up so his hand could grasp the part of the tube protruding from his lips. A bright light shone down on him from above, and around his head were the straps of a soft white eyeshade. He was nude, lying on a tiny diaper. Two plastic tubes, connected to syringes and IV tubing, emerged from his navel. He was breathing rapidly and with exertion. His skin was smooth and quite transparent, a dark red color, and he had thick dark hair on his head and fine hair on his shoulders and upper arms. He moved often, kicking his tiny feet, his arms making large, jerky motions. Aral mentioned many things about JJ, his hair, his skin, his movements, his breathing. He wondered about JJ's lungs, since he was on the respirator: "Does that signify something about age or lung development?" And he was interested in his physical activity and the fact that JJ had just been born.

> I'm very curious about his activeness. What's controlling all that? And then also his brain development. . . . All of a sudden I was curious about going from an environment where you're in the mom to now where he's out on his own, just the idea of his reaching for [the tube] to hold on to. And whether he's doing that knowingly or whether that's just something he does. Even as a 2-day-old baby, even though he is so small, I feel like, especially compared to Christian, he's doing so much more. He's so much more active. He seems to be doing a lot more stuff that I imagine a baby to be doing. . . . I remember comparing Dominic to [Christian] and saying that [Dominic] looked so much more alive. And that's what I felt again with [JJ]. . . . From what he's doing I feel he's more mentally active.

In here, Aral struggled with the fact that JJ was 2 days old, but "so small." I think he was comparing him with a 2-day-old term baby. He also returned to the idea that mental development is related to what the baby can do. Aral identified birth—the transition from the *in utero* environment to *ex utero*, where the baby is "on his own"—as an important landmark.

We returned to these points over and over again in subsequent sessions, and they were building blocks for his eventual ideas.

We stopped back to see Dominic for a minute before leaving and had the following conversation:

> *Aral:* Seeing him after the other baby, I feel you can see so much of development between these two babies. When you look at [JJ], [Dominic] looks like a normal baby.
> *IK:* What do you mean by a normal baby?
> *Aral:* Normal sized.
> *IK:* Like a newborn baby?
> *Aral:* I'm not thinking about [Dominic] as a 2-month [-old]. When we saw him the first time I noticed right away he seemed really small. But I feel like it looks to some extent like he's catching up. He's not as skinny. His body proportions are much better. A normal baby his age would be a lot bigger, in terms of weight, wouldn't he? How much would he weigh?
> *IK:* What kind of baby?
> *Aral:* One born at 7 pounds.
> *IK:* They say you double your weight at 3 months.
> *Aral:* So a normal baby could be 8 to 13 pounds? I keep forgetting he's 2 months old now and so he appears like a normal newborn baby in a lot of ways, not in what he does, just his size and stuff.

Again Aral was struggling with the discrepancies between age, size, and "what he does" that occur in a premature baby compared with a term baby. In my comments, I tried to point out distinctions—"What kind of a baby?"— to keep him open to the many parameters that are important in thinking about a baby.

Aral had had lots of other ideas and observations besides what I've described here. Our conversation had ranged over many topics as I tried to let him articulate his thoughts without direction from me. In my reflections on the session I was excited about two of Aral's ideas in particular: (1) His observations of JJ's breathing and his questions about lung development and (2) his questions about age versus size versus "what he does" and his comparison of Dominic to a term newborn. I felt that this second question related to a critical way of thinking about premature babies, one that I use every day in the NICU: As a neonatologist it is important for me to think about the gestational age (age from conception until birth), the postnatal age (age since birth) and the postconceptual age (total age since conception, which is gestational age plus postnatal age), because each provides different information about what to expect for the infant's development.

Session 4: March 29—We Try to Feed Dominic without Success, but Holding Him Raises Lots of Questions and a Focus for Aral

Feeding a baby was one of the experiences that I thought would relate to Aral's interest in development, since the ability to suck, swallow, and breathe in a coordinated enough way to take milk from a bottle is one that a baby develops at about 35 weeks postconceptual age, regardless of whether she or he is in utero or in the NICU. Bottle feeding a baby also involves holding her or him and would get Aral more physically engaged than he had been able to be before. Dominic, now 9 weeks old, was scheduled to be fed at the time of our session.

We got instructions from the nurse, and Aral held Dominic and tried to feed him. I sat close by, helping him hold the baby in a comfortable position and offering suggestions. Fortunately, we had been warned that Dominic was not a very good feeder, because our attempts were unsuccessful. Afterward we sat, Aral holding Dominic, and Aral talked about what he was noticing. He brought up a question that he had had about each baby so far: What is the baby noticing about his environment? "He must notice something." I brought up Dominic's gestational age (26 weeks), and Aral said that Dominic was "getting to the age where he'd almost be a normal—he'd be close to 35 weeks now if he hadn't come out early." When I asked what he meant by 35 weeks, he said it came from 26 plus 9, which confirmed to me that he was thinking about total postconceptual age, gestational plus postnatal, although we weren't using the terms. He wondered about the development of the body of a baby born 13½ weeks early and how it compared with that of a baby who stayed *in utero* until 40 weeks.

> That 13½ weeks is under a different kind of environment that he's not in any more. How does that change the development of different parts of him? . . . I wonder what's the difference between him and a fetus in his 35th week? I feel that he should be much [more developed], because he was put in that stressful situation of coming out. . . . My big question is, How does his growth compare to what's happening in the womb? And compared to a normal baby that's 9 weeks old now?

I mentioned the lungs, and Aral said, "I'm curious whether his lungs are still undergoing development that would have gone on in the womb."

Then, as we watched the nurse feed Dominic through the feeding tube, I said, "Feeding's another thing that you could compare at different ages." This led to Aral's wondering if tube feeding were part of the reason that Dominic's own sucking wasn't developed. As we talked about the reasons that a baby would not be able to feed at 26 weeks, I continued to ask questions to keep the discussion in the area of comparisons between postnatal and postconceptual ages. To Aral's comment that Dominic was fed by tube after birth, I asked, "What if he'd stayed in utero instead?" Aral said, "He wouldn't be feeding at all. . . . When it comes out at 26 weeks, does it catch up really quickly or is it doing two things at once, catching up but also moving forward?" I asked him to clarify "moving forward," and I concluded that he thought that on the one hand there is normal development after term birth and on the other hand there is development from 26 weeks to term, and that in Dominic's case elements of both might be occurring simultaneously:

> A normal [full-term] baby moves forward, developing. A lot of its body is formed when it comes out. . . . [A premature baby]'s getting bigger but it doesn't seem as much developmental as if a baby's born normally. . . . It seems like there's got to be a reason for 40 weeks. Between 26 and 40, something's got to be going on. How much is going simultaneously? What's the combination? Are certain things not going to happen because he didn't have the 13 weeks?

Aral was continuing to develop his ideas about how to think about age in a premature baby. He thought that the development that normally happens after a term birth allows the baby to learn to do new things. The development that occurs from 26 weeks to term might be more physical, "getting bigger." He wondered how these two fit together in a baby born prematurely.

Aral said that holding Dominic, hearing his sounds, "adds a whole element." I sensed that his fascination with the baby, to whom he was relating now more than he had through the walls of the incubator, increased his interest in knowing more about him.

Session 5: April 8—I Give a "Lecture" on Lung Development, and Aral Says, "It Makes Perfect Sense"

When Aral and I were scrubbing, I asked him if there were anything particular he was interested in or wanted to focus on. He said he was interested in stages of development, such as learning to sit or walk, but that he didn't have any kind of landmark for premature infants. As he was talking he seemed to remember something, and he said, "Yeah, that's what I'm really interested in: How do you think of how old they are?" I asked him to tell me what he meant by that. He said, "You know, they're born at 26 weeks, and they're 9 weeks old, which makes 35 weeks, so how old are they really and how do they develop?" So I said that we'd talked about several different parts of the body whose development we could look at— the lungs, the skin, the feeding—and we could look at X rays of babies' lungs today, to think about just that question.

I decided I would give Aral a "lecture," not in the traditional sense of talking for an hour, but in the sense of a directed exposure to some new ways of looking at a subject, at the end of which I hoped he would have reasoned through a specific idea. Of the two areas we had touched on that seemed to me to illustrate aspects of age-related development—feeding and lung maturation—I chose the latter, because I thought that I could use X rays of infants' lungs at various stages to show how and when changes occur. Lung development, in particular the development of the ability to make a substance called surfactant,[3] is an example of something that is undeveloped in most babies born prior to 35 weeks, but that develops rapidly after birth. I found X rays for us to look at from three babies: (1) JJ, who had, at birth (27 weeks), a typical X ray of surfactant deficiency and whose second X ray at 3 days of life showed much clearer lungs; (2) Jason, born at 35 weeks, who also had had an early X ray with collapsed lungs from surfactant deficiency and a later one with clearing; and (3) a full-term newborn with normal clear lungs, for comparison. We looked at the X rays and saw whiter lungs in JJ's and Jason's first films, which meant less air in the collapsed, surfactant-deficient lungs. Aral was able to observe the similarity between the patterns on JJ's first day and Jason's first day, and the similarity between the follow-up films on both babies. After that seemed established, I brought up surfactant—he'd mentioned the word in an earlier session so I knew it wasn't completely unfamiliar. I told him that surfactant deficiency is common in premature babies, and that the pattern we'd seen on the first X rays of the two babies was the typical X-ray pattern for surfactant deficiency. Several times I set up the comparison of the two babies in terms of their initial situations and their recoveries. I said things such as "OK, so [JJ's] 27 weeks and he doesn't have surfactant, but he gets born, . . . and here he's 3 days old—27 weeks and 3 days, look at what happened. . . . So then how about this baby who is 35 weeks and then 35 weeks and a day. Comparing his lungs? . . . If you saw this pattern in a brand-new 35-weeker and a brand-new 27-weeker?"

There were lots of fairly long pauses in our conversation, and after one of these, Aral said, "It makes perfect sense." He proceeded to explain his idea that "surfactant production" wasn't going on at 27 weeks *in utero*, but that birth was a stress that signaled the need to begin production. "There must be signals from the body, that he's no longer getting oxygenated blood from the umbilical cord." He thought this could happen at 35 weeks also, because "it's still not expecting to be born." He had figured out that the lung pattern we looked at, surfactant deficiency and its resolution, was an example of an aspect of development that was not present at birth but that develops rapidly after birth regardless of the gestational age. Aral was very pleased with this idea (as was I).

We then went to see Dominic, JJ, and Jason. Aral's comment on Dominic was, "He looks so much better. So much more normal." I asked what he meant by "normal," and he said he meant like a term baby. He tried to articulate the two separate developmental trajectories that he had talked about last session: (1) the *ex utero* development from 26 to 40 weeks, which can exhibit "catch-up," by which he meant accelerated maturation such as we had seen with the lungs and surfactant; and (2) the normal development that occurs in a term baby after birth.

With both JJ and Jason, Aral noticed the breathing. JJ's was more labored than the last time we saw him. Aral saw his whole chest and stomach as "working," and he talked about the movement of the chest and sides and abdomen that were "pushing." With Jason, Aral remarked that his abdomen was moving: "I noticed it right away, now that I know about it." Indeed, both babies were working hard to breathe.

My initial reaction to this session was that it went so well, that Aral had synthesized so much, that I couldn't imagine what to do next. At this stage I found this project both exhilarating and nerve-racking. I was excited by what my student had put together, although in this report it seems clearer than it did at the time. There were many stops and starts, many unfinished sentences, and many unclear ideas in our sessions, and at times I wondered if he were really "learning" anything. At other times I felt his enjoyment of the process and wondered why all teaching isn't this way.

Session 6: April 15—Aral Has Read about the Sucking Reflex and Still Has Questions. We Feed Jacob, Who Eats Well

While we were scrubbing I asked Aral what he'd been thinking about since our last session. He said he'd done some reading. He'd looked up sucking and had read that the baby first sucks at 14 weeks gestation and that sucking is "really strong" by 34 weeks. Another thing he'd looked at in the books was about the effect of experience on the development of the baby—namely, What is the effect of the time spent out of the womb on the development of premature infants compared to babies who stay *in utero*? He remarked that the book said that it probably doesn't make much difference, but Aral sounded as if he weren't sure he believed that. (I wish I had asked him.) He'd tried to find the answer to the question of how you should consider a baby's age—postnatal or postconceptual. The book he'd read brought up both as possible ways of looking at it. I asked what "it" was. He said, "Development." I asked if there were any particular aspects of development, and he said, "Like feeding."

I was pleased that he'd chosen to focus on sucking, as I had planned our day's activity to be feeding a baby. Baby Jacob had been born at 28 weeks and was now 10 weeks old and reportedly a good feeder. Aral held him and fed him two ounces from a bottle. A lot of our interactions were with Jacob, rather than with each other. He was very alert, looking around wide-eyed, smacking his lips and tongue. He hiccuped and was very wiggly. Aral noticed Jacob's sounds and was interested in figuring out how he was making them; Jacob's hands and why he held them as he did; his changing level of alertness as he dozed off after taking the bottle; the way Jacob grabbed a finger of Aral's hand holding the bottle. He found Jacob very compelling and talked to him a lot. He said,

> (To me) I don't know why, but I've noticed his hands more than I've noticed in other babies. . . . (To Jacob) Are you OK? What are you doing? (To me) What he's doing now, it seems that he's very much more . . . active. I don't know if it's the fact of holding him, I feel like he's relating a lot more to me, than I felt some of the other times, especially when they're inside [the incubator]. . . . I feel that he's observing his surroundings. . . . The way he's moving his eyes seems more inquisitive, not just random movement, but rather purposeful, in terms of what he's taking in.

One of Aral's first comments as he sat down to feed Jacob was, "So we know nothing about him, right?" I was pleased that he thought there were important things to know about the baby's past in order to understand his current state. After Jacob was sound asleep in Aral's arms, I pulled out the medical chart and gave Aral the note written by the doctor who attended Jacob's birth. This contained information about the mother's condition and the reasons that Jacob was born early. Aral immediately noticed the gestational age: "$28^5/_7$.[4] He was pretty early." He then calculated Jacob's age since birth (9½ weeks) and commented that he was now 38 weeks, or term. He seemed facile with his calculations of postconceptual age and with using them to think about Jacob.

At the time I wondered if we'd accomplished anything in this session, because we didn't have the kind of deep discussion of ideas that we'd had before. This was true of the next session, also. I remembered, though, that experiencing the subject is an integral part of this work. Without it, there's nothing to talk about! As Aral and I had these experiences together, we built a foundation for further discussion.

Session 7: April 24 and 25—Aral Sees a Newborn Baby and a Birth. He Spends Several Hours in the NICU with a New Baby and Gets to Know Firsthand What We Do for Small, Sick Preemies

One of the experiences I'd been trying to arrange for Aral was for him to see a birth. The moment of birth had turned out to be an important point in our discussions of premature babies. Aral had wondered about the intra-uterine environment where the placenta supplies all the baby's needs, compared to the NICU environment. He agreed that a birth would be wonderful to see. Unfortunately, births are not something you can schedule, but on my on-call weekend, Aral agreed to come in and do our session whenever a baby was born.

The session took place in two parts, because the first birth of the weekend occurred before I could call Aral. He arrived when the baby, a 6-pound, 35-week infant who was very healthy, was 15 minutes old. We spent about an hour with the baby. There were so many things to see. The baby was lovely, pink, and wide awake, looking around, moving his arms and legs. He made sucking movements and occasional noises. Lots of black hair, big black eyes. Aral noticed the baby making sucking movements and occasionally bringing his hand to his mouth. He was interested that he would do that even though he had never eaten. He said it could be a "totally neurological thing," but that after the baby had experienced eating "there must be some learning." I asked him to say more about how he was thinking about learning. He thought that taking a bottle, feeling hunger, and getting full would be related for the baby after the experience of feeding. As a countersuggestion to the idea that the baby had never fed before, I asked if he had read any of the articles I had given him (no) and told him that in one of them it says that a fetus in the last trimester swallows 450 cc of amniotic fluid each day. He said, "Well, that completely blows that idea," meaning his idea that drinking was a new activity for the baby. "I have to rethink the whole thing now." I left it at that.

Aral said that the breathing looked "good," that he felt the baby wasn't using as much of his body in the breathing. When I asked him to compare this baby's breathing with the others we had seen, he said, gesturing to chest and abdomen, that the others were using their whole bodies. Then he looked at this baby and said that the abdomen was still going up and down but it seemed more relaxed, easier.

The next evening there was another birth. Aral met me in the hospital, and we put on jumpsuits, hats, masks, booties, and gloves so we could go into the delivery room. It was a Cesarean section delivery at 31 weeks, because the mother was severely ill with high blood pressure. I found Aral a place to stand to watch the surgery. The surgeon pulled the baby out head first and suctioned out his mouth, and the baby cried. They handed him to me, and Aral and I went into the resuscitation room, where the residents and nurses were waiting for us. The baby cried a little and then was quiet, breathing quite hard. We began our routines, drying him off, suctioning his mouth, listening to his heart rate. As one or two minutes passed, we made the decision to put him on the respirator. We brought the baby into the nursery, and Aral and I stayed there for the next 2 hours, he watching what was happening to the baby, and I doing my other work, but spending some time talking to him. He noticed that the baby was breathing hard and heard me discussing the infant's lung disease with the residents and nurses, adjusting the respirator, ordering and looking at the chest X ray. The X ray had a mild version of the pattern Aral and I had looked at in our fifth session, and he heard us discussing whether or not we should administer surfactant.[5]

Looking at the baby, Aral said, "It's hard to believe that there's only 4 weeks between him and the baby we saw yesterday morning." Indeed, the difference was amazing: This baby, born at 31 weeks, weighed 2½ pounds; the other, born at 35 weeks, weighed 6 pounds. We didn't discuss the other contrasts, but there were many—and I am sure Aral noticed a good number of them.

Session 8: April 29—Aral Has Done More Reading. We Talk about What He Has Seen in the Past Two Sessions and His Ideas about Development and Prematurity

I felt that a lot had happened in the past two sessions that Aral and I needed to talk about. He had just finished the reading I'd given him. He said that it "made sense" to him why a premature baby has a difficult time feeding, since the capability to suck has to develop at a time that the baby is also under stress from other conditions.

> There is this innate reflex, that they do start sucking. . . . And combining that with a positive reinforcement, so what's learned on top of what's innate. The whole idea of stamina fits into this be-

cause if a baby's working really hard to breathe or to do other
functions then it's not going to have the energy or the desire [to
feed]. So from a learned aspect and from an aspect of physical
capabilities, what is it actually going to be able to do? Putting all
those together, it seems like it fits why a premature baby would
have more trouble. And all of these things are very interconnected,
and definitely seem very developmentally controlled. Just having
been that little and young and not having been able to develop
physically, as well as having these extra stresses. Other things are
going to take precedence over the idea of working on something
like [feeding].

He has expanded his earlier notion of "voluntary or involuntary" (see
session 1) to a more complex one that has distinctions between "innate"
and "learned" and *in utero* and *ex utero*. He has also added the notion of
stamina.

There are so many things that [premature babies are] working on.
[There's] normal [physical] development, since they were born
much earlier than they were supposed to be. Normally they would
not be needing to expend any effort for most of the functions like
breathing, eating, all these things. The normal things that would
have been developing create even more of a stamina problem. . . .
Just purely on an energy-consumption level, you have two things
going on that wouldn't necessarily be going on [together]. Evolu-
tionarily, humans aren't meant to do that, and that's why they're
given that 13 extra weeks. Normal babies have the normal shock of
coming into the world and having to deal with all the things going
on, and this premature baby has all the systems that would normally have this time to just be growing plus all the things that it
needs just to survive on top of that.

This is a very rich, complex picture of what a premature baby faces as
it grows through the time that it should have spent *in utero*. The baby has
to accomplish the development that would have occurred *in utero* at the
same time as she or he must adjust to extrauterine life by becoming able to
breathe and digest milk. This combination stretches the energy reserves of
the baby, and further energy drains, such as sucking to get its milk, may
be too much.

I asked him what he meant by one activity "[taking] precedence,"
whether it was the baby's or the doctors' doing that feeding is less of a

priority during the early days when the baby is sick with lung problems. Aral said:

> The baby isn't even asked to do something like [take a bottle], because there are all these other pressing needs. And at the same time, internally there are all these pressing needs, so it's working on those. . . . With the lungs it seems like those two things are working together for the baby to catch up, . . . us giving surfactant and giving oxygen and making its environment easier, and at the same time the baby's under stress so right away it's [developing its lungs].

Here Aral is contrasting the two systems we had focused on, breathing and feeding. The former is a greater priority for the baby's survival. We who care for the baby can take the stress of feeding off of the baby, by giving the milk by feeding tube.

Aral told me that the reading helped him look back at the babies we had observed with a new eye, one that I think could see more complexity.

> There was one interesting thing I got out of the lung readings. It had to do with how the lungs develop—the idea that it wasn't until 24 or 26 weeks that [air sacs in the lungs][6] start being produced. A lot of babies that we were looking at [were that young]. JJ was 26½ weeks at birth, and the other baby was 27. I didn't know physically that their lungs were *so* immature at that point. Basically they had very little gas-exchange ability because of just how old they were. That was kind of amazing, that they're able to do anything.

I asked Aral about the births he had seen.

> The birth itself was so fast, it happened so quickly, that it in itself had less impact on me than I thought it would. I guess it's also because you think of birth as this magical event. . . . That few seconds was really intense but then it's over. . . . [It was] sort of a continuum. It happened like it was a natural thing. The baby came out and cried.

In his expanded view of gestation, birth, while an important event in a fetus' life, is no longer the beginning. It is now part of a "continuum."

In the last part of our conversation about the births, we compared the two babies from session 7 after plotting their measurements on a growth chart. I wanted to do this because of Aral's comment in the last session about the amazing difference 4 weeks made between the two babies. Referring to the smaller baby's growth chart, we had this exchange.

> *Aral:* If you plot him, he seems so classic for what he was.[7] . . . His weight was very low, because he wasn't getting nourishment, but yet its head is normal [sized], because the body [shunts nourishment to it]. The length is sort of on the low side.
> *IK:* Yeah, he's absolutely classic for a growth-retarded baby.
> *Aral:* [The chart] seems perfect for that kid.

What he saw when he looked at the baby made sense of the chart (why the plot came out as it did) and the chart helped make sense of the baby (why he looked the way he did).

I asked him what the smaller baby would have weighed if he had not had the problems that resulted in poor growth in utero (in other words, a normally grown 31-weeker). Aral said,

> So you would think that he [would weigh] probably about 1,500, 1,600 [grams, 3½ pounds or so]. . . . And on top of that, even if he'd been [growing normally], he still would have [gained] almost 1,000 grams in 4 weeks, [from 31 to 35 weeks]. . . . That's interesting in terms of what we were talking about before. If you're looking at babies born at 26 weeks, and between 30 and 35 is where you have the most [growth], that adds more into the idea of normally what would happen to this baby. . . . Under normal situations *in utero* [fast growth] would happen by itself. And outside, the stress might be put on by the intensive care unit where they are trying to make sure the baby gains the amount of weight. It's not going to be able to do it passively any longer, so that's going to be very harsh stimulus.

I said, "Neat idea. I have a new respect for that particular period of gestation." He had constructed an idea of what happens as a premature infant tries to get through those weeks that was beautiful to me as someone who has been intimately involved in the struggles. It was a new way of looking at it for me, too.

At the end of this session, he talked about this way of teaching and learning.

> It makes you realize how much you can learn without just being presented something. Seeing all this stuff first, and then putting it together afterwards, you have a frame to put it all together.

Reflections

This kind of teaching and learning is unlike any I experienced as a medical student or a medical teacher. I think it is richer and deeper. What did I do that allowed Aral to have this experience?

I believe that Aral learned more from this experience than he would have if I had given him eight traditional lectures on neonatal intensive care. I can see, in the way he talks about premature infants, a complex set of ideas with many interconnections among them. I believe there are several advantages to this kind of knowing. It provides a frame (to use Aral's term) into which he could fit new information, as he did with what he learned from his reading about lung development, that then enriches the entire structure. This is different from how the word *frame* (or *framework*) is sometimes used. Often it refers to an overview or outline that is presented to a student, into which she or he is supposed to fit the details that come later. Aral's use is the opposite. His "frame" came from his actual experience with the subject, in this case interacting with premature babies. His observations of babies informed his reading about lung development.

The work Aral did in this project generated a tremendous interest on his part. He found time to read about babies even though he carried the full course load of a first-year medical student and had three exams during the weeks we were working together. He came into the hospital late at night to see a birth. He asked me if he could continue to observe in the NICU during his 2nd year.

What did I provide that made this possible for him? I provided him access to a rich and fascinating subject. My knowledge of the subject matter enabled me to make choices of what we were going to observe or do, as I tried to understand what he was understanding and what his thoughts might connect to that we had seen or could see. I also brought a kind of empathy; both intellectual empathy, in that I tried to understand what he was thinking, and emotional empathy as I tried to understand how it felt. The latter was especially important since this was an unfamiliar process. We who have experienced traditional education and its judgmental nature look for judgment from our teachers, and it usually comes quickly and predictably. Since I wasn't going to tell him if his ideas were "right" or "wrong," I had to be sensitive to the fact that he was probably used to someone's doing that and would be expecting it. Indeed, Aral made several self-deprecating remarks ("Do I sound completely clueless?" "I'm going to embarrass myself badly") that let me know that he did feel this at times. In our last session, he said, "You rarely have that opportunity to just think about things and not necessarily be right about them."

In allowing our direction to emerge from what he noticed, I had to trust both Aral and the subject: Trust that what he noticed would be important; trust that the important aspects of the subject are noticeable. These sessions were not structured the way my previous teaching has been, with the session's direction generally mapped out before we began. Rather, trusting my subject matter to show its important aspects, I structured our curriculum by my choices of material for us to observe.

My first thought about applying this kind of teaching more broadly in medical education is that there couldn't possibly be time. One way to look at this project is that I spent 8 hours teaching Aral one small concept; how could he possibly learn all that a doctor needs to know at that rate? However, I think elements of what we did together could become part of medical education, and that the benefits to both the amount of learning and the process of learning would be significant.

If medical teachers would ask students "What did you notice?" instead of "What did you find?" as they debrief after the student has seen a patient, it would make a difference to learning. First, it would mitigate the notion that there is one right answer (that a student often assumes she or he will be reviled for not being privy to). Though there are surely answers that are more right than others (and what we are trying to teach is how to discern them), seeking only *the* answer reduces attention to the richness of what is in front of you, and may well distract you from the very aspect that will guide you to where you need to go. For example, a student who describes noticing that a baby's chest X ray has white lung fields, small lung volumes and a grainy appearance to the lung pattern is more prepared to consider the physiology of the labored breathing that the baby shows than a student who says "respiratory distress."

Second, asking the student what she or he noticed helps the teacher learn some of the details of what the student knows and can better guide the student's choices of what to study next. A medical term (e.g., surfactant) stands for (and often stands between the student and) a huge and complex set of understandings about cells, the mechanics of breathing, age, and the physics of surface tension. The details of how a student evaluates (notices things about) a baby with breathing problems helps the teacher assist him or her in what to do or read to learn more about surfactant deficiency and respiratory distress syndrome. The closer the teacher's suggestions for further learning are to what a student is already trying to figure out, the more likely the student is to follow through on them and to retain the information.

The third benefit I see of starting with students' noticings instead of their conclusions is that it acknowledges to all that the student is the one ultimately who determines what is going to be learned. We forget that often in medical schools, believing that if we (teachers) have "covered" a topic, they (students) have learned it. Students are just as prone to this belief as are faculty, and it stifles a necessary element in dealing with the massive amount of learning required in a short time: their own efforts in making sense of it all. If they are asked to put their own noticings in front of themselves, they will see more clearly what they do and don't understand, and they will want to improve.

In paying attention to what our students notice and think, each of us can learn how novices experience our subject—precious insights which are otherwise inaccessible to us, being, as we are, far from novices ourselves. And if many of us put together our observations of many students' noticings, we will enrich our collective teaching capability.

As a final word, I need to say that an additional result of this teaching/learning research was that I myself was able to spend enjoyable time with babies. This gave me time to re-explore my subject and renew my own interest. I became a learner again, and, in a self-sustaining cycle, a more committed teacher.

Notes

1. Full-term gestation is 38 to 40 weeks.
2. Connected by long pieces of tubing to a respirator.
3. Surfactant is a substance made by the lungs to maintain inflation when one exhales. Premature babies usually are unable to make surfactant at birth and often have very collapsed lungs. However, they develop the capacity to make it within a few days, regardless of when the birth occurs. That is, after birth at 26 weeks gestation or at 35 weeks, it takes a few days for them to start making surfactant. The chest X rays of babies with surfactant deficiency show a characteristic pattern, very white lungs, which clear up (get blacker on the X ray) as surfactant is made and the lungs inflate better.
4. Gestation of 28 weeks and 5 days.
5. One of the treatments for surfactant deficiency is to inject a preparation of surfactant directly into the baby's lungs.
6. The air sacs are where exchange of oxygen from air to blood occurs.
7. This baby's placenta had not been functioning well and thus the baby received an inadequate supply of nutrients. We had discussed earlier the fact that in such conditions the nutrients that the baby does receive are preferentially used by the brain, so that the head circumference continues to grow, at the expense of the weight and length.

7

Looking at Learning to Understand Teaching: A South African Case Study

Namane Magau

This chapter focuses on the experiences and learning of one teacher, Bonolo, one of six teachers who participated in a seminar on teaching/learning research that I conducted in 1990. Through the seminar I created an environment for the teachers to explore and extend their thinking and knowledge about teaching and learning. The seminar was based on Eleanor Duckworth's Teaching and Learning course, referred to in the Introduction, in which, among other things, students are engaged in exploring various subject matter. The students are encouraged to be aware of their thoughts and how they come to understand things. They also engage other people as learners, attending to their different ways of approaching the same phenomena. In this capacity they seek to extend the learning through inquiring into the learners' thinking and reflecting on their own interventions and understanding. Therefore both teacher and learner learn in the process.

My seminar involved four teacher educators, one primary school teacher, and Bonolo, a secondary school teacher. The 6-week seminar consisted of 16 sessions of 2–3 hours each.

The seminar created an opportunity for the teachers to engage as individual learners as well as an opportunity to learn from one another. Projects included reading poetry, figuring out mathematical formulas, and coming to know a drawing (this last project is not described in this chapter). The teachers worked on the subject matter themselves, and also with other learners outside the group, trying to understand how those individuals developed their thoughts and how to assist them in developing their understanding. Group activities also included reflections on specific words, following Pat Carini's work (see Avidon, 2000), and readings, particularly Eleanor Duckworth's *The Having of Wonderful Ideas* (1996), Lisa Schneier's "Dancing in the Hall" (1986), and articles by David Hawkins (1973, 1974). The participants kept journals about their experiences and thoughts on teaching and learning. I also interviewed each of the participants three times to capture development of their learning: once at the beginning of the seminar, once in the middle, and finally at the end.

The seminar took place just before the end of apartheid, and the teachers' responses speak to the potential of this work in situations where inquiry has been restrained. I find it still enormously relevant within the context of the continuous challenges of change that we are facing in South Africa. We are all living in an ever changing world demanding continuous solutions and new ideas for meaningful existence. In addition to meeting the challenge of democratization, South Africa has to align new policies initiated by the democratic government with broader thinking and practice in society. Paving ways for new thinking and learning requires even greater emphasis on inquiry than was present in the apartheid era.

In South Africa we are feeling the extent to which diverse areas of the world have been brought together and are working toward common goals. Interdependence is key for success in different settings, highlighting the importance of working across boundaries, harnessing the richness of diversity, and making synergies work across race, gender, culture, and types of skills. In this environment, understanding how to engage others in learning is crucial for success. It is important for learners to know how to relate in a meaningful way to what others know, how they came to that understanding, and the role that they as individuals play in shaping the experiences. The work described here can promote understanding of how teachers themselves learn from experiences, as well as how teachers can facilitate this responsive kind of knowledge.

Introducing Bonolo

Bonolo was a young secondary school teacher who was on study leave during the time of the seminar. She was an English teacher interested in writing. In the initial interview she indicated that she viewed student participation as important in learning and that in her teaching she had involved her students in finding more information relating to topics they were dealing with in class. She considered her teaching to be successful, as she had enabled her students to get good results on the external examinations. What concerned her, however, was the tension she encountered with her matric (Grade 12) class, when they complained that she was giving them more work than the syllabus required. She was also uncomfortable with the fact that some of the teachers in the school sided with the students. Even though her class got the best results in her area, she was still concerned about the disappointing experience and felt that her hard work was not appreciated.

In the seminar she came to realize, with some difficulty, the value of inquiry into other people's ways of thinking. This began in her very first journal comments, which relate to the group's reflection on the word *writing*: "The brainstorming on the word 'writing' was interesting. It showed me that people operate at different levels and have different points of departure."

Experiences during the First Project

Her concern for connecting with other ways of thinking continued in the group discussions as well as in her investigations on learning. Bonolo readily engaged in the initial project on Keats's *Endymion,* because she liked the poem. (In retrospect I realize that this poem was much too long for the close study that is most productive; see Schneier's work in chapter 2. Nonetheless, it served us well with Bonolo.) She explained that she had read the poem as an English student as well as an English teacher. During the group's initial work on the poem, she gave a detailed interpretation. She emphasized the importance of understanding Keats and the times in which the poem was written. She expected the poem to have a specific interpretation and disagreed with some of the interpretations from other teachers. Later she raised concerns in her journal about what she perceived as her lack of patience with other people's ideas. Reflecting on her response to how others made sense of the poem, she wrote:

> I am angry with myself because I still want specific interpretations or nothing. This I picked up as I disagreed with Ms Q as she was talking about "nature" and the poem. I just felt I was being pushy.

She continued to find it difficult to deal with views and responses that conflicted with hers. In the presentation of her first fieldwork she reported that she had invited her niece, a student teacher, to interpret the poem for her. She expressed surprise that her niece "went into a shell," and was reluctant to read the poem. The niece explained to her that she had last studied poetry in standard 9 (Grade 11). Bonolo explained that in interpreting the poem, her niece had said only that the poem was describing the beauty of daffodils. She was not able to get additional ideas about the poem from her. Noting that the response could be explored further, I asked

Bonolo if she thought it could be helpful to find out how the niece had picked the idea of daffodils. After a brief silence, she indicated she would try to probe her niece more extensively on the idea. Bonolo described her niece's English to be "in a desperate state" and said that her niece did not want to acknowledge her limitations. Because Bonolo had indicated, in our initial interview, her concern about the disappointing experience she had had with a high school class that challenged her teaching, I found Bonolo's criticism of the niece noteworthy, as it made me wonder if she might also have been critical of her students.

Bonolo next did the investigation with her 9-year-old daughter, Neo. She explained that she worked with Neo because she had not been satisfied with how she had fared with her niece. She asked Neo to read the poem and to tell her about it. Noting that some of the words might be too difficult for the child, she had wondered whether to use a dictionary, but decided not to, as she thought it might have been "more like teaching" rather than trying to understand how the child was making sense of the poem. Neo told her that the poem spoke about the beauty of nature and that people are destroying the beauty. This interpretation Bonolo linked to television advertisements advocating nature conservation. With a beaming face she explained to the group how surprised she had been at the child's interpretation, and that, puzzled by the child's ideas, she had found herself listening, wanting to understand how the child came up with the ideas. Subsequently she wrote in her journal that she was realizing that "there are several interpretations to a situation and that no particular answer is necessarily right." Bonolo was reconsidering the idea she held earlier, that there is one best interpretation. She was conflicted, however, between this new open-minded listening and her difficulty in keeping her own ideas from interfering with understanding the ideas of the learners she worked with. She stated, "I find it very difficult not to interfere, because I think I know more." Further on she indicated how she tried to control the urge to give her own interpretation: "Each time when I feel like giving my own interpretation I remind myself that . . . I may think I know what is contained in this only to find there is so much I missed."

In presenting her fieldwork with Neo to the group, she said, "I stopped to think" about the unexpected response she was getting. Previously, during the initial group discussion of the poem, she had questioned why the investigation of learning the poem was open to learners in lower grades, and she indicated her doubt that people in lower grades could understand the poem. The interpretation from Neo was thus a surprise. At the end of her presenting her work with Neo to the group, she indicated a concern: She wondered if Neo had left feeling good about her ideas.

The next group activity was a reflection on the word *look*, which seemed to have raised further questions for Bonolo and extended her sensitivity to other people's ways of thinking. Commenting on this experience, she wrote in her journal (addressed to me):

> It is always fascinating for me to realize that in each brainstorming we have done, not one comes with the same idea. A word like "look" can come with different ideas and thoughts from different people. What I find odd also is that people come with these ideas, some of which I quietly think are off the track, but to my amazement you seem to accept anything. This acceptance of everything makes me wonder if that is what education and learning is about.

She not only raised a question, but she further indicated how the reflective session had affected her thinking about teaching.

> This session made me look at my past teaching experience and I [felt] bothered that there are many children I have not attended to in the past. I also worried that I had lost so much in terms of growth from not giving each person attention.

In her subsequent fieldwork she appeared to pay particular attention to the learner's feelings about her investigation.

For her next fieldwork on the poem *Endymion* Bonolo worked with a medical student. Her fieldwork report was detailed. In her presentation of it to the group, it was evident that Bonolo had engaged the learner in making sense of the poem, and through the process she had gained insight into how he did this. He had come up with ideas she had not anticipated but that she found interesting. It was also clear from the presentation that she had pursued his ideas to get clarification on the issues he raised. When he indicated that the poem presented beauty as "a permanent feature that can be overcast by gloom or shine" and that "life must be overcast by both or we die," she engaged him in clarifying his idea by asking, "Do you experience these at the same time?" He responded that it depended on circumstances, and that people can see things differently depending on their moods, attitudes, or circumstances. She further asked him if people's situations actually changed whether things were beautiful or not. He indicated he was not sure, and she still persisted in probing his ideas. She told us with excitement how she liked his interpretation "that which shines over beauty becomes clear itself" and she was amused by his interpretation that poets see beauty where there is none. Remembering that he had said that beauty was a permanent feature depending on who is looking, she asked him to explain why he said poets see beauty when there is none. To the amazement of everyone in the group, she explained that he stated that the "beauty that poets put before us haunts us until we also see it and end up liking *it* like the poet, whereas we did not see beauty in it before." It was evident from the presentation that she had found the experience enriching.

In this fieldwork, Bonolo had also paid attention to how the learner experienced the investigation. Remembering her concern after her work with Neo, she wanted to understand how her approach affected how the student had experienced the session. She asked him, "How do you feel about the discussion?" "Who spoke more?" The student indicated that he thought she was interested in seeing how he was interpreting the poem, and that he spoke more than she did. It pleased her that he indicated that he liked the experience and that he learned better through such participation, even though he had never come across this way of questioning at school. I should have asked her if by "school" he included even his experience at medical school.

As she had been critical of her niece's English, she was critical of an oversight made by the medical student. I believe that her disapproval when their behavior did not fit her expectations limited her inquiry into their ways of making sense of experiences. Even though she noted in her presentation how enriching her investigation with the medical student was, she expressed in her journal her surprise that the student initially read only the first part of the poem and seemed not to realize that the poem continued on the next page. Indicating her impatience about this response, she noted: "I was shocked by this because I could not see how anyone cannot see that the poem continues. This made me think of students who do not read instructions or miss part of instructions."

This difficulty with situations that did not coincide with her expectations was also reflected in Bonolo's response to views from other teachers that conflicted with hers. On one occasion when she wrote in her journal about her problems with the views on nature of a teacher she identified as Q, I responded that I was sorry about her concerns, and I suggested that she also explore how the other teachers came up with differing interpretations. Following up on the comments from her journal, I asked her in an informal interview to tell me about the concerns she had raised regarding the poetry interpretations in one of the group sessions. She explained that whereas she had initially thought Q was monopolizing the discussions, she was now wondering if she was simply too impatient with the different approach Q was using in interpreting the poem. She also commented about Q's presentation on the investigation she had done with two teenage boys. She had found the way in which Q engaged the reluctant boys remarkable. The conversation indicated to me that Bonolo was becoming more engaged in the process of inquiring into learning and in examining her expectations.

It also appeared that the challenge of expressing her thoughts and confronting her deeper feelings was not easy for Bonolo. She felt tension during the group's discussion of David Hawkins's "What It Means to Teach" (1973). She explained in her journal her sense that the other teachers did not like her criticism of the Christian National education perspective in South Africa. She argued that the approach absolutized knowledge, basing her views on Hawkins's criticism of a teacher's role, which can reflect a "master and slave" relationship. Her journal entry after the incident indicated concern that the other teachers seemed to view her as confused, and revealed her discomfort about opening her ideas to the group. She wrote:

> There was even a feeling that I was confused. In my quiet moments I have even contemplated leaving [the seminar]. It is the first time that I have had to be so open with a group of "strangers" and that sometimes tends to unsettle me. The research is opening me up and does not seem to be giving me any answers, and this can be terribly frustrating.

Reflecting on the experience also triggered thoughts about her disappointing experience with her matric (Grade 12) class. Revealing how she examined her teaching experiences she noted:

> Another problem is that I have become quite self-conscious. This whole weekend I spent with flashes of thoughts about how I approach my teaching. I have been bothered about my own arrogance as a person and as a teacher. For instance that episode at the school about my teaching—I wonder if I made an effort to explain to other teachers what I was all about. All of a sudden I am wondering if—whether—if I had created some understanding with the teaching staff, would I have received the same kind of treatment? I feel after I finish studying I must go back to make up.

Toward the end of the poetry project, Bonolo indicated an appreciation of her experiences in exploring how others approach this learning:

> It seems that by the end of this exercise I will be a lot richer not because I have looked at John Keats's *Endymion* a thousand times, but because I will then be able to probe, listen with interest not because I was told to do that at college but because I sincerely want to know how my students interpret and reach their conclusions on issues.

Bonolo's thoughts throughout the poetry project indicate her grow-ing awareness of the importance of listening to participants' ideas. As she became engaged in observing other people's thoughts, she began to exam-ine her own ideas and attempted to keep her own thoughts from interfer-ing with her inquiry.

Experiences during the Second Project

Toward the end of the poetry project, Bonolo's increasing appreciation of other people's ideas seemed to focus her attention on what knowledge is. Commenting on the unexpected insights she gained during her investiga-tions, she said, "I am afraid of knowing," referring to her awareness that what she believes she knows with certainty could be perceived differently by others. Following this insight, Bonolo's focus in the math project seemed to be more on learners' thinking and her own learning.

I gave each participant a couple of dozen of each of four different colors of sweets, and asked them to arrange the sweets in rows, with one of each color in each row. They were to find all the row-arrangements they could and to construct their reasoning for why they thought that there couldn't be any more and that there were no repeats (see Duckworth, 1996, pp. 131–135).

Bonolo's initial reaction to the project indicated her discomfort with math. At first she did not take the exercise seriously. She explained in her journal that she thought it was a game and did not anticipate that anything would come of it. However, when she started realizing that it was math-ematical, she was concerned. She wrote:

> I was not very happy because I was being confronted by math which, as I stated earlier, had been written off in my life. So when-ever anything mathematical comes my way, I simply push it to the side. Then here I was obliged to work.

This comment indicated the initial discomfort Bonolo felt about the exercise and her lack of confidence in her knowledge of math. The initial feeling, however, disappeared as Bonolo became engaged in figuring out the problem. She took some time to make her arrangements and was encouraged by the fact that even though it took her such a long time to finish, she had done the problem successfully, and in her own way. In the beginning she seemed to work without having in mind a complete pattern; using the four kinds of sweets, she had placed one kind of sweet in the first position four times and placed the rest in alternative positions to make her first four arrangements. Using letters, she represented her arrangements as follows:

```
Y  G  O  R
Y  O  G  R
Y  G  R  O
Y  R  G  O
```

As she continued, she moved the Y's to the second row, and she used the other sweets to start the new arrangements, using the same sweet twice:

```
G  Y  O  R
G  Y  R  O
O  Y  R  G
O  Y  G  R
R  Y  O  G
R  Y  G  O
```

This led her to discover the pattern of sixes, and she went back to the first set of four where she had started with Y's four times, and added two more, making them six. She was the second, after Lerato, to feel convinced that she had found all the possible arrangements, and she felt good that she had managed the exercise. She explained that figuring out the problem shed light on her understanding of the nature of math. She felt that she had developed her own system of solving the problem, and that gave her confidence that she could improve her knowledge of math. She commented in her journal:

> What amazed me here was that *I* had dealt with a math problem successfully. I have since seriously contemplated learning math privately with Damelin [a correspondence college in South Africa].

Bonolo further indicated that she learned from other teachers' experiences.

> I was fascinated to see that people could come out with patterns from the exercise. Lerato arranged the sweets in triangles, Ms. Q and others started with [each one] six times and so on.

It also appeared from Bonolo's comments at the end of her investigations in this project that she discovered another dimension to understanding how others learn: She shifted her focus from her initial challenge of appreciating other people's thoughts to an attempt to get a deeper understanding of how others organize their thoughts: "On a more serious note, this approach does not only allow you to get information *from* the learner, it also gets you to know more about the learner."

During the poetry project, I had suggested that Bonolo pursue her niece's ideas further. Instead, Bonolo worked with her again on the mathematical permutations, and the experience seemed to alter the initial negative perception Bonolo had had about her niece. She was surprised that her niece seemed not to have problems in figuring out the permutations and that she made 24 arrangements in a short space of time. Bonolo also indicated that she admired her niece for having found it easy to work out the exercise—much more easily than she (Bonolo) had. This suggested that she now viewed her niece in a different light from that in her first presentation. What was missing from her presentation, however, were the details of how her niece figured out the exercise. When I asked Bonolo if she was able to explore how her niece came up with the arrangements, she indicated that her niece worked very fast, and she had responded to Bonolo's question to explain her approach by giving her a mathematical formula ($4 \times 3 \times 2 \times 1$).

It occurred to me that Bonolo was impressed with the niece's answer and did not yet see the need to explore how deeply the niece understood the problem. But I noted with interest Bonolo's change of perspective about her niece's capabilities as a learner.

Bonolo was more observant and more probing in her investigation of the arrangements with her daughter. When her daughter, after making 12 arrangements, indicated that she was through, Bonolo managed to encourage her to continue working. When her daughter seemed to get stuck, she stretched her thinking by asking her to explain the arrangements that she had already done. She wrote in her report:

> I looked at her work and realized that she had started with "O"s six times and that she had not exhausted the other[s]. . . . I then asked her to count how many times she had started with the "O." She counted and said six times, and as if a bright spark had lit, she remarked, "oh $6 \times 4 = 24$."

Bonolo's experiences during the permutation exercise also led her to reflect further on the nature of learning. In her reflection she cited an article by Lisa Schneier (1986) and indicated what seemed to be a new insight to her:

> In all, this method says there is no better way but there are several different ways of doing the same thing and even that which seems

"wrong" as in Schneier's lesson on fractions is "right" and definitely has logic.

This statement indicated a deepening awareness in Bonolo of the importance of the unique ways in which individuals organize their knowledge.
The permutation exercise extended both her thinking about teaching and
her knowledge of the nature of math, and as a result it triggered her anger
that she had not been given the opportunity to continue studying math after
standard 6 (Grade 8). (It was normal practice in South Africa that only a
limited number of children were selected at around the 8th grade to continue with math and sciences.) "By the way the math issue still leaves me
very resentful because along the way some teacher made a decision for and
about me that I was not going to make it in math." Bonolo felt that it was
decided that she could not take math lessons before she herself could make
an informed decision about it.

Bonolo's feelings of disappointment about a past learning experience
brought to my mind a comment she had made earlier during the group's
reflection on the word *curious*. Bonolo pointed out that it reminded her of
how active and curious she had been as a child, and how she was dis-
couraged by teachers from being open and active. Subsequently, she had
learned to keep her ideas to herself and decided to use writing as an outlet
for her ideas.

Bonolo was also learning from the other teachers' investigations. The
comments Bonolo made after one of Selina's presentations serves as an
example. Selina had indicated to the group that the experience of watching her daughter struggle with the arrangements indicated to her the importance of patience in teaching. Acknowledging that people see things in
different ways, Selina raised the question, "We fail to see things within
ourselves, what more about others?" indicating that it was an even more
complex challenge to understand others. As the word *patience* was pop-
ping up in several of the journals at the time, I wanted to explore the idea
further with the teachers. So in a conversation with Bonolo, Thembi, and
Selina, I indicated that I found the idea of patience as explained by Selina
in her previous presentation interesting—the idea of how much patience
it takes to understand others. In response, Bonolo indicated that she also
was struck by Selina's idea. She indicated that she was sensing a change in
the way in which she was relating to other people, including her family
members. She commented that she and her husband had decided to post-
pone a family trip that they were supposed to take that particular weekend, and she had to inform her children about the decision. She noted that
in the past she could have just told them about the decision, without taking the time to consider their opinion concerning the matter. This time she

found herself more concerned about what their thoughts were concerning the trip. Then she explained to them the difficulties that necessitated the postponement of the trip and asked them what their views were about the matter. She was surprised by how considerate her children were and how she had changed. Bonolo stated, "I marveled at the way I had the patience to go through the logic of it all."

It is evident from the ideas Bonolo raised and explored that she took the experience in the seminar seriously and that it was enriching for her. The following journal entry made by Bonolo toward the end of the seminar (after the third project, which is not reported here) indicates what the experience in the seminar meant to her:

> Watching myself learn has opened my eyes a lot. I have come to realize that deciding in advance and coming with a "tailored" lesson for children is limiting. This method has also through your way of doing things, taught me to be less interfering in the learner's life. To lay back and observe what happens and just trigger thinking. This approach demands patience. Schneier [1986] exercises a lot of patience with her pupils. She deals with the real world—answers come from pupils. If she thinks pupils still have confusion, she works with them until they sort that confusion out.

Last Group Session and Final Interview

In the final session I engaged the teachers in expressing their feelings and thoughts about the whole seminar. They responded to one another's ideas by raising questions or connecting their ideas to issues brought up during the discussion. Bonolo was one of the key actors during the discussion, and she developed her ideas on the issues raised by the other teachers, and in that way helped to stimulate the process. She attempted to connect sensitively with the ideas expressed by the other group members.

Bonolo's comments during the final session were centered on her idea of what she perceived as the "power of not knowing." In her deliberations she recalled particular experiences and cited from articles by David Hawkins (1973, 1974) and Eleanor Duckworth (1996). When Selina quoted one of Duckworth's students about coming to appreciate the excitement of "not knowing," Bonolo supported the idea by citing Hawkins's notion of a master-slave relationship. She pointed out that a teacher who assumes that she or he can learn from students will listen more, and that a teacher who assumes she or he "knows" is limiting her or his experiences. She made the group laugh by quoting one of her previous teachers at college who used to say repeatedly to them as student teachers, "A teacher must know. . . . a teacher must know." The idea was that they should present themselves to students as people who know everything.

Supporting a point raised by Thembi that listening to learners requires patience, Bonolo indicated that it not only requires patience, but also engenders patience. Her following comment indicated the point effectively:

> As teachers we learned to be learners, and by experiencing the problems of learners, we learned to be sympathetic to learners' feelings. As Thembi was saying—You start being more sympathetic. You start being more interested and curious, and even when a person talks and speaks English the way it is not supposed to be spoken, you listen to the idea—to what the person is saying, you explore the idea, until you come up with things in the midst of confusion.

The final interviews were private times for me to discuss with the individual teachers their experiences in the seminar. In the interview I had with Bonolo, I wanted to know more about the issues she raised in the final group session and to follow through on the concerns she raised in the initial interview.

Explaining what the seminar had meant to her, she suggested that the experience of exploring learning and examining her thinking about learning had changed her as a person and as a teacher. She explained:

> One thing. . . . I used my children for the work, and the closeness that it brought me. I felt so close to them. I felt the closest that I've ever felt to them. And if I am going to take that to a classroom situation, I actually imagine myself being a much closer teacher. It's a remarkable experience, it really is a remarkable experience because all of a sudden, I'm just imagining if I had used this method before, that my students would have grown so much, so much. . . . This method, if I had used this, we would be talking [about] something else.

She further indicated that as a result of her experiences she was now going to relate differently to students from how she had before, and that the seminar had already made her more sensitive about how she relates to others. She explained that she had found herself dealing differently with conflicts and that in a recent disagreement with someone she had noted the change. Bonolo described how, instead of arguing with the person, she decided, "I must try and understand her ideas and help her understand my ideas, too."

She reflected on the other teachers' views and noted how they had contributed to her development:

> I thought just a simple thought; and then the other people around me say things that reinforce what I've said and actually make it a dramatic thing; so then it makes me realize the power of other people, the power of people around.

And she was struck by reading "Teaching as Research" (Duckworth, 1996) at the end of the seminar. During the interview she read a passage from that article:

> "By contrast, most students—adults and children—believe knowledge to be an absolute which some people have caught onto, and which they, if they are smart enough, will be able to learn from someone who has caught on." Do you know what I mean?

She continued to explain how the statement had clarified her questions about knowledge as an experience. I viewed the realization in the light of the issues she had raised concerning knowledge in the seminar and thought it indicated a deepening understanding of knowledge as an experience. Bonolo further went on to describe her newly acquired view of knowledge.

> This is what I have learnt from this exercise. . . . Knowledge is something you come across. And the way you come across it is your way, and it's unique and it's good. There's nobody that's got the right to come and say your way of looking at things or your way of finding that knowledge is inferior and someone else's knowledge is better.

In the initial interview, at the beginning of the seminar, Bonolo had indicated that she had implemented an alternative curriculum to suit the needs of her students, so I wanted to know if her experiences in the seminar had any impact on that. As she seemed to be struggling to articulate how it had impacted her thinking, I asked her if she thought her experience in the seminar connected with her idea. She responded with an explanation that I found illuminating, as it seemed to capture her idea of what she had learned in the seminar and to relate to the experience of all teachers and learners under apartheid.

It does not only connect, it extends. For instance, we live in South Africa with the apartheid system that has so much affected people's lives. . . . I mean our people are highly possessed people so that when you teach in class you teach people, but my teaching was to relate people [to their situations]; to take them outside the classroom. That was my teaching. But this [the teaching/learning] was dramatic. It does not only take people outside the classroom, it deals with the person, so that you are not only saying "look at your conditions." . . . [I]t is just the opposite. . . .

I was saying, "Education for you is about things that are happening around you." But I had never thought of education as something that's not only around you but as something that is within you . . . . something you must take out of you. I think that's where the whole drama is. . . .

You're taking something out of the child. So at the end of the day now, we'll be having children who know the power that is within them. Not just them having the power to go out and change the world but the power of knowing that they can change themselves and in the process, change their world. And I think it is a dramatic thing.

This appeared to be very significant for her, and as if to ascertain whether or not I had understood her idea, she paused, and then proceeded once more.

I don't know if I am coming across nicely. When you think that power is outside you, then there is a very strong chance that you will think that there are so many odds against you. But when you think the power is within you, then it's another issue.

References

Avidon, E. (2000). Reflective conversation on a word: ENOUGH. In Himley, M., & Carini, P. (Eds.), *From another angle: Children's strengths and school standards: The Prospect Center's Descriptive Review of the Child* (pp. 36–38). New York: Teachers College Press

Duckworth, E. (1996). *The having of wonderful ideas* (2nd ed.). New York: Teachers College Press.

Hawkins, D. (1973, September). What it means to teach. *Teachers College Record, 75*, 7–15

Hawkins, D. (1974*). The informed vision: Essays on learning and human nature.* New York: Agathon Press.

Schneier, L. (1986). *Dancing in the hall.* Unpublished manuscript, Harvard Graduate School of Education, Cambridge.

8

Teaching/Learning Research

Eleanor Duckworth

In chapter 1 of this book, I describe a class I was teaching. I made notes about it, as I often do, to help me think about the teaching. I had ample time that year, and I became particularly intrigued with this search for density, so my notes became more and more complete.

In the other chapters, authors describe work that was done for the purpose of understanding the learners. The authors became teachers, in order to follow what was involved for learners in coming to understand their subject matter.

I point this out because I find no difference in kind between the work I did, as discussed in chapter 1, as a teacher, and the work carried out by the other authors, as research. The two are inseparable. We sometimes call this work teaching/learning research—research on learning that can be done only by someone who is committed to helping someone else to learn.

The approach can be thought of as an extension of the kind of interviews Piaget and Inhelder did with children to uncover their thoughts. We authors do not think of our work as interviews, but it does share with those interviews the following: The idea is to listen, to have our learners tell us *their* thoughts.

Our extensions of Piaget and Inhelder's interviewing practice are of two sorts. First, as these chapters show, we often involve more than one learner at once. In this way the work can reveal the interaction of ideas among two or more people engaged in trying to understand the same thing. And second, these sessions are, most often, extended in time. Instead of just finding out what someone thinks at a given moment, we are interested in following the *development* of understanding, over weeks or months.[1] Taken together, these two forms of extension provide opportunities for a dynamic account of the development of ideas, confidence, engagement— rather than a description of a static moment.

So this has given us an approach in which one person is both teacher and researcher.[2] We consider that this kind of teaching is the *only* way to learn some things about the development of human understanding: Engage people in trying to understand something, keep their interest alive while they try to make sense of it, and follow the development of the sense they are making. We learn the details of what is entailed in this development, both in specific domains and across domains. We learn about the interactions between feelings and thoughts. We learn about interindividual construction of understanding.

It is very different from much of the work in cognitive psychology, looking at single sessions with individual learners. There, interviewees in fact are not usually thought of as learners, but rather as informants about their current thoughts.

In order to help deepen our understanding of teaching, the fundamental research that is needed is methodical inquiry into learning in all of its interpersonal, feeling-laden, time-demanding, situation-dependent complexity.

Doing Teaching/Learning Research

Since doing this kind of research involves a kind of teaching, it is clear that we must know our subject matter well. But since we do not simply tell the learners what it is that we know, what do we do with our knowledge?

One essential is that we try to know our subject matter in the most flexible ways possible. Throughout our relationship with it we try to be tuned in to areas or encounters in which our subject matter surprises us, puzzles us, excites us, intrigues us; these are precious indicators to us of ways our students might connect with the material. We try to catch ourselves in moments when we make what we might consider a "foolish" misjudgment, quickly corrected; we want to understand what led us to think this even for an instant, as a way of understanding what some of our learners' ideas might be. We work at phrasing, for ourselves, any technical term in nontechnical language, so we do not fool ourselves into thinking we know something that we don't, and so we can more readily recognize our learners' articulations of their ideas when they are not couched in conventional language. We are alert to times when we encounter our subject matter unexpectedly, in case they might help us to fashion encounters for our learners.

We call on this knowledge of our subject matter in recognizing the potential in the paths that the learners take, and to offer materials, questions, activities, and comments that enable the learners to realize some of that potential.

We call on it in order to engage learners with that subject matter, and to keep them engaged. To some degree, this is what we are trying to learn about—how learners engage with the subject matter, and how we can deepen that engagement. But it takes nimbleness in the moment even to recognize ways to try. This is one reason that we tend to do the research with small groups of learners. We want to know what we can learn in these small groups that will be of help to us and to other teachers when numbers are greater.

Capturing and maintaining interest usually means taking the lead with suggestions of activities to do, or things to look at, or questions to discuss. We do not by any means leave to the students all decisions about what they are to do. We give them materials, instructions, questions (loose though these may be), that we hope will offer them ways to engage with the subject matter. We choose for discussion those of their activities or ideas that we think have a chance to engage them further. We continue to propose specific activities, situations, and questions, though often these are based on questions that have arisen from the learners. The point of what we propose is not that they come up with any particular thought, but that they keep their minds on this until they encounter something that captures them again, when they will again take off on their own. Some of the activities we propose do not work very well from this point of view; others do.

Our approaches to the initial engagement take many different forms. Sometimes we try to honor what the learners already know about, as a starting point. Sometimes it is the opposite—we try to surprise them with aspects of what they thought they knew. Schneier (chapter 2) gave her students a poem that contradicted all their thoughts about poems and uses of language. Cirino (chapter 3) gave her students empty books, which honored anything they might choose to write or draw and which invited their participation in the adult world of writing books. Quintero (chapter 4) built on the children's existing knowledge and interest in their neighborhoods.

Sometimes we ask a specific question. Sometimes we invite the learners to notice what they will.

As the work proceeds, we take people back to the subject matter to pursue their own questions. This means providing a testing ground that is other than our own authority. In chapter 1, the learners checked their ideas by trying out what actually does float on what. In chapter 2, they checked them against other lines in the poem. In chapter 4, Inés checked her maps against her view from the balcony and her daily walks. We take pains to accept all responses—all that are offered with serious intent. We encourage people to say things (or write stories or make maps) that they are not sure about. We find it essential for people to express their understanding and their questions as much and as freely as possible, and one of the things we constantly work at is finding ways to encourage people to do that. So we ask questions that do not have a single answer, questions for which everyone would have something to say: "What do you notice?" "Show us what you did." We notice when a person seems to want to say something, and we ask what is on his or her mind. We ask for comments on what the others in a group have just said. And we never disparage what a learner says. Aral, in chapter 6, and Bonolo, in chapter 7, both comment on how unusual an experience this is. "You rarely have that opportunity to just think about things and not necessarily be right about them," said Aral.

So we encourage students to say what they think; to express ideas in their own terms in ways that make sense for them; to take their ideas seriously and see where they lead; to listen to each other.

Encouraging the learners to say what they think has three main purposes. First, and most obvious, it is a good way for the rest of us (teacher and fellow students) to learn what is on their minds. Second, as they try to say what they think about something, their thoughts often become clearer. Third, it encourages them to take their own ideas seriously. We have found that most people, and adults in particular, are nervous about expressing their own ideas, especially in a realm where they are quite sure that there is some appointed wisdom to which they are not privy. They think, then, that their own ideas are not worth attending to; they should drop them, and catch on to the real, authenticated knowledge. We believe, on the contrary, that one's own knowledge—tentative and incomplete though it may be—is all one ever has; and that the only way to develop it further is to pay attention to it, figure out what needs to be further thought about, modify it, and keep striving to make it more adequate to one's experiences. But it takes work on the part of a teacher to convey that view of the importance of one's own knowledge. We work hard at helping learners feel willing to say what they think. And when they do express themselves, then we try to make it absolutely clear that what they think is OK with us; that we will attend to it carefully and help them to do the same. This, too, is difficult when ideas go against ones of our own which we find important. In chapter 5, Delaney writes of her own responses to some of Tim's and Mark's ideas. We do not always do this well. But it is always what we strive to do.

About Learning

In the stories in this book, it becomes clear that different individuals come to their understanding in different ways. Once a person has constructed her or his own understanding, she or he can make connections with the different ways others have made theirs, but it is clear that another person's way of understanding can interfere, rather than help, while the learner is putting things together in her or his own way. This is especially true if a teacher insists on a given path to understanding.

On the other hand, it also becomes clear, however, that when no one idea is presented as the official path, learners are often able to build on one another's ideas and learn more as a group than they could if each were working alone.

We see how difficult, and even painful, it can be to change our ideas. This depends on how entwined they are with other ideas, beliefs, wishes, and thoughts. The more entwined, the more difficult, because changing ideas means giving up ones that may have been important to us. Note how hard it was for both Mark and Tim in chapter 5 to think that a photo session might be set up to make a world leader look good—when everything that they said indicated that they saw all the reasons why this might be the case. Note also in chapter 7 Bonolo's pain—profoundly understandable—in accepting thoughts about teaching and learning that were different from those behind her whole life's work until then. In chapter 1, note Henri's attachment to the air hypothesis, beyond the point where he needed it.

We see the futility of trying to impose a desired end point of learning without attending to the learners' own coherence. "Critical" experiences are seen to be critical only to a person who has already developed a network of ideas that give the experience meaning. The same is true of any idea that does not connect with the ideas a learner habitually uses.

In many of the stories we see how early experiences, only partially understood, over time contribute to the construction of large ideas.

We see the importance to a learner of feeling that his or her ideas will be taken seriously. This feeling of safety turns out to be essential if one is to take the risk of trying out an idea—that is, to take the risk of trying to learn.

And we see how similar adults are to children. Adults are by no means "finished" products of cognitive development. It is clear that for adults, ideas develop just as slowly and painfully—and joyfully and playfully—as they do for children, through construction on the basis of currently held ideas. For real learning to take place, at any age, there is no short cut for starting where the thoughts are and helping learners take their own thoughts further.

About Curriculum

We believe that this work contributes both to curriculum theory and to specifics of curriculum development. The ways of engaging learners enough to want to talk about the sense they are making, so we can follow that sense, double as ways of engaging learners enough to learn. And of course, what the work can reveal about people's untutored ways of making sense of the subject matter additionally offers precious indications for curriculum development.

At the most explicit level, the curricular lessons of these stories are the specifics of the networks of ideas and points of engagement that people use to come to understand this or that subject matter. This is where their power lies.

At the same time, there are other levels of interest. This work leads us to the following seeming paradox: If fields of knowledge are to be accessible to learners, they must be presented in all of their complexity. When we oversimplify curriculum, we eliminate the very specifics with which learners can connect. Aral, again, in chapter 6, spoke of the babies themselves as the "frame" on which to hang generalizations that he read in his textbooks. We need to make use of, take advantage of, the complexity of a subject matter if we are to help in the creation of classrooms where significant learning can take place.

Our work depends on making a connection with the learners' concerns, and it takes into account whatever influences come from whatever sources. We believe through systematically following specific learners of specific subject matter in specific learning situations, a collection of stories such as these can serve as the basis of curriculum development. And stories written by classroom teachers, it seems to us, could serve as the curriculum outline itself. One teacher writes for interested colleagues, far and near: Here is my situation, here is what I used, here is what I did, here is what happened, here is what I noticed, here is what I would do again, for these reasons, and here is what I would do differently another time, for these reasons; here is what I did the first time I did it, here is how I changed it the second time. And so on.

We think it is possible that such stories themselves would be the most directly interesting, informative, and useful kind of curriculum.

We hope, in any event, that this body of work can contribute both to the most general questions of the nature of learning, and to teaching and curricular decisions of schools and teachers.

Notes

1. After Piaget's (1951, 1954, 1966) enlightening early studies of his own children in their first 2 years, he never again did longitudinal studies. He and Inhelder studied many different children at different points in time (Piaget & Inhelder, 1967, 1974, 1975), rather than following individuals as their thoughts developed. Inhelder did do some lovely studies that followed individual children over several sessions (Inhelder, Sinclair, & Bovet, 1974).

2. It is close to the work that Michael Armstrong describes in *Closely Observed Children* (1981). The work of other researchers inspired by Piaget and Inhelder, and committed to education, also shares some of this focus: that of Emilia Ferreiro (see, for example, Ferreiro and Teberosky, 1983); Androula Henriques (see, for example, Henriques, 1990); Constance Kamii and the teachers who write with her (see, for example, Kamii and DeClark, 1985).

References

Armstrong, M. (1981). *Closely observed children: The diary of a primary classroom.* New York: Writers & Readers.

Ferreiro, E., & Teberosky, A. (1983). *Literacy before schooling.* Exeter, NH: Heinemann.

Henriques, A. (1990). Experiments in teaching. In E. Duckworth, J. Easley, D. Hawkins, & A. Henriques (Eds.), *Science Education: A minds-on approach for the elementary years.* Hillsdale. NJ: Erlbaum.

Inhelder, B., Sinclair, H., & Bovet, M. (1974). *Learning and the development of cognition* (Susan Wedgewood, Trans.). Cambridge, MA: Harvard University Press.

Kamii, C., & DeClark, G. (1985). *Young children reinvent arithmetic: Implications of Piaget's theory.* New York: Teachers College Press.

Piaget, J. (1951). *Play, dreams, and imitation.* New York: Norton. (Original work published 1946).

Piaget, J. (1954). *The construction of reality.* New York: Basic Books. (Original work published 1936).

Piaget, J. (1966). *The origins of intelligence.* New York: International Universities Press. (Original work published 1936).

Piaget, J., & Inhelder, B. (1967). *The child's conception of space.* New York: Norton. (Original work published 1948).

Piaget, J., & Inhelder, B. (1974). *The child's conception of quantities.* London: Routledge & Kegan Paul. (Original work published 1943).

Piaget, J., & Inhelder, B. (1975). *The origin of the idea of chance in children.* New York: Norton. (Original work published 1951).

9

A Schoolteacher's View

Lisa Schneier

Schools are fast-paced in many ways, ridden with pressures to teach certain curricula in a certain length of time. The investigative work recounted in this book is slower, able to conform to the true pace of a mind, to follow where a student's mind leads. Public school structures require that we teach 25–35 students at a time. The stories in this book describe close, ongoing attention to individuals or small groups. School curricula and assessment are often structured to get students to reach a certain statement of knowledge in a certain length of time. In the work presented here, the development of new knowledge follows to a significant degree the movements of the students' thought. How can the work detailed in these stories, which seems so luxurious in its use of time, in its focus on what is happening for individuals, and in its freedom to go where an exploration leads, speak to the challenges relevant to schools and particularly to teachers in schools?

For me as a schoolteacher as well as a practitioner of the kind of work put forward in this book, the question of the implications of such work for schools has long been a compelling one. On the one hand, such stories of learning—their close focus on the intricacies of what is involved for learners as they deepen their understanding, and their illustration of a practice that provokes this learning and brings it to light—are obviously and profoundly relevant to school practice. But how, specifically, do we make use of these?

The stories consist of the specifics of people learning certain subject matter, and each chapter therefore has particular implications for teachers of that subject matter in that it portrays some of the possibilities for learners' developing thought. Chapter 1, "Inventing Density," for example, shows some of the possible questions and connections that can happen as people develop their ideas about floating and sinking. What I will focus on here, however, is not the implications that are particular to each subject matter but rather those that the chapters have in common. What these chapters share is a practice that was developed by Eleanor Duckworth and adapted by each author to the age group and subject matter with which the author worked. This practice, developed over years, embodies Duckworth's (1996) conviction that "the essence of intellectual development" is "the having of wonderful ideas," by which she means developing ideas of one's own that are forged from the work of trying to make previously held ideas adequate to new situations (p. 1).

Both using this practice and studying what it reveals about people's learning in my own and other's work has given me a vastly enlarged view of the capacity of the human mind. It has done this by bringing me, again and again, face to face with the living movement of students' thought. For my purpose here, it doesn't matter whether the students whom I am facing are 3-year-olds, or teenagers, or adults: The nature of the mind is the same. When my student Marco decided that the speaker in "miss rosie" could be talking to a decaying farm rather than to another person—that the "you" in the poem could be inanimate—he was in the act of grasping a new possibility for the working of language. His idea came out of need—this poem was challenging his expectations of language—and it also came out of previous experience that led him to an awareness that language can "exaggerate," that it can move beyond literal meaning. It is because I had followed in some part the history of his idea—the story of his learning—that I could see his idea in the fullness of its intelligence.

Throughout this book we see acts of intelligence being made visible by their contexts, by the stories of learning into which they are woven. We see recounted the history of belief, question, insight, confusion that can give to any one idea its sense, its essentially purposeful quality. We watch as a new idea is born out of a previous one. It is this history of ideas, the story, that lets us see the intelligence of the students' work.

It is the practice that the authors employ that leads to the chapters' narrative form. This practice calls forth and relies on the singular history of a learner's ideas. It embodies the belief that each person's ideas have an integrity that to a significant degree determines its own route or pathway. But this belief, which is a characterizing force for this work, is also where the work can seem problematic for schools in two ways: The first is that teachers must work with large numbers of students; and the second is the question of bringing students to "right answers." I will attempt to describe several insights of my own that served to clarify for me the relationship of this work to my school practice.

Working with Large Numbers of Students

It might seem that the implication here for teaching practice is that teachers follow the individual understanding of all students all the time in order to help them develop their ideas. This, of course, is impossible. I began to make some headway on the question of how to make such a seemingly individualized practice relevant to groups when I did the work that is the basis of my chapter on "miss rosie" (chapter 2). I had begun the work thinking that, even though we were working in a group, I was going to write separate stories about each student's developing ideas. Before long I realized that I could not write separate stories—that what was happening was the story of the group. It included in significant part the following of individuals' developing ideas, but the central development was the group's understanding as students worked with one another's ideas. Sometimes this was the story of conflicts that grew into dramatic new insight for everyone; sometimes it was one student's idea serving another student's insight; sometimes it was one student articulating something with which the rest of the group agreed or disagreed. There were many times when ideas ceased to be attributable to one student or another, so central were they to the whole group's ongoing study. It was striking to see the degree to which the students were interested in one another's questions and also found their way to common questions once each of them had taken some time to become familiar with the poem and with his or her own initial thoughts.

The point here is that it is not necessary to follow every student's understanding all the time in order to catalyze and follow the significant development of a group's ideas. When students talk about their ideas, they excite other students' ideas. (In chapter 5, Delaney also talks about this.) The teacher of the group does not have to hear them all at any one point. In hearing what others say or seeing what they do, students will get more conscious of—more alive to—their own ideas, beliefs, noticings, feelings on the subject and have those to work with as the work proceeds. The teacher need not know of every insight or every development in order for members of the class to experience them.

As a teacher I now often see my role as helping a group to develop a history of ideas. By "a group" I mean every individual in the group, but I also mean something more. I mean the individuals in relation to one another. Sometimes this role involves highlighting one or a few individuals' ideas for a time so that the group can get familiar with them and participate in the ways that they develop. (In chapter 2 I referred to this as moving an idea to the center of the table.) Sometimes it means finding out from everybody what they notice about something or how they would respond to a particular question and then moving on to a discussion from there. It all depends on the matter at hand and what I think will best serve the group exploration. This takes the same balancing of individual and group welfare that is familiar to anyone who has taught in a school and that is one of the hallmarks of a teacher's work. It also opens the way for various configurations of individual, small-group, and large-group work that can inform and lead into one another.

Bringing Students to "Right Answers"

The second question or tension point with school structure that I mentioned is that of leading students to "right answers" within a fixed space of time. As I see it, the work presented in this book *is* committed to helping students eventually reach a "right answer," if we mean by that to develop adequate knowledge about something. But it is committed to doing this with full understanding on the student's part. The tension point here is deep and many-layered, involving questions of what knowledge is and how people develop adequate ideas, what an adequate assessment is, what is most important for students to learn. For me, experiencing the kind of work presented here leads to questioning about the very nature of the structures of knowledge that we present to students, and therefore to questioning the structures of curriculum and of schools. As a result of my experience of this kind of work, it has long seemed to me that knowledge as it is conceived of in much of school curricula and textbooks is a thin shadow of what it might be, a verbal repetition rather than a true development of ideas, damaging in its standing in for something that the students then lose sight of.

But what I want to focus on right now again involves an insight about my position as a teacher with a class of students. It has to do with what I'll call the substantiality of the students' minds. Or I could call it the trustworthiness of their minds—the fact that they can make sense of subject matter by using the power of their own ideas. This takes me as the teacher out of the role of translator of knowledge—using my knowledge of a subject matter to tell them what they need to know about it, to bring them to an answer—and into a role that facilitates their direct contact with the subject matter. This is a fully active role on my part: I choose and often construct the form in which to present the subject to them, I take an active role in exciting their interest (this is, as I see it, perhaps the most challenging and important facet of the work, because if the subject has caught their interest it means that they are at their full power, that they have really entered the work), in keeping them engaged, in supplying support for and challenge to their ideas, but I don't often paraphrase for them the subject matter that they are studying.

Part of what I'm describing is an insight about the potential of the mind—we can trust it to find its own way—and partly it is an insight about the potential of subject matter. It is really about the two together—how the mind meets subject matter when the way is cleared for the direct contact between the students and the material under study. The insight that I had about this was a long time in coming to me. It had many facets and had to revisit me many times before I held on to it in a way that affected my practice. The time I most remember was when I was taking a class with Eleanor Duckworth and starting to use the practice of eliciting and following learners' thinking that she was teaching us. As part of the work for that class, I was involved in a study of poems with two high school students. I chose one of the poems for its unusual syntax, hoping to get the students interested in thinking about how in a poem aspects of language can be used differently from how they are used in prose. In my written report on one of my meetings with the students, I described how I had tried to focus the students on the interesting grammar and punctuation in this poem. Duckworth wrote in reply,

> Here is my belief: once you have chosen a poem, the poem becomes the focus, not its punctuation or its vocabulary or its spacing. You can choose a poem for its interesting punctuation, but the object of study is the *poem*. What gets focused on, then, is what the student notices.

I was confused about that comment for quite a while. I remember going back and forth between a vague sense of what she was saying on the one hand, and on the other, saying to myself, "but I *have* been focusing on the poem! I've been showing them something that's right there in the poem!" After a while of this, I realized that I had been holding on to my belief that I had to show them what I wanted them to see in the poem, that the only way students would ever recognize the depths of it was if I showed them. What I began to realize was that I was not the best source of their knowledge of the poem. The *poem itself* could guide them through its features, once they were caught up in it. It was the poem that would both allow them and compel them to develop their own knowledge of it. As I came to realize that I did not need to be the translator of the subject matter to the students, I had the feeling of something lifting, a physical shifting of weight from my shoulders onto the poem. I saw my own place in the work as shifting from leading the students through my sequence of ideas toward creating circumstances in which they could explore the poem directly and build, from their own responses, individually or collectively, their own route of access into it.

And then an extension of this realization: This kind of work, which might be seen as burdensome, demanding the impossible in terms of individual attention to students, profoundly unrealistic regarding the time that teachers have to devote to any one topic, in fact does not demand any particular teaching practice so much as it is gives us *something to lean on* in the classroom. It gives us the potential *reliability* of the students and the subject matter in ways that we are often not challenged to think about by prevalent curriculum.

This reliance on students' minds can take many forms in teaching practice. I have seen it take different forms in my own classroom and also in those of colleagues whose teaching styles are very different from mine and from one another's. One consistent form that it takes for me is that my first curiosity and focus when I think of teaching something is on what the students already believe. What are their current questions, what have they noticed about this topic that even they themselves might not yet be aware of? My first work is to elicit their awareness of those existing ideas. Most often, I do this not by asking them directly but by using my own knowledge of the subject to choose materials that will spark their awareness of what they think about something (for example, choosing poems that challenge their expectations of poetry so that they will talk about these expectations). *It is at this level of current belief that their interest lies.* I always go after that interest as the motor of what we will do together. Subjects that it might seem students would have no real interest in because these are not clearly or dramatically related to their most obvious concerns become the source of passionate debate when I reach their real beliefs. This is as true of the relationships of fractions or the workings of electricity as it is of a topic that is more clearly on their minds.

Another implication for my practice is my consistent choice to give students the subject matter in its full complexity (as Eleanor Duckworth recommends in chapter 8) rather than to simplify it for them. I look to the complexity of a subject or a skill to provide a variety of inroads for the variety of students that I teach, and I look for materials that will embody that complexity. This leads to using as the objects of study the real stuff of the world, primary sources, the poem itself rather than an account that tells them what to pay attention to before they have read it.

One of the striking common features of the chapters in this book is how clearly the students come to care about what they are thinking and about saying what they mean. This brings me to what, for me, is the heart of the matter, in terms of the question of the usefulness of this work to schools. As it shows us the potential of students at work with real and complex facets of the world, as it shows us the power of students' own ideas as the means of deepening their knowledge, it shows us also the potential of each teaching decision, even the most seemingly minute, either to enlarge or to diminish a student's access to the power of his or her own mind. It shows us what is at stake, what depths of possibility are present in a classroom, pooled there, waiting. It highlights for us as teachers something important about the nature of our work, the essentially political nature of our choices to support our students' reliance on their own powers of thought. Because of the presence, the substantiality, of their minds and their ideas, there is no neutral ground. We are always either supporting or diminishing their reliance on their ability to think.

These choices are often not easy or clear for teachers. The fact remains that schools are structured to bring students to fixed points of knowledge in a certain length of time. Teachers and students are accountable to elaborate structures of assessments that are wielding more and more power. These assessments carry with them assumptions about learning and knowledge that exert a constant narrowing force on the work of schools. Often the decision as it confronts teachers is whether to short-circuit substantive work that is happening in their classrooms in order to prepare students for these tests. How to balance these forces against the deeper knowledge that we want for students is a continuing question for me. How to create more-adequate means for setting standards that demand equitable education and for supporting schools in the work of creating it is also a continuing question.

Even with the disturbing questions that come with my increasing awareness of the ways in which school structures do not support students' intelligence and its expression in their active thought, this awareness also lets me see more instances of my own success as a teacher, because my measure of this success now includes how well I do at casting the students back onto their own minds, calling forth their reliance on one another and on the power of their own intelligence.

Reference

Duckworth, E. (1996). *The having of wonderful ideas* (2nd ed.). New York: Teachers College Press.

Index

Academic levels, 43, 93, 97, 99
Anna (inventing density participant), 2, 11, 27, 28
Anne (young writer), 79–92
Apartheid, 167, 179, 180
Aral (medical student), 147–65, 184, 186
Attention span, 93
Avidon, E., 167

Benedict, Susan, 195
Bilingualism, 93–94
Bipolar thinking, 142–45
Bonolo (South African teacher), 166–80, 184, 185
Butler, A., 90

Carini, Pat, 167
Cirino, Hallie, xii, 79–92, 183, 195
Claire (inventing density participant), 2–3, 6, 7, 9, 11, 13–16, 19, 23–26, 29, 33–35, 40
Clifton, Lucille. *See* "miss rosie" (Clifton)
Colette (inventing density participant), 2, 3–4, 6, 7, 9, 10, 11, 15, 22, 23, 24, 27–28, 29, 31, 35, 40
Complexity, of subject matter, 193–94
Critical barriers to learning, 141, 142, 144
Curriculum, xiii, 126, 141, 163–64
  conflict and resistance as basis of, 145
  and disengagement/engagement of students, 78, 93–94, 102, 104, 122, 124
  and materials, 145
  students' experience as basis of, 93, 95, 121–22, 123

students reactions, questions and noticings as basis of, 145
  and teaching/learning research, 185–86

Danielle (inventing density participant), 2–3, 7, 9, 12–15, 22, 29, 34–35
Delaney, Mary Kay, 125–46, 184, 190, 195
Details, 164
Drawing
  and journals of young writers, 80, 81, 82–83, 84, 85, 86, 87, 88, 90, 91
  and mapping neighborhoods, 99, 100, 101, 102, 104–20
Duckworth, Eleanor, 1–41, 4, 166, 167, 173, 177, 179, 181–87, 189, 192, 193, 195
Dyson, A., 90

Elementary science study, xiii
Ernst, Karen, 90, 195
Ethnicity, 43–44
Evelyne (inventing density participant), 2, 13, 14–15, 21, 23, 24, 26, 28, 31, 32, 35–36, 40, 41

Families
  and learning, 94
  See also Parents
Ferreiro, Emilia, 91
Floating and sinking study
  air hypothesis in, 5, 8–9, 10, 11, 12, 14, 15, 20, 22, 28, 29, 32, 33, 37
  and Archimedes, 24, 35
  balloons in, 10–11, 23, 27, 32
  and bearing surface, 4, 6, 9, 18, 35

Thinking
  bipolar, 142–45
  and encouraging students to say what
    they think, 183–84
  implications for teaching in thinking
    about, 141–45
  and South African case study, 167
Trust, importance of, 164
Trustworthiness of minds, 191–92
Turbill, J., 90

Understanding children, xiii

Words in lieu of ideas, 164

Young writers study, xii, 79–92
  and alphabet, 85–86, 87, 90
  and "copying", 88
  "official" equipment for, 80, 90
  parents's role in, 84, 86, 89, 90
  rituals during, 86
  sentences, 81–83
  teacher's role in, 90–91
  words, 81–83
  See also Journals

About the Contributors

Hallie Cirino first became interested in young children's writing when she was a student teacher in Susan Benedict's kindergarten classroom. Fifteen years a preschool and elementary school teacher, she has taken part in teacher-research groups, and, with her colleague Karen Ernst, learned about helping children incorporate art into their writing. Currently on leave from her teaching, she is tutoring children in language arts and working as a parent volunteer in the classrooms of her own two young children.

Mary Kay Delaney is assistant professor of education at Meredith College in Raleigh, North Carolina, where she teaches undergraduates who are preparing to be teachers, and graduate students who are seeking deeper understandings of teaching and learning. She has taught social studies, government, and politics in high school and middle school.

Eleanor Duckworth is professor of education at Harvard University. A former student of Jean Piaget and Barbel Inhelder, she teaches with a focus on helping teachers think about how people learn, and what anyone else can do to help. She has worked in curriculum development, program evaluation, and teacher education in the United States, Europe, Africa, Latin America, and her native Canada.

Isabella Knox is associate professor of pediatrics at the University of Connecticut School of Medicine. She teaches residents, fellows, and nurses while taking care of sick newborns in the neonatal intensive care unit. She also teaches various courses to medical students; this work includes developing and running courses in clinical problem-solving. In her role as associate dean for faculty development, she works with faculty in curriculum development and in improving teaching and learning at the medical school.

Namane Magau is currently vice president for human resources at the Council for Scientific and Industrial Research, in South Africa. As such she is part of an executive team working on organizational learning, leadership development, and the development of Black professionals, in science and technology institutions. She is an executive member of the South African Council for Higher Education. A former high school language and history teacher, she also taught teachers for 11 years at the Soweto College of Education.

Ileana M. Quintero is assistant professor of education at the University of the Sacred Heart, in San Juan, Puerto Rico. She is director of a pilot teacher-education project that integrates theoretical courses with practical experiences, starting during the students' first year in college. The project is part of a larger one with the goal of systemic change in one entire school district.

Lisa Schneier has spent most of her career teaching and working on curriculum development in the Boston public schools. She has also worked as a curriculum developer for a television network that broadcasts live, interactive programs to schools. Currently she is on the faculty of the Harvard Graduate School of Education, where she teaches prospective teachers.